The Forbidden Sky

The Forbidden Sky

by Endre Marton

Little, Brown and Company

Boston - Toronto

To Ilona

The prisoner is entitled to a daily walk. He should take the walk with hands clasped behind his back and eyes turned to the ground.

Excerpt from the AVH prison regulations

Preface

Fourteen years ago today, on November 4, 1956, Russian tanks rumbled through the streets of Budapest and the Hungarian revolution died in blood.

What happened in those weeks in the fall of 1956 is history — and unique: the first and thus far the only armed national uprising against Communist oppression. It cost the lives of at least thirteen thousand Hungarians, and in the aftermath over two hundred thousand Magyars fled their country, more than thirty thousand of them to the United States.

The revolt broke out on October 23, 1956. It was not planned, it was a popular rising, and it spread like a forest fire. It was neither organized nor made by an army; and it was not an ideological revolution, because it was fomented by Communists against Communism.

The great and noble words, epitaphs in memory of those who died, were spoken long ago. The House Committee on Foreign Affairs said the West's failure to help Hungary constituted "the lost opportunity of our generation," and Dwight D. Eisenhower, then President of the United States, said that Budapest, the Hungarian capital, "is no longer merely the name of a city. Henceforth it is a new and shining symbol of man's yearning to be free."

The words were resounding. More than a decade later there is no need for great words. Fourteen years is long enough for historians, politicians, and other contemporaries to answer the questions: was it in vain? and, if not, what did it achieve? As one of the contemporary witnesses, I try to answer the questions in this book.

Why so late? one may ask. Because I heeded the friendly advice of John Foster Dulles, who told me one evening in the spring of 1957, shortly after I came to Washington, to wait for what he called "the necessary perspective." In the summer of 1968, after the invasion of Czechoslovakia, I felt the time had come, despite the differences between the two bare aggressions: Czechoslovakia 1968 could not have happened without Hungary 1956.

Reminiscing about 1956, I have had to speak about the eighteen months I spent in the prison of the Hungarian Communist secret police, while my wife was in another isolated cell in that House of Horrors. Our crime was the treason and espionage we had committed, so the state contended, as Hungarian citizens and correspondents for American wire services. This is not a prison story, although our arrest, trial, and early release before the revolt were in integral and logical connection with the events of 1956.

This book is neither a scholarly assessment of the Hungarian revolution, nor does it attempt to give a chronological account of those weeks. The pages which follow contain the recollections of a reporter who happened to be the only Western correspondent to cover the revolt from its first day to the bitter end. Other colleagues from the West came late or left early.

I do not use footnotes nor do I require the reader to look for information in appendixes at the end of the book. Instead I use what I consider the more convenient, though admittedly less scholarly way of giving the required information in the text. And because it is not a historical study, I have taken the liberty of omitting a name here and there, usually but not always, the name of a Hungarian. Though times have changed in Hungary and the Stalinist terror, one may hope, is a memory of the dreaded past, *plus ça change, plus c'est la même chose,* and this book should not jeopardize anyone who chose to stay in my old country.

I dedicate this book to my wife, who for years has prodded me to put into writing my recollections and my thoughts. She was my brave colleague who shared without hesitation the dangers of underground life during the Nazi occupation of Hungary, of Russian "liberation," and of the revolt. Never did she try to persuade me to cower but joined me to live the life of an outcast: the life of an American reporter behind the Iron Curtain. No man could ask for a greater partner.

My thanks go to two friends and colleagues at the Associated Press: John M. Hightower and Sam Summerlin, both of whom spurred me to write.

My daughter Kati, now a graduate student, should not remain unmentioned for her grooming of the manuscript, and her grumbling over my clumsy grammatical errors.

My thanks also go to the Princeton University Library for permission to study the personal and private papers of John Foster Dulles; to Alexander P. Clark, curator of manuscripts, for the quiet days I spent in the library; and to the distinguished men, including President Nixon, who gave me permission to use their confidential remarks on 1956, deposited among the Dulles papers.

There is a photograph over my desk in our suburban Washington home. It shows Dulles at one of his press conferences in the east auditorium of the State Department, with me among the reporters bending over their notebooks. The date was November 1958, two years after the revolt. Dulles must have remembered it when he sent the picture down to the press room where I have worked for more than thirteen years. The caption, in his characteristic handwriting, said: "To Endre Marton, whose able reporting of the Hungarian freedom revolt provided a solid basis for free world judgments of that important event."

Since 1958 the picture was a constant reminder that I, in a way, promised this man that one day I would write. With this book, to change slightly the Latin saying, *scripsi et salvavi animam meam.*

E. M.

Contents

The Forbidden Sky

I

I See the Sun Again

August 15, 1956, started as just another day. After eighteen months prison life in my solitary cell had become routine. For weeks I was left alone, except when the jailer pushed my meals through a small opening in the solid iron door three times a day.

I was a convict, sentenced originally to thirteen years in November 1955 after nine months of pretrial detention and interrogation. This term was reduced to six years by the Hungarian Supreme Court one month later. Yet I had never been transferred to a prison, as I should have been, but was kept in the sinister fortress of the secret police, alone in a small cell.

For weeks after the trial before the Supreme Court, I had been wondering why they were keeping me in Fö utca (Main Street), the secret police fortress on the Buda side of the Hungarian capital. Nothing is done without a reason in a Communist country and the secret police usually discard people whom they have squeezed dry of information and for whom they have no further need. But by August 1956 I had given up pondering. The prisoner's isolation is perfect in the prisons of the secret police in every Communist country and I could not know what was going on in the outside world. Probably nothing. Changes are rare in Communist countries, and if they occur, they are usually for the worse.

I knew that my wife had been freed on parole in April and reunited with our daughters, then nine and ten. I knew this because they had let her visit me once in the spring. We had been tried together and she, as a lesser "spy," a mini–Mata Hari, was sentenced to six years by a lower court, and to three by the Supreme Court. That she had been released on April 4 made sense to me: even a hard-core Communist must have smiled over the charges against her. Her release date was the principal Communist holiday in Hungary, commemorating the country's "liberation" by the Russians in 1945. Even in the early years there were limited amnesties on that day.

Though by August 15, 1956, I was living in luxury, I was more depressed than usual and annoyed whenever I felt the jailer's eyes fixed on me through the peepholes of the Judas. The joy over the many privileges gradually granted to me since my trial had slowly faded away. I had my pipe, even my typewriter; I could get books from the prison library. I had a small table and a wooden chair, all unheard-of pleasures in that building of draconic military discipline.

About noon, the door was unlocked and the jailer motioned: "Jöjjön!" He escorted me through deserted corridors and stairways to the front of the fortress, to the office of the secret police major who had interrogated me before my trial.

How well I knew this route. For nine long months in 1955 I had traveled through the same corridors at least twice a day to sit before him and others. But since the trial the authorities had lost interest in me and when I was summoned by the major — an infrequent event — it was usually for a chat with no apparent purpose. The major was a simple but friendly little man with thin reddish hair and pale blue eyes. He looked uncomfortable on the rare occasions when he wore his uniform, which hung on his slight frame in a rather unmilitary fashion. I liked to think that he had saved my life in May 1955 when he took over my case under dramatic circumstances. I was then close to breaking down and surrendering to the tough guys who were doing their best to extort a "confession" from me.

I knew, of course, that Major Kretsmer had played a prescribed role in my interrogation, that he had taken over my case not because he pitied me but because he had been ordered to do so when those who had desperately needed my confession suddenly lost interest. Yet I was grateful.

It was easy to make Kretsmer talk, though he was careful not to talk about what interested me most, events beyond the walls of the fortress. He talked about himself, with unmistakable pride about his role in the "rehabilitation process" of Noel Field, the mysterious American who had spent five years without trial in prison, and about a Colonel Maléter, a partisan in the resistance against the Nazis whom he had met in a Russian prisoner-of-war camp. Then the name meant nothing to me. A few months later the same Maléter was to become the military hero of the Hungarian revolution.

"Comrade Major, prisoner 530," my jailer, a secret police sergeant reported, saluting stiffly. Major Kretsmer, standing at his desk, nodded and the sergeant disappeared. The major was not alone. There was another man in civilian clothes sitting in an armchair in a remote corner of the room, right under the only picture on the wall, an enlarged photograph of Felix Dzerzhinski, the Polish nobleman who became Soviet Russia's first secret police chief and ultimately the idol of all Communist secret policemen.

During the rough period of my pretrial investigation several "tough guys" were frequently present, but there was no need for such reinforcement when Major Kretsmer took over my case and especially not now when, I thought, I had become a forgotten convict serving his time. It was immediately obvious, though, that Kretsmer had not called me because he was bored and wanted to chat. His face was solemn as he motioned me to sit down.

There is one simple wooden chair in every interrogator's room for the arrested man; all the other chairs are comfortable, upholstered armchairs. I sat down, careful not to let my face reveal my curiosity.

"This is Colonel Jámbor from the ministry of the interior," the major said. I nodded in the man's direction and he returned the nod.

"To begin with," the major said, "I will read an announcement of the government of the People's Republic which will be made public tomorrow." Then, standing behind his desk, he read a few sentences. Their essence was that I was pardoned and would be released.

I can only remember sitting there, with my head bowed, trying to understand what the major had said. I did not say a word. Then Colonel Jámbor rose and began to talk matter-of-factly. There were certain formalities to arrange; I would have to wait another twenty-four hours. My wife would be notified and asked to fetch me. Clothing would be returned, papers signed.

"We want you to continue your life where it was interrupted when you were arrested," he said, and I pricked up my ears. This was something that had to be clarified at once. Many months earlier in the same office, Kretsmer had asked what I thought I would do when I was released after serving my time. Obviously, he said, I could not go back and work again as an American correspondent. I had sidestepped the question by telling him that there was no point in speculating on what I would do so many years later.

"You mean," I now asked the colonel, "that you would have no objections if I continued to work for the Associated Press, provided, of course, the AP is still interested in my work?"

"Exactly," he said. I sensed a trap and rose from my chair,

something a prisoner is not supposed to do without being so ordered.

"Colonel," I said, and I still remember how calm my voice was, "what do you want from me? Is there a price you expect me to pay for letting me go? Because if there is one, you had better send me back to my cell."

Both men smiled. "I understand your suspicion," the colonel said, "but you don't know what is going on outside these walls, you don't know about the changes of recent months. Go and see them for yourself. And then we expect you only to report the truth. It will be exciting, I assure you."

That was the end of the audience. Escorted back to my cell, I felt my heart throbbing in my throat. Though a prisoner is never supposed to talk to a jailer, I could not resist whispering to him, "I'm going home tomorrow." The sergeant, one of the friendlier types, nodded with a grin. This was sensational news to me, but he was accustomed to it. In August 1956 dozens of political prisoners were released every day.

The colonel was right. After eighteen months it took me a day to realize that Hungary in August 1956 was an entirely different country. Communists denounced Communism, they demanded reforms, and the Communist-run newspapers and magazines, intoxicated by their unprecedented freedom, spearheaded this strange, almost feverish trend.

This was the climate, but I had to learn the facts and my wife became my principal tutor. She was an experienced newspaperwoman who had been released in time to watch and to report how this wave had begun and surged to reach its peak two months later on October 23, the day the revolt began. For me, however, the change occurred in Fö utca on the day I was released.

It was probably the longest day of my life. In the morning the barber came, himself a secret police sergeant — and one of the most unpleasant ones in the building — to free my face from the week-old stubble. My shirt, socks, underwear, and necktie were returned to me, together with my watch and everything else I had in my pockets on the night of my arrest. Then, shortly after lunch, which I could not touch, I was escorted for the last time to Major Kretsmer's office.

Ilona was there, radiant and beautiful, with Kretsmer and another major who had interrogated my wife before our trial, and with the prison doctor, a major himself, who had always been nice to us, even during the first months of terror. The whole scene was unreal. Here I was, in my once elegant dark suit which I had been wearing on the night of my arrest on my way home from a friendly dinner-and-bridge party in an American home. I had worn this suit for eighteen months — inmates of the secret police prison wear their own clothes until transferred to an ordinary prison, and my poor suit looked accordingly.

The three majors were smiling and appeared to be happy. My wife, always the center of any gathering with her quick wit, was bantering with them; only cocktails were missing. As I entered, Ilona had just told the three what had happened when she gave the prison's address to the cabdriver and then, arriving there, asked him to wait.

"Oh no, lady," the cabby replied. "You call another one when you leave, provided they let you go. Many people go in here, not many come out," and he drove away.

The three thought this was very funny. Maybe it was. It was not so easy for me to join this merrymaking. I was still trying to solve the riddle: what could have happened, what was Colonel Jámbor talking about a day earlier, how was it possible that the same men, or at least men wearing the same uniform as those who not so long ago had assured me every day that I would be hanged, were now pumping my hand and repeating, "Go out, you'll see . . ."

I warmed up only when Kretsmer solemnly produced a carefully wrapped package which contained two cartons of

American cigarettes and a large tin of pipe tobacco. Christian Ravndal, the American minister to Hungary — the diplomatic mission was then on the legation level — had sent them to Ilona and me before Christmas 1955. They were not returned but neither were they delivered, though by then we were convicted and theoretically entitled to get packages from the outside. I did not ask why they kept them and they did not offer any explanation. I knew the reason. During the terror period of the months I spent in Fö utca, one of the favorite torments of my interrogators was: "You think the Americans will help you? Don't be a fool. They don't care about you. You are just one of many unmasked spies, forgotten by everyone." It was a trite argument, but often used to break the spirit of a man they wanted to confess — and it sometimes worked.

Ilona was in a generous mood: she gave one pack of cigarettes to each of the three majors. They were heavy smokers and American cigarettes were luxuries obtainable only on the black market.

The change must be great indeed, I thought. There was no other explanation for this strange scene, three fairly high-ranking secret police officers and two American "spies" standing together in a happy group in the dreaded House of Horrors.

Then, as a possible but implausible reaction to Ilona's funny story about the suspicious cabdriver, Kretsmer offered an official car to take us home. We needed a car. In the major's closet, there were two large, worn suitcases, filled with every piece of paper they had taken from our apartment when I was arrested, including copies of thousands of dispatches I had sent during the eight years I worked for the Associated Press.

When Kretsmer opened one of the suitcases, I began to laugh. The first thing I saw in the chaotic mélange of old photographs and copies of stories, were dozens of airmail envelopes, neatly opened. They contained my so-called mailers: features or lengthy analytical stories which I had sent by mail.

"That was a mistake, wasn't it?" I asked, pointing at the envelopes. I had always known that our telephones were tapped and our mail opened, but according to the rules of the game, after having read my stuff they should have closed the envelopes and forwarded them to the addressee. The three majors laughed with me, but no apologies were offered.

A black, unmarked Mercedes, which may have been the same in which I was brought in eighteen months earlier, took us home. Our house stood on a hillside and about two dozen steps led up to the entrance. I will always see my daughters — how small they were then! — running down the stairs in the warm summer afternoon, with their arms stretched out toward me, and crying in my arms.

I was at home. I had to find out what the colonel was talking about.

To understand what happened in Hungary in 1956 one has to go back to 1953, the year Stalin died.

Mátyás Rákosi was then the unchallenged ruler of Hungary. He wore two hats, as first secretary of the Hungarian Communist party and as president of the council of ministers (prime minister). As a man of great intelligence with excellent connections in Moscow, he must have sensed that the days when his loyalty to Stalin was appreciated and rewarded, were over. Yet he made a last desperate attempt to prove to Moscow's new leaders that he alone could be trusted as their proconsul in that satellite country. On May 10, 1953, about one hundred thousand Budapesters were herded into the enormous square in front of the Hungarian Parliament to hear Rákosi boast about how successfully he was "building socialism."

But Stalin's successors in Moscow thought otherwise. A few weeks later, shortly after the June 17, 1953, revolt in East Berlin, Rákosi was summoned to the Kremlin. He was ordered to bring with him two of his top lieutenants, Ernö Gerö, the economic czar of Hungary, and Mihály Farkas, who was defense minister. Imre Nagy and István Dobi, figurehead president of the People's Republic, were also ordered to come.

Nagy was one of several who held the empty title of deputy premier. He was a veteran Communist who between the two world wars had spent many years in exile in Moscow. After World War II Nagy was in charge of the long overdue land reform in Hungary, but in 1948 he disagreed with Rákosi's ironfisted methods of forcing farmers to give up their independence and to join the cooperatives. Nagy then withdrew from politics to teach the science of modern farming.

President Dobi later told me what happened in Moscow. He was a man I had known since 1944, the year the German Nazis occupied Hungary. This simple, honest, landless peasant had belonged to the small group of men who actively resisted the Nazis and who made up a strange mixture of Communist veterans of the Spanish Civil War and aristocrats, of Catholic priests and Protestant pastors, of Jews who had escaped deportation and patriots who simply hated Nazism.

Between the two wars Dobi had been a member of the Smallholder party, a liberal opposition group in the Hungarian Parliament. In 1944 I attended one underground meeting at which Dobi was instructed to tour Transdanubia, the western part of Hungary between the Danube and the Austrian border, and to organize farmers to resist the Nazis.

"You need money, István," he was told.

"I don't," Dobi replied quietly. "I have a friend in every village. I'm at home everywhere," and he walked out of the room.

In the 1950's, after the Smallholder party ceased to exist and its leaders were jailed or exiled, Dobi became a lonely, sad, fat puppet, a man the Communists used to prove the clumsy lie that proletarian dictatorship meant the holy union of the workers and the peasants. By then he was a heavy drinker, a man unhappy and uncomfortable in his high post as figurehead president of the republic. On the rare occasions we met he preferred to remember the romantic times when only one thing counted: to resist the Nazis.

The manner in which Rákosi and his group were received in the Kremlin was unbelievable, Dobi said. He alone did not speak Russian, but was aware of the tension before the words were translated.

The Soviet leaders, especially Beria, were particularly rude to Rákosi. There were tactless references to his Jewish origin; vitriolic questions were asked about whether he planned to establish a Jewish dynasty; accusations were made that he had lied to Moscow when he had depicted a rosy picture of Hungary's economic progress. Finally Rákosi was bluntly told to vacate the premiership, though he could remain as the party's first secretary. And to add insult to injury, Rákosi was told that Imre Nagy was to be his successor as head of the government.

That year, in 1953, July 4 became a holiday for the Hungarians too. And what a July 4 it was, as Parliament convened.

This rubber-stamping body of handpicked deputies met once or twice a year for several days to hear routine reports of cabinet ministers and to approve whatever the government had done between sessions. For years it had been a dull affair, but not in 1953.

The handful of foreign correspondents had a separate box in this oversized neo-Gothic building on the Danube, built under the Hapsburgs when Hungary was three times as big as the territory left to her after World War I. The reporter working in a Communist country must be quick with his pencil because there are no advance texts of speeches; in fact, there are no texts available at all.

First it was announced that Rákosi had resigned as prime minister and that Nagy had been nominated to replace him. This, alone, was no great surprise. By then in the Soviet Union the "separation of power" had been carried out: Nikita Khrushchev was the party boss and Georgi Malenkov, the head of government. It was clear that Moscow would not tolerate a different practice, the same man ruling the party and the government, in its satellites.

Parliament, of course, voted for Nagy by acclamation. They would have voted for Caligula's horse with the same apathy. But the apathy did not last long. There was already drama in the air when the two men changed places, the stone-faced Rákosi rose from the number-one, red velvet armchair in the row of ministers and took the seat right behind it, in the first row of deputies.

Then Nagy delivered his first speech as prime minister and I filled a notebook with what he said. He was not a good orator, though he had a pleasant baritone. But it was what he said, not how he said it, that counted.

For the first time in the Communist orbit a high-ranking party member publicly denounced virtually everything that had been done since the Communists had taken over the country. He did it quietly, but without hesitation. He did not blame any individuals, but blamed the system and promised amends. It was a long speech and Nagy touched on all wounds. He assailed the insane policy of forced industrialization in a country with few natural resources, especially the stress on heavy industry and the neglect of consumer goods. He promised to end the forced collectivization of farmers, the end of deportation of "unreliable" elements to the countryside, and the dissolution of internment camps. He spoke about the "consolidation of legality" and about the need to review the cases of political prisoners.

My right hand began to ache as I tried to record every word. I had to force myself to concentrate on what he said and suppress my personal questions: how was this possible? what was behind all this? would Rákosi, who represented all the evil things his successor was denouncing, take this sitting down?

When it was over, we ran to the telephones. Outside, on the wide corridor overlooking the Danube, we bumped into the

new premier, surrounded by friends, on his way to his office in
the building.

Ilona stopped him. "Mr. Prime Minister . . . this is a sensation —" she burst out. Nagy looked at us through his glasses,
with a faint smile around his lips under the heavy moustache.

"Sensation, maybe, but don't make it appear greater than it
is."

I dictated for about an hour. The editor on the other end of
the line recognized the immense importance of the speech; its
significance extended far beyond the narrow confines of Hungary. He requested more and more details and finally I was
ordered to get the full text, translate it, and cable it to New
York.

It was late in the afternoon when we drove to Christian
Ravndal's residence to celebrate the Fourth of July with the
American diplomats and their guests. I had the impression that
by then everybody had partaken of one glass more than he
would have normally, perhaps because of the excitement of the
one topic of discussion: Nagy's speech and its implications.

I am convinced that history will record July 4, 1953, in
Hungary as the day when "socialism with a human face" was
first proclaimed in a Moscow-bloc country. This was fifteen
years before Alexander Dubcek made his effort to introduce it
in Czechoslovakia, but neither Dubcek nor Nagy succeeded.
Nagy had to die for his ideas, Dubcek is a non-person in his
country. One may have been killed, the other has suffered humiliation, but it is impossible to wipe out the ideas for which
they lived. Communism in Hungary reached a turning point on
that July 4 and despite tragic lapses, has never been the same
again.

Hungary's experiment with Nagy's humanistic socialism
lasted only nineteen months. It was a honeymoon, short but
sweet, despite the fact that Nagy could not fully carry out the
ambitious program he announced on that unforgettable July 4,

because Rákosi, with the party apparatus in his iron grip, countermanded Nagy's orders.

In addition to the apparatchiks who helped Rákosi, the difference between the characters of the two men played an important role in frustrating Nagy's well-meaning efforts. Rákosi was a ruthless dynamo whose boundless energies were not sapped by sixteen years in a Hungarian prison between the two wars. Nagy, on the other hand, was a typical Hungarian peasant offspring who became an intellectual. Rákosi, short, rotund, his oversized bullethead sitting on broad shoulders with virtually no neck in between, was quick and unwavering, a workhorse one rarely meets in central Europe. Nagy liked to stop and reflect, and in comparison seemed almost lazy.

Once near the end of 1954, when the two men were engaged in a life-and-death struggle for political survival, they returned very late at night together from Moscow. Rákosi immediately left the Budapest railroad station and headed for the headquarters of the Communist party, where he spent the night working at his desk. Nagy went home.

The fight between Rákosi and Nagy started just after the new premier proclaimed his "new course." It was fought in typical Communist secrecy, behind the scenes. Nagy's great disadvantage was his complete loyalty to the party of which Rákosi was the boss. Rákosi skillfully avoided public opposition to Nagy's program; instead he "explained" it, saying for instance, that of course Comrade Nagy was right in permitting the peasants to return to individual farming, but this did not mean a change in the party policy supporting agricultural collectives. Such interpretations, or misinterpretations, of Nagy's program provided encouragement for the lesser party functionaries to translate the government's orders into practice as they pleased.

Nagy's decisive mistake was that he did not purge the government of elements who remained loyal to Rákosi's Stalinist line. In fact only few of Nagy's supporters received important posts in his administration. But even so the "new course" limped along. There were more consumer goods and less was spent on heavy industry. There was a greater variety of foods on the market and, most importantly, men who were thought to be dead reappeared slowly from the depths of the prisons.

Most of the returnees were Communists, or former Social-Democrats. One of them was János Kádár, the man who was to become Hungary's Quisling when the Russians crushed the 1956 revolt.

Rákosi fought against the rehabilitation of his former comrades who had miraculously escaped the gallows and survived prison. He knew well that those now being released would revenge themselves. But Nagy remained firm and at that point he still had Moscow's backing. His chief supporter was Malenkov, whose program was largely identical with that of Nagy: more emphasis on consumer goods with less police terror.

The process of rehabilitation had two phases, and both were slow. The man picked for return to life was brought back to Fö utca from the prison where he was held, all his former "confessions" were put on the table, and the case was reopened. It was not enough that both the policeman and the convict knew that all the confessions were extorted lies, that the convict was neither a traitor nor a Titoist spy. They had to go through every page of the confession and rewrite all of them, a procedure which lasted for months.

After release came the second phase. The man was free but usually owned nothing except the one suit he wore. I know of several cases where "good" Communist wives turned their backs on their convicted husbands, divorced them, and remarried. The rehabilitated man surfaced years later and found neither family nor home, and had no job and no money. Then, slowly, apartments were found, money was given, and jobs too, usually less glittering than before, but jobs. Kádár, for instance, became the party secretary of a large Budapest industrial district, a far cry from the high posts he held before his arrest.

The second half of 1954 marked the beginning of the struggle between the two Soviet "collective" leaders, Khrushchev and Malenkov. There is a theory, accepted by many who witnessed the Hungarian "new course," that Nagy's first downfall in 1955 was closely connected with the ouster of Malenkov, his erstwhile guardian angel in the Kremlin. Their almost simultaneous exit in February 1955 could not have been just a coincidence.

Yet neither I nor anybody I knew sensed before a certain day in December 1954 that the "new course" and Nagy, the man who symbolized it, were in danger. On December 21, 1954, official Hungary celebrated the tenth anniversary of the country's so-called liberation by the Red Army, and Parliament was summoned to a commemorative session in Debrecen. This city in northeast Hungary was the site in December 1944 of the first provisional postwar government when Budapest was still in German hands.

As a result of a rare courtesy of the foreign ministry's press section, foreign correspondents were invited to ride on the special train which carried members of Parliament and of the government to Debrecen. We were but a handful and were carefully isolated in a passenger car specially reserved for us. We really did not mind being by ourselves, the atmosphere was relaxed, it was a festive occasion, and no one expected more than a color story to come out of it. How wrong we were.

Rákosi was the keynote speaker when Parliament convened in the centuries-old Calvinist church. It was clear at the outset that he was once again the omnipotent boss of the country. It was a vicious, mean, belligerent speech and the legislators listened like a flock of frightened sheep. It meant only one thing for everyone: "I am back, I am the master, and nobody should forget it."

The same evening the government gave a reception and buffet dinner in Debrecen's famous old Bika (Bull) Hotel to which all the reporters were also invited.

Three of us decided to talk to Rákosi outside the hotel, where the sidewalk had been carefully cleared of curious onlookers.

"Why should I talk to you? Whatever I say, you will not report it truthfully," he said, and looked us over with contemptuous eyes. He hurried away and we had no choice but to follow him inside. The reception was under way, the tables were packed with whatever delicacies Hungary could offer, and Rákosi was the center of interest, surrounded by large groups, sycophants from the party apparatus and a Catholic archbishop, peasant members of Parliament and renowned writers. He moved around the huge hall in a triumphant procession. Nagy made no rounds. He was sitting at the head of one of the tables with only a few of his devoted adherents around him. He withdrew early in the evening and the word was passed that he did not feel well.

A day or so later *Szabad Száj* (Free Mouth), a Budapest comic paper, appeared on the stands with an enigmatic cartoon on its front page which showed a young man and a woman sleighing down a very steep slope. "Careful, Malvin, we are approaching the curve!" the man warned his obviously frightened partner. Everybody understood the message the cartoon tried to convey: Hungary was approaching a dangerous curve and nothing could be done about it. The next couple of weeks were devoted to speculation. The nation's sleigh reached the curve early in March 1955, but I was not on it any more: I was arrested at dawn on February 25.

2

De Profundis

My wife and I went on the evening of February 24 to the American military attaché's house for a family dinner and game of bridge. Returning home shortly after midnight we parked the car in a garage we had rented in a neighboring apartment house. The next minute we were surrounded by six plainclothesmen. They did not talk much and I did not need much explanation. They hardly gave me sufficient time to kiss Ilona good-bye before the black Mercedes — who else had Mercedes cars behind the Iron Curtain but the secret police? — began to roll quietly down the street with its headlights switched off, taking me to the Fö utca prison.

Csaba utca, the street where we lived, was in a quiet residential section of Buda. The French ambassador's residence was next to the apartment house garage. The street was deserted when they drove me off and, strangely, it occurred to me how beautiful it was, covered with snow glittering in the moonlight. For eighteen months I saw neither the sun nor the moon. My only contact with nature was a tiny blade of grass that grew in a crack in the asphalt of the prison courtyard, where I walked alone for ten minutes a day with eyes turned to the ground and

hands clasped behind my back, under the watchful eyes of a
guard.

The street was deserted but there had been one witness,
Donald Downs, counselor of the American legation, our next
door neighbor and a good friend. Don had been walking his
German shepherd, Duke, in his fenced front yard and had noticed men lurking everywhere. As he told me much later in
America, he immediately sensed what was going on and kept
watching. A few minutes later he witnessed my kidnapping.

During the ten-minute drive to Fö utca I sat motionless,
wedged in between two plainclothesmen in the back seat, feeling nauseated and asking myself the questions: why? why
now? I remembered a telephone call in 1953, shortly after
Stalin's death, when one of the leading editors of the country
called to congratulate me for having survived the years of
terror. And I also recalled the question some of my American
and British diplomat friends had asked me with understandable
curiosity: "How come you managed to remain free?" What
would they say tomorrow morning when they learned that I
had indeed been arrested?

The two who flanked me in the car did not speak to me, nor
to each other. The big gate was shut with a bang when the car
stopped in the prison courtyard. I was led to a room on the first
floor and handed over to two uniformed jailers. They curtly
ordered me to undress completely, went thoroughly through
my pockets, and finally returned to me my suit and shoes together with prison underwear. A few minutes later the door of
a cell on the third floor was closed behind me.

The cell was cold and I was shivering. I took off my shoes
and lay on the bunk, pulling the smelly blanket over my head
to escape the light of the naked bulb, which burned day and
night above the door. Instantly the door opened and an old
guard entered, explaining in a whisper that I must lie on my
back, with hands above the blanket, so that he could see my
face and hands through the peepholes.

I had been lying wide awake for about ten minutes when the door opened again and the guard motioned me to come. He explained tersely the basic rules: I would have no name, but would respond when the number of my cell was called; no questions should be asked because none would be answered; I could lie on the bunk during the night but only sit on it in the daytime; whenever the cell door opened I must spring to my feet and face the wall; and outside the cell I should walk quickly, with my hands clasped behind my back. And so we walked, quickly, I with my hands behind my back, up and down stairs, through endless, empty corridors to the front of the building. There he opened a door and I entered a spacious office room where five young men in civilian clothes were waiting for me. One of them, a lanky man in his early thirties, stood behind his desk; the rest were in the far end of the room, staring at me with apparent curiosity.

"Mr. Marton, at last! For years I have been waiting for you," the man behind the desk said. The first thing I noticed was the sickly yellowish color of his skin. His name was Captain Zoltán Babics.

When my first interrogation ended, it was already day and I had been accused of being "the" master spy of the United States. Yet that broad generality was the only thing they accused me of.

The victim of a Communist secret police organization is never told what the specific charges against him are. He is expected to confess "voluntarily." I was told the first night that I was a spy and traitor and that my profession as a newspaperman was only a flimsy cover for my real occupation. But that was all. I was supposed to furnish them with the evidence.

My first three months in Fö utca were rough. Babics was my main tormentor, but frequently he was assisted by others, and Colonel Balázsi, head of the investigative branch, also participated in the grilling. They usually left me alone during the night, but one evening, around ten o'clock, I was escorted to

Balázsi's office. There was another man sitting in the back of the darkly cavernous room. The single glaring light on Balázsi's enormous desk was turned toward my face so that I could hardly see the colonel or the other man who was completely shrouded in darkness.

Balázsi, a former butcher, a rude, pompous, and short bundle of muscles, asked some general questions without inquiring into specifics, so it was obvious to me that the whole performance was arranged for the benefit of the third man in the room, to introduce me to him in this peculiar way. I did not know, of course, who this man was, and in that period of my life it did not really matter. Only much later, after my release, did I find out that the silent man in the corner was Colonel Ivancov, the "special envoy" of Moscow's secret police, sent to Budapest to stage the planned show trial of the Martons.

The daily séances with Babics lasted virtually from morning till evening, with only one brief interruption for lunch, and often not even for that. Babics, it soon became clear, had to deliver me and my confessions by a certain date in May. He increased the pressure as the deadline approached, making dark hints that he would get what he wanted one way or another, including my wife's arrest if I continued to refuse cooperation. Babics was an experienced interrogator and his name, as I was told in 1957, was well known to the American security personnel at the embassy in Vienna. The men who occasionally assisted him were the same tough brutes who enjoyed inflicting physical terror in the Stalinist times. There was little of this when I was an inmate of Fö utca, yet there should be no mistake: they can break a man, and after three months I was close to breaking down, too. One example will perhaps illustrate what I mean.

I was afraid only of being forced into incriminating others, my nonexistent "accomplices," since every spy must have a spy ring, as I was told every other day. One morning Colonel Balázsi came into Babics's office, together with another of his men, an extremely rude major who found special satisfaction in ordering me to stand face to the wall while shouting obscenities into my ears. Balázsi started the battle.

"Tell us how you tried to enlist one of our leading economists," he began. I was really puzzled. Firstly, I did not know any economists, leading or not. True, I had gotten my Ph.D. in economics some twenty years earlier but since then I had had no contact with the academic world. Furthermore, I had never enlisted anyone, I explained.

A whole day was spent with this issue, with the three shouting together or taking turns, ordering me to sit or to stand at the wall. I first requested, then asked, and finally pleaded with them to give me a clue, to lead me, as they must have known what they had in mind and I did not. Finally, after eight hours without interruption and without lunch for me, while the three took turns in munching what their secretaries brought in, Balázsi gave me the clue: a name. Then I remembered.

At the university there had been a professor's assistant, a bright young economist. We knew each other because I read several papers on international economic problems at a seminar his professor held. After I got my diploma in the mid-1930's I did not see him again. Many years later, in the early 1950's, he stopped me on the street and I hardly recognized him. This always impeccably dressed man was shabby, he badly needed a dentist, and my first impulse was to buy him a meal. I was in a hurry and he was obviously not, so I asked him to accompany me. While we walked he told me briefly his sad story: he had left the university before the war to accept a high post in an industrial enterprise, and became what in the United States would be a vice president. When the Communists nationalized industry, he lost his job because, as he said, he was unwilling to compromise and to work for them. I felt sorry for him and asked what I could do. He said he did not need money but a job. I told him that being an outcast myself I knew of no jobs, but suggested that maybe one of the Western legations in Budapest could use a man with his background and knowledge of several languages. I told him that I did not know of any vacancies, but he should inquire and if one of them was interested in him — all legations had Hungarian translators and other clerical personnel — I would gladly put in a word for him. With this we parted and I never heard from him again.

So this was my role in "enlisting a noted economist into my spy ring," and three high-priced secret police officers spent a whole day grilling me about this ridiculous episode. How did they know about it? The answer is simple. They had either followed us (they usually shadowed me) and picked up the wretched man afterwards, or he was one of their agents provocateurs, probably forced to play this unsavory role.

It is ridiculous in retrospect; then it was not. When finally, late in the evening, without lunch or dinner, I was sent back to my cell, my body was covered with sweat and I fell on my bunk, completely exhausted, into a dreamless sleep. But they got their "confession." Yes, I talked to this man, who was not a "noted economist" but an economist of some sort, and I advised him to seek employment at one of the Western legations if, as he said, it was impossible for him to work "for them." The confession did not do them any good; it was not used against me at my trial.

There were sometimes, very rarely, more amusing episodes. One of the plainclothesmen who had arrested me frequently attended my interrogations during the early period. His name was Lieutenant Budai, or so he was called by Babics, and he looked strikingly different from the others.

The average Communist secret police officer rarely dons his Russian-style uniform. He usually wears the most inconspicuous civilian clothes and is anxious to look exactly like any other petty bourgeois. Budai certainly did not look like one. The tall young man with a crew cut looked exactly like an American college football player used to look. His six-foot-five frame was tucked into an American-style overcoat and he wore a multicolored shawl around his neck. He was, I learned much later, in counterespionage, and his job was watching the United States and British legations in Budapest, to make contacts with diplomats, plant microphones in their homes, and force their maids to spy on them.

In the early 1960's, when I was already in Washington, there were sensational reports in Swedish newspapers about the training of agents in the Soviet Union — how they are kept in an artificial little town near Winniza in the Ukraine, built exactly like Middletown, U.S.A. There they live for years the lives of Americans, speak only English, talk baseball, eat and drink as the average American does. I do not know whether such a town exists in Russia, but Budai certainly looked like the product of such a special institution.

Budai did not participate in the questioning, but watched. One afternoon when Babics was urgently summoned to Colonel Balázsi, we were left alone. The young man was pacing up and down the room, and when the silence became awkward, he started to talk — in English, with an unmistakable Midwestern drawl. What he said was unimportant, he parroted the same trite arguments I had heard so often, that I was doubtless a spy who became an easy prey of the CIA because I was blindly devoted to everything the West produces, ranging from democracy to loafers. By then I had gotten used to not listening. Budai did not ask questions, nor was he threatening; it was obvious that he just wanted to kill time and found nothing else to talk about. But while he delivered his sermon, I could not restrain a smile. Reprimanding me for preferring Western products, Budai automatically fumbled in his pocket, took out a pack of American cigarettes and lit one with an unmistakably U.S.-made lighter.

The whole scene was unrealistic. Here was a young man who dressed, talked, and behaved like an average American, smoked American cigarettes — something no ordinary Hungarian could afford — in a room decorated with the picture of

Dzerzhinski. Despite my misery, I had to smile, and Budai, I am sure, was smart enough to recognize the irony of the situation. I never saw him again.

This, however, was probably the only time I had reason to smile. The closer we came to May, the stronger the pressure became. The few hours I was left alone in my cell did not help and I was driven every day closer to desperation. The few "privileges" of a prisoner are really rewards for good behavior, meaning cooperation and confession. They include permission to get books from the prison library, a daily ration of ten Kossuth cigarettes, the cheapest brand that existed in Hungary, and better-quality food. At the time I had none of them, but curiously, I missed only the books. Though I was a heavy cigarette and pipe smoker, it did not bother me that I had none in this period. Babics was a chain smoker and once, during an exceptionally heated argument, he threw his pack of cigarettes in front of me in a crude gesture to have one and calm down. I threw the pack right back to him without taking one, which obviously surprised him.

Other inmates were less lucky. I was usually in solitary, which Babics considered a punishment; I did not enlighten him that I preferred to be alone, but for short periods I had cellmates. Some of these temporary partners suffered immensely, dreaming and talking about women and wine, a meal served on a plate, and a good cigar. I was lucky, I had no such desires.

During the brief hours when I was left alone in my cell between interrogations, I paced up and down trying to find the missing answers to the tormenting questions: what do they want? why now, two years after Stalin's death? I thought there must have been a political motive behind my arrest and then, suddenly, I remembered the cartoon in *Szabad Száj*, and Rákosi's spectacular comeback in Debrecen.

Nagy must have been ousted, I speculated. He is probably in this building, being prepared for trial. If the pattern of the late 1940's still held good, there would be a list of charges against him, one of them perhaps that he was a CIA agent. This would explain why I was there: they needed somebody with known American connections to testify that Nagy was an American spy.

That was not the sick imagination of a man grilled to exhaustion. Such things have happened before. For instance, there were dozens of witnesses at László Rajk's anti-Tito show trial in 1949, appearing before the court as seemingly free people to incriminate the defendant with their testimony. The next day the Hungarian papers would report that this or that witness confirmed that Rajk had met secretly with Rankovic, Tito's minister of the interior, plotting Rákosi's overthrow. The innocent reader would never suspect that the "witness" was a prisoner himself, to be tried subsequently in a secret trial.

The longer I thought, the more logical this scheme appeared to me. It was around the end of April 1955 and by then I was in bad shape. The expert team, headed by Captain Babics, was close to breaking me and after two months I would have gladly given them whatever confession they wanted if it would have incriminated only me and nobody else. There comes a point in a prisoner's life when all he wants is peace, even if it is the peace of the grave, and I had reached that point by then. One day Babics, screaming as he frequently did, accused me of having been disrespectful to Rákosi, "the greatest Hungarian of all time," when I tried to interview him in Debrecen. I thought that my feverish speculation about Nagy was correct and decided to try it out.

The same night I volunteered to make a confession. Babics took a piece of paper and I started to dictate. I told him a fantastic story about my intimate connections with Nagy, how I was in effect a liaison between him and the American legation. I kept it in generalities and the captain did not ask for specifics. He jotted down every word I said and dismissed me around midnight without commenting on my performance. Back in my cell I tossed around pondering on what this gamble would produce. It had already produced one precious thing, some quiet hours at the interrogation, instead of the usual screams.

The next morning Babics was unusually quiet. "This of yesterday," he said, pointing at my testimony, "was a lie from the first word to the last. Why did you do it?"

"Because you would not tell me what you want. You won't even tell me the charges against me! If this is not what you want, then tell me what is! Of course it is an absurd lie, but I will go on lying and then revoke my confession in court, which you won't like, if you don't tell me what you are accusing me of." By then it was my turn to shout, with some effect. Babics looked at me with curious eyes but did not respond. For several days I was ignored.

My "logic," of course, was all wrong. Nagy was not under arrest. Shortly after Malenkov was ousted in Moscow, early in March 1955, the Central Committee of the Hungarian Communist party severely censured Nagy, then still prime minister, for having permitted "rightist deviations." A month later, at another session, he was stripped of his membership in the Central Committee and in the Politbureau, and simultaneously discharged by Parliament from the premiership. His "new course" had come to a sudden end, but he was not in jail, and for Rákosi this was a fateful mistake.

Captain Babics and his team were determined to break me and they made sinister hints that by May 1955 my life would be even more miserable than it was if I continued my stubborn resistance. Why the May deadline, I did not know then.

From the very beginning of my daily séances with Babics, I had the feeling the secret police knew more than it should have known about what Ilona and I had discussed with our American friends at the legation. I was not too surprised, but the extent of their knowledge was greater than I could explain to myself. During our years as American correspondents in Budapest, we always had several friends among Western diplomats.

We were invited to their homes and they came to ours, and once a week, on Tuesday mornings, there was a regular get-together with the American minister at the legation.

These regular meetings were proposed by Alexander Kendrick of CBS when Robert Vogeler, the American businessman, was arrested and tried in Hungary. Kendrick suggested that the minister, Nathaniel P. Davis, should receive Western correspondents regularly, and these Tuesday meetings continued when the number of foreign newsmen dwindled to a handful. There was nothing clandestine in what we discussed at the legation or in private homes. It was the usual give-and-take between newsmen and diplomats. There was always some talk about what was happening in Hungary or what the government in Washington believed about developments behind the Iron Curtain. Everybody familiar with American diplomats knows how careful they are when talking to reporters and my American friends in Budapest were no exception. They sometimes went overboard, which I considered slightly ridiculous, when for instance they insisted that whenever we "talked shop" we should walk in the gardens around their homes, even in ankle-deep snow in wintertime, hoping that there were no microphones hidden in trees. It was no secret, though they rarely talked about it, that their homes were "bugged," and the most annoying — though also hilarious — case was when a microphone was found carefully planted in an electric fixture in the bedroom of a newly wed American diplomat.

I had no doubt that microphones were also planted in the legation. There were no "secure rooms" in those times in the embassies (there are now everywhere, not only in Communist capitals), but I was not worried in the least because, so I thought, there was nothing in what I said or what was told to me that anybody, even a Communist, could have interpreted as espionage. I was obviously wrong.

Robin Hankey, now Lord Hankey and retired, the British minister to Budapest during the dark period of Stalinism, used to switch on a decrepit radio on his desk on the few occasions I visited him. The little monster produced nothing but noise, and Hankey, one of the most able diplomats I have ever met, had a good laugh when I did not conceal my annoyance, protesting that I could not hear my own voice, much less his, under these circumstances. With the radio blaring, the microphones were useless, or so Hankey believed.

The Communists apparently did not need planted microphones to listen in. Once they kidnapped my former secretary and released her only after she signed a "contract" to spy on me. One of her instructions was to talk to me close to the telephone which obviously served as a microphone even with its receiver lying quietly in its cradle. The poor girl, when they let her go, came to me immediately and confessed in tears what she was forced to do. I was not surprised and consoled her. The whole affair was stupid, I thought. To believe that I, the "master spy" in their judgment, would reveal any secrets in a friendly chat with my former secretary showed the childish imagination of the secret police. They asked more of her. She was ordered to submit regular written reports about our conversations, which she was to direct in such a way that I would talk about my views on Hungarian politics. The game had to be played according to their rules, so for about a year I diligently wrote the girl's reports for the secret police each week, disclosing faithfully my views, which were known to them anyway from my news dispatches. The whole thing was too clumsy and after a year or so they cut off connections with the girl. She was, however, arrested soon after I was and kept in the same prison for several months, until they let her go without trial.

My former secretary was of course not the only "spy" forced by the secret police to work for them and to report on the Martons. Each of our maids was approached by the boys of Fö utca, but each of them, one sooner, the other later, broke down and told us what they were forced to do. Living in a

Communist country one must get accustomed to such things and good maids were rare treasures, so Ilona did her best to assure them that we did not care as long as we knew what they were doing. Still, one of them, a dear peasant woman, said she could not do it and would rather return to her village. The way the plainclothesmen from Fö utca approached our maids revealed how self-deceptive the Communist mentality was. My former secretary, a girl with a "bourgeois" background, had to be kidnapped and threatened, but the maids were "proletarians," so obviously they hated their capitalist exploiters — at least this was how things should be, they were told. The Martons were enemies of the dictatorship of the proletariat — what they were — consequently it was the patriotic duty of their employees to spy on them. It is still hard for me to believe that at least the more intelligent secret police officers did not know the fallacy of this argument. If they did not know then, they must have learned in 1956 that the sympathy of the proletariat was not on their side.

As I said, right from the beginning I had the strange feeling that Babics knew more about what was going on inside the American legation than he should have, and that his knowledge went beyond what he could have learned by listening in with the help of planted microphones.

What Babics knew did not compromise me, according to Western standards, but according to the Communist standpoint virtually every word exchanged with the "enemy" was espionage. Major Gerö, Ilona's interrogator, took the trouble to explain the Communist philosophy to her. A mosaic, he said, consists of many small pieces. If one little piece is missing, the whole picture is worthless. Her "crime," however ridiculous it sounds, was to have provided the "enemy" with such small pieces. One example, and that was a serious charge against her, was that she talked about food prices in the market as any good housewife would. Sure, Gerö admitted, the American diplomat's wife could have found out how the price of eggs fluctuated — there was nothing that could have prevented her — but to tell her or her husband was "aiding the enemy," a capital crime.

The charges against me were slightly more serious, though in retrospect some of them were ridiculous, too. Time and again the Communist papers in Hungary published colorful reports about the plight of Negroes in the United States, trying to make the reader believe that the Negro in America was still a slave, wearing shackles. Knowing my countrymen I was not bothered; nobody would believe such nonsense anyway, but the Americans at the legation were slightly annoyed. There is nothing simpler than to counterbalance this clumsy propaganda, I told Christian Ravndal at one of the Tuesday sessions. There are Negro diplomats in the foreign service: let the State Department assign one to Budapest. Ravndal liked the idea and asked whether he could forward this recommendation to Washington, mentioning that it came from me. I had no objection. The story would not be complete without telling how disappointed I was when, some months later, the Negro diplomat arrived. I was expecting a six-foot-five pitch-dark giant, preferably with a red Cadillac convertible, but Rupert Lloyd, whom I learned to respect as a skilled diplomat and highly cultured man, was five foot five, café au lait, and, to add insult to injury, he drove a small Simca car which he brought from Paris, his previous post.

Well, Babics knew about my advice and I readily confessed that the charge was true, after two days of shouting, threats, and grilling. The Communist interrogation technique still does not make sense to me. Instead of confronting me with the evidence — in this case telling me "we know that you advised the Americans to bring a Negro diplomat to Budapest to give the lie to our newspapers," in which case we could have disposed of the charge amicably in five minutes — the question was, "Tell us, what defamatory advice did you give the Americans?" Even if I had wanted to cooperate, which I did not, I could not associate the question with this minor incident which had happened many years earlier, and we battled for two days, until Babics lost his temper — and he made a major mistake.

From the many thick folders in his safe which obviously contained all the compromising "evidence" against me, Babics produced a sheet of paper. "On June 16," he said, "the legation sent a report to Washington. It was signed, in the minister's absence, by the chargé and the political officer" — and he mentioned their names — "submitting your recommendation. You still pretend not to know what advice you gave?" The date did not mean anything to me and I still did not know what Babics was talking about, but suddenly I became alert.

Back in my cell that night I tried to think hard. It was entirely possible that Babics was bluffing, that he wanted to impress me with his vast knowledge of the legation reports. On the other hand, there might have been a report on that day, and if there was then there must be a serious leak in the legation, because no microphone could have supplied that information to the secret police. I decided that if I ever came out alive, and my chances then were rather slim, the legation must investigate this possible leak.

I did not forget my decision. After my release I immediately shared my suspicion with Tom Rogers, my best American friend at the legation and, incidentally, one of the signatories of the alleged report. Then came the revolution and both Tom and I had other, more important things to worry about. But in Vienna, in January 1957, when I was debriefed at the embassy, I told the security officers to concentrate on this alleged June 16 report. I repeated that I still did not know whether Babics knew something or whether he was bluffing.

In Vienna, where we spent nearly three happy months — I was working in the AP office — I again forgot the incident. The night we left Vienna (in a car Ambassador Llewellyn Thompson placed at our disposal) to catch a plane in Munich for New York, many old and newly acquired friends came to see us off. One of them was Keirn Brown, head of security at the embassy.

"By the way," he said, as he took leave of us in front of our hotel, "there was such a report on that day, and there was a leak." I had no time to ask questions, the car was ready to leave and, I assumed, Brown would not have answered them anyway. But on the long flight from Munich to New York, approaching the Promised Land which was to become my country, I felt depressed. Maybe I was naive — as an experienced newspaperman should not be — but until then I never thought that somebody working at an American mission overseas could have betrayed to the Communists what was said in confidence in the legation.

The story is almost always surprisingly the same. The foreigner has an affair with a local woman who is either on the payroll of the secret police or was pressed into serving it. Then they are photographed in bed, through a one-way mirror, as happened in the case of the man who betrayed me, and the foreigner is blackmailed. There is no risk for the secret police; it either works or it does not. Their man either cooperates, or he refuses, goes to his superior, tells him that he is in trouble, and is shipped home in twenty-four hours, probably with only a bad mark on his record.

This simple scheme is as old as diplomatic relations with Communist countries, yet sometimes it works. Everybody sent to a post at an American diplomatic mission behind the Iron Curtain is thoroughly briefed about the possibility and warned. He is instructed to report immediately if he is blackmailed. And yet, however incredible, it happens time and again that some weakling chooses treason when he clearly has an honorable alternative.

The picture would not be complete without adding that the man who played this despicable role in my case was neither a foreign service officer nor a local Hungarian employee of the legation in Budapest.

Anybody under constant pressure must become irrational at times and suicide attempts in Fö utca were not uncommon, though they rarely succeeded. A dead man was of no use to the secret police because a dead man could not confess. In 1956, when I was over the worst, I was surprised one day when instead of the usual single jailer, two came to escort me to Major Kretsmer and both gripped my arms firmly while we walked through the endless corridors and stairs to his office. This was unusual because by that time I was a veteran known to all the jailers and they permitted me to walk in front of them on such occasions. I was curious and asked Kretsmer what the reason for this unusual attention was. It turned out that somebody, while being escorted to interrogation, had thrown himself headlong down the stairs in a desperate attempt to kill himself.

Every precaution was made to thwart such an attempt. The new prisoner had to undress completely and nothing was left in his pockets, not even a handkerchief. In addition his necktie, shoelaces, suspenders, and belt were taken away and his towel was hung on a nail outside his cell. The only cutlery he got was a soft-metal spoon and if he could not eat the little meat he was given without a knife, that was his problem.

Yet, despite every precaution, some tried, and so did I, twice. The first was a clumsy, desperate effort, during the period of utmost pressure. One evening, after an unusually long and stormy day with Babics, I staggered back to my cell. It was a cold night and sticking my hands, covered with cold sweat, into my pockets, I pricked my fingers on something. It was a small pin. How it got into my pocket, and why I discovered it only then, I could not explain.

That night on my bunk I tried to pierce the vein on my left wrist. It was, of course, a hopeless effort. The pin was too small. I could not hold it firmly between my fingers. I tried it again and again, always watching the Judas on the door for the jailer who made his rounds on the corridor. I struggled for an hour, then I gave up.

But I did not give up the idea. Suicide, according to psychologists, is either an escape or intended as a punishment for those who are left behind. In my case it would have been both. I wanted to escape because I was dead tired and endless sleep was all I desired. I was ready to confess to everything involving myself, but refused day after day to incriminate anybody else, and by then it was Babics's primary aim to "unmask the spy ring" which, he insisted, worked under my command. And obviously I wanted to punish Babics and his comrades. I vividly imagined how they would curse finding me dead before I had complied with the scenario they had written for me.

The needle did not work, but something else could. The prisoner of the secret police is a valuable asset and therefore he must be kept alive and reasonably healthy. Fö utca had a physician and an unusual supply of medicines, including things not then available in the state-run pharmacies. One day I asked for the doctor and when he came I complained about being nervous. He prescribed two tablets daily of Sevenal, a medium-strong sedative.

Every morning a medical corps subaltern made his rounds along the corridors carrying a large tray suspended from his neck with all the medicines the doctor had prescribed and with a list showing who should receive what. The procedure was that the jailer opened the little window on the door, the prisoner stood in front of it, the man with the tray handed him the medicine, the jailer gave him a cup of water, and the prisoner had to swallow the medicine right there, opening his mouth and showing his hands afterwards to prove that he had done so. Well, I had not. It was an easy trick, and it worked for months. I took the two pills in my left hand and pretended to throw them immediately into my mouth, grabbing the tin cup with my right. But I kept the pills in my left hand, and while drinking from the cup, I quickly pushed the pills into the pocket of my overcoat — showing immediately, as required, that my hands were empty and opening my mouth for inspection.

For storage I tore a little hole in the pocket of my overcoat and collected the pills in the lining. Though I had never taken sedatives before, I had a notion that a dose of about a hundred would be enough, and that meant fifty days of deceiving. I had about eighty of the small pills when Kretsmer took over my case. The pressure ceased immediately, but I remained suspicious. This, I thought, might be just one of their tricks, the well-known hot-and-cold-water treatment, and Babics or one of the brutes might come back one day. I decided to continue my collection, but a few days later I was found out.

One morning there was an unusual search of the cells. Whether it was routine or whether they had a special reason, I did not know. I was ordered to leave my cell, stand in the corridor wearing only my prison-supplied underwear, with one jailer guarding me, while two others ransacked the cell. It was no problem; there was nothing in it, just the two bunks cemented to the floor, with one coarse blanket each, and my suit and overcoat. When they left, taking my overcoat, I knew they had found the pills.

An hour later I was taken to Kretsmer. The pills were on his desk in a neat heap. I told him why I did it and why I had not discontinued my collection. He made no fuss about it and the case was closed.

By then I was living on easy street. The change came suddenly one day around noon. At that time — it must have been about mid-May 1955 — for a number of days a man attended my sessions with Babics. He was slightly built, unassuming, with thin reddish hair. He usually came in when my interrogation was under way and I knew his rank only because when he entered, Babics, a captain, sprang to his feet and greeted him in true military fashion as "Comrade Major."

Unlike the others, however, the major did not take an active part in the grilling, but sat for hours somewhere in the corner behind me. The going got rougher and rougher and I really did not care much about this silent witness.

One day I thought I was coming to the end of my wits. By then, for weeks Babics had been hammering on the question of my "accomplices." He wanted names, many names, and dismissed my suggestion that yes, I was a most important spy, but a lone wolf. Then, on that day, I had a desperate idea which might give me some badly needed time to regain my composure. What if I incriminated someone who was dead?

About a year before my arrest, Ilona and I gave a dinner in honor of an American couple, reassigned from the Budapest legation to Washington. We had invited three couples, two American and one British — all three men were diplomats — and three attractive young Hungarian intellectuals who spoke faultless English. This was the year of Imre Nagy, when things appeared to be so incomparably easier and when, I thought, it was harmless to bring Western diplomats together with a few Hungarians. One of them was a Count Eszterházy, a scholarly young man who was then making a living by working as a translator. Shortly after our dinner Menyhért Eszterházy was stricken with polio and died.

That day in Babics's room, for the first time in my life I was afraid I was going to faint and fall off the chair I was sitting on. I grasped the edge of the chair with both hands and tried not to listen to the earsplitting noise that came from Babics's direction. It was of no avail. I saw red rings dancing in the air and felt dizzy. I knew I was defeated.

"All right," I heard my almost unrecognizable, hoarse voice, interrupting the flood of abuse which came from Babics's mouth. "I did enlist someone, Menyhért Eszterházy . . ." Suddenly there was dead silence in the room. Babics looked at me with his large eyes — their whites, I remember, were always sickly yellowish — and then quickly grasped his pen. Finally he had what he wanted, a confession on the spy ring. Whether he was aware that Eszterházy was dead and out of his reach, I did not know. But the minute I made my "confession" I regretted it. It was not only the weakness of flesh and nerves, giving in to terror to gain some relatively peaceful hours, even days. Babics wanted a spy ring, he would not be satisfied with one name, and if he did not know that Eszterházy was dead, he soon would. Then he would press for other names. What could I invent the next time?

When Babics started to write, I shrugged in desperation and my aching head was hanging deep on my chest. Then suddenly I heard a quiet voice from the back of the room: "Comrade Captain, I want to talk to you . . ." I looked back — something I was not supposed to do. The major was standing there, ignoring me but looking at Babics. The captain, seemingly surprised, looked up too.

"But Comrade Major," he said, "he just started to make his confession."

"Captain, I said I want to talk to you," came the reply. The voice was still composed, but there was the tone of authority in it. It was Babics's turn to shrug. He picked up the telephone and called for the jailer. Until the subaltern entered to take me back to my cell, no word was spoken.

Back in my cell I left my lunch untouched. Defying the regulations that no prisoner can lie down on his bunk during the day, I threw myself on the old, smelly blanket. My head was empty and I tried not to think. Strangely, the jailers left me alone, though they must have seen through the Judas that I was violating the rules.

A few hours later they came for me again. I was escorted back to Babics's room. Despite my miserable condition, I observed one change already when I passed through the little room which led to the captain's office. The girl secretary was not the same. Inside the room, behind Babics's desk, the slightly built man with the thinning red hair was standing.

"My name is Major Kretsmer, I have taken over your case," he said, and motioned me to sit down. Before him, on the desk, were dozens of folders, my so-called confessions, the yield of about three months. "These," he said, pointing at the folders, "these are lies, aren't they?"

"They are," I acknowledged, and my voice was as calm as his. He nodded.

"We will start from scratch. I am interested only in the truth, not in lies," Kretsmer said, and pushed aside the folders.

I do not know and never will know whether all this was prearranged, whether Babics's surprise was genuine. But this, at that moment, was irrelevant. What counted was that the room was quiet, that the man on the other side of the desk talked in low tones, almost casually.

"This nursery tale about Eszterházy . . . you invented that, didn't you?" he asked. I nodded, and he took his pen, crossing over the page on which a few hours earlier Babics jotted down the first words of my confession. The second, long, but peaceful phase of my interrogation started.

The prisoner in an American jail is indeed "behind bars"; he can see what is going on outside his cell. The prisoner in Fö utca is behind an iron door and he can never see the other inmates unless he gets a cellmate, usually a stool pigeon. The result is that much like a blind man, the prisoner develops an extraordinary sense of hearing, grows a sixth sense to interpret the noises. For a brief period there was somebody in the cell next to mine for whom the jailer came twice a day, often during the night. There were no words exchanged on such occasions; the jailer motioned and the prisoner followed him. Yet on the second day I had the feeling I knew who the man was because of the unusual shuffling gait which I heard during the brief seconds when he passed my cell. I racked my brains to remember where I had heard this hesitant step before. And then suddenly I remembered: a Hungarian employee of the American legation, a quiet, scholarly man, who is now, as far as I know, a librarian at one of the American universities. This must be K., I thought, though he was free and working at the legation when I was arrested. But I could not be mistaken. Much later, shortly before my release, I suggested to Major Kretsmer that we prisoners probably know more than we should and told him that I had recognized K.'s particular gait and knew that at some point he was kept in a cell next to mine. The major acknowledged that I was right.

It was much easier to notice extraordinary preparations on the third-floor corridor of Fö utca than to recognize K.'s shuffling steps. One evening, after the hours of interrogation, there was unusual coming and going, opening and closing of cell doors. This always meant some reshuffling of men, but it was on a large scale this time. I was left alone, however, in my cell at the end of the corridor. The next morning, let out to fetch my usual basin of water, I looked around hastily.

Our corridor was obviously reserved for important prisoners because until the day before almost all were in solitary, meaning that there was only one towel and one cup outside each door. But not so this morning. Most of the towels and cups were paired and there were neither towels nor cups by the doors of at least half of the cells. The inference was obvious: prisoners were being doubled up to provide vacant cells for a large group of new inmates. This meant that an important political plot had been discovered and a mass arrest was to be expected soon. That happened early in 1956 and I had, of course, no basis to speculate who my new colleagues on corridor three were to be. Only after my release, weeks after Rákosi's final downfall, was I told that he had been preparing to arrest four hundred writers, journalists, and other rebellious intellectuals to nip in the bud the ferment which that fall led to the revolution. But it had been too late. Not even Rákosi was able to afford such a Stalinist move so late in the game, after Stalinism had been renounced by his master in Moscow.

Good hearing, or this sixth sense, had also brought me into contact with my wife in prison. For months after my arrest I had been interested only in one thing: to keep her out of this sad business. Captain Babics tried every trick in the book to make me incriminate her, to admit that she had been my partner in my nefarious espionage activities. Were we not in the same profession, didn't we visit the American legation together, didn't we entertain other spies disguised as American, British, and other Western diplomats? Babics once tried a cheap trick. For reasons I was not familiar with, the prisoner testifies orally and the interrogator makes his notes in longhand; then the typewritten testimony is ready next morning for the prisoner to read and to sign every page.

The testimonies, so-called, rarely reflected the prisoner's thoughts, nor even his words. At the beginning I protested against this practice, declined to sign one testimony after the other and was sometimes permitted to make minor changes. Later, however, I lost interest. The whole thing became a Grand Guignol, terror mixed with comedy. What I had actually said bore no relation to the contents of the pile of papers neatly typed and prepared for my signature. Yet my eyes, trained to discover errors in galley proofs, could not avoid a gross misrepresentation of my words however bored and uninterested I had become. And so one morning I found that when Babics had written down that I had confessed to having done this or that, he added to the first person singular confession the words ". . . and my wife."

It was my turn to scream. "How dare you put words in my mouth!" I shouted and threw the bundle of papers onto his desk. Babics, caught red-handed in cheating, had obviously expected such an outburst, but he remained calm.

"All right, take it out," he snapped, and I struck out the words "and my wife," writing on the margin of the paper: "Untrue! I did not say this."

Often they threatened to arrest Ilona too, if I continued to insist that I was a reporter and not a spy. I told them I did not believe them, that even they would not dare to arrest a woman who was a mother with two small children to look after. I told them to leave her alone, that I was willing to admit I was a spy if only they would tell me what I had done as a spy — for whom was I spying? Derisive laughter was the only answer.

Some weeks after Major Kretsmer took over my case from Captain Babics and there was no longer pressure on me to confess to crimes I had not committed, there was a bolt from the blue. One morning, going through the daily opening routine of reading my testimony of the previous day, I found a page among the others which obviously did not belong there. I glanced at the bottom: it was signed by Ilona.

For the first time in those months of misery I broke down and cried like a child. "Why did you do it? Why did you do it?" were the only words I could mumble. Kretsmer was embarrassed. "We had to," he said quietly. The major acknowledged that he had slipped the page purposely among the transcript of my testimony because he had been ordered to inform me about Ilona's arrest and, he admitted, did not know how to do it. Kretsmer tried to console me. Ilona was in great spirits, she was being interrogated by a Major Gerö, a good friend of Kretsmer's whom I knew, too, because he used to come in and watch me during my interrogation. She was kept in a corridor reserved for women prisoners where the jailers were women, too. The children were all right, taken care of by friends. I could hardly hear what he said.

Many months later, sitting on my bunk during the quiet hours between reveille at six and breakfast around eight, I thought I heard a familiar cough, Ilona's. If my ears were not deceiving me that could only mean that she had been removed from the women's ward and was now here, somewhere on the same corridor. Staring at the door I listened and heard the familiar cough again. Then I started to cough, and there was an answer. From then on, every morning and every evening before the nine o'clock "taps," we communicated by coughing to each other.

I don't know whether love and affection can be expressed in coughs. We tried, and we understood the message.

3

General Péter of the AVH

For months before Stalin's death in 1953 Hungarians sensed that something sinister was going on in Moscow. News dispatches from the Russian capital published in the Hungarian newspapers were full of the usual trite stuff about new heroes of production or some kind of a new "victory" over the dark forces of imperialism. They revealed nothing.

But even a Communist party hack is human, and in those months before Stalin died, few Hungarian Communist officials could conceal that they were worried: the instructions from Moscow were not as clear as they used to be, which meant to them that something unusual was going on in the capital of world Communism. Then came the strange news about the doctors' plot, Stalin's insane charge against a group of Jewish physicians who were accused of having murdered prominent Communists. The leaders of the Hungarian party were now obviously ill at ease because they too were Jews, though all of them were atheists.

Mátyás Rákosi, Hungary's undisputed Communist boss, reacted swiftly. This cunning man of exceptional intelligence and a remarkable ability for survival always knew how to please his aging master in the Kremlin. In January 1953, shortly after the charges were made against the doctors in Moscow, General Gábor Péter and the top-ranking officers of the Hungarian secret police were arrested. The great majority of them were Jewish. The same day Lajos Stöckler, president of the Jewish community of Budapest, disappeared. Rákosi had interpreted the news from Moscow correctly. Anti-Semitism was again the order of the day and Hungary could not lag behind its masters in "vigilance" — one of the favorite words in the Communist vocabulary — against Zionism. Rákosi, Ernö Gerö, Mihály Farkas, and József Révai, the quadrumvirate of the Hungarian party, did not wait to be sacrificed on the altar of Stalin's senility. They chose others of lesser rank to play the involuntary role of sacrificial lamb.

Two years later, in the summer of 1955, I heard the voice of General Péter, shrieking like a wounded animal. The sound still haunts me.

I stared at the solid iron door of my cell. After six months of silence this was the first time I had heard the voice of another prisoner. I jumped to my feet not believing my ears: somebody was daring to break the rules. He was screaming desperately: "You are driving me crazy. . . . What do you want? This has been going on now for a week. . . . It's enough . . . it's enough!"

The place was the Fö utca prison of the secret police in Budapest. Passersby only see a block-long red brick building shaped like a U. Inside, in the courtyard, stands the grim prison. Like all other secret police institutions behind the Iron Curtain, Fö utca copied its operations from Moscow's ill-famed Lubianka. The main building facing the street housed hundreds of offices for interrogators, prosecutors, and judges, all of them on the payroll of the secret police, and several courtrooms. The Soviet officers of the MVD (Ministerstvo Vnutrykh Del, the ministry of internal affairs) assigned to Budapest also had their offices there.

Inside the prison, regulations were strict and the furnishings meager. Each cell was outfitted with two wooden bunks and nothing else. The bedding consisted of a dirty, coarse, bad-smelling blanket. A gray daylight filtered faintly through the tiny window just below the ceiling, with iron bars on the outside and a wire screen on the inside. Once a day, and only once, the prisoner was let out of his cell to go to the washroom. He needed no orders. He picked up his towel hanging on a nail outside his door, rushed to the washroom and rushed back with water in an aluminum washbowl. He had to rush because not until he was safely locked back in would the prisoner of the next cell be let out.

No one had a name, only a number, the number of his cell. The jailers spoke only the minimum of words, and those in a whisper. The floors were covered with rubber. The guards walked through the corridors in felt boots.

The blanket of silence was a Soviet idea too, based on the theories, as it was explained to me, of the great physiologist Ivan Pavlov. Prisoners, grilled every day for long hours, should not be distracted by any sound between interrogations as this helps them to "concentrate on their crimes."

I had been an inmate of Fö utca for about six months when I was unceremoniously booted out of my cell. Moving from one cell to another was no problem: I had nothing with me, not even a handkerchief or a toothbrush, no stockings on my feet and of course no shoelaces. Stockings and handkerchiefs were considered dangerous because the prisoner could use them to commit suicide, though I could not understand how, as there was nothing on the walls by which one could have hanged one-self.

The cell which I was ordered to evacuate was on one end of the U-shaped corridor. I was led to the other end of the U to my new cell, which was opposite the one I had left. The next morning when I was let out to fetch water from the bathroom next to my former cell, I saw a guard in front of the one I had left the day before, peering through the Judas. That morning I thought the guard was only curious. But whenever I left my cell during the daily water-fetching ceremony, or whenever I was escorted to the interrogator, I saw a guard doing the same: watching whoever was inside through the peepholes. One day I was amused to see on this special duty an extremely short jailer who had to stand on a footstool.

For a week I wondered who this man could be. I knew he must be "important." The jailers who watched him were obviously under orders to report everything they observed. They made notes and kept their diary on a chair placed between the door of the cell of their man and the door of the washroom. One morning coming from the washroom I pretended to be clumsy and put down my bowl of water to close the door behind me. Picking up the bowl I took a furtive glance at the open notebook.

"7 A.M.: the prisoner shook his head," the last entry said.

Then one morning came the desperate scream, and two days later in the evening the mysterious man introduced himself. His shouts must have pierced the stillness through all seven floors of the silent prison:

"They will kill me. . . . Tonight they are going to kill Gábor Péter. . . . They will kill Gábor Péter tonight. . . ."

I defied regulations by clinging to the iron door to hear better. There was a brief shuffling sound from the corridor, the creaking of a cell door, then silence again.

Gábor Péter in his heyday was probably the best known and most hated Communist secret police chief outside the Soviet Union. For the eight years he headed the Hungarian secret police he was undoubtedly the most feared man in Hungary, until his sudden disappearance in January of 1953.

Péter's real name was Benö Auspitz. He had left school at the age of fourteen to become a tailor and soon joined the outlawed and insignificant Communist party; but he had achieved little eminence by the time World War II broke out. After the Nazis invaded Hungary in March 1944, the underground party entrusted him with the hiding of its mimeograph machine, a priceless treasure of any underground movement. Péter and his machine found refuge in one of the Budapest university clinics headed by Professor Antal Babits, a renowned physician and idealistic Communist.

Early in 1945 the Russians occupied only half of Hungary but they had already set up their secret police terror organization generally known as AVH (Államvédelmi Hatóság, or State Security Bureau), and installed Péter as chief with the rank of lieutenant general. Hungary's Red boss, Mátyás Rákosi, subsequently wrote in the party's ideological monthly: "There was one single organization where our party demanded leadership and admitted only Communists: the State Security Bureau. We held this organization thoroughly in our hands from the first day of its existence and saw to it that it remained the reliable and sharp weapon of the fight for a people's democracy."

The AVH was organized in accordance with the Soviet pattern and was run almost entirely by Soviet advisers, though they remained well in the background.

Under Péter the secret police became the real power throughout the land, a state within the state, feared even by the Hungarian Communists. Like other Communist secret police organizations during Stalin's reign, the AVH developed an army of its own. It set up watchtowers, minefields, and barbed wire fences along the borders. This military array was the visible evidence of AVH power. Undercover, thousands of other secret police officers penetrated every nook of Hungarian life. They spied, reported, kidnapped, imprisoned, and murdered countless thousands of their fellow citizens. No outsider knew exactly how many men Péter had under his command at his peak. One accepted figure was eighty thousand, not counting thousands of occasional agents and informants. This was a huge force in a country smaller than the state of Kentucky, with fewer than ten million Magyars.

The AVH set up its first headquarters in the building once used by the Hungarian Nazi party on Andrássy ut, Budapest's main thoroughfare, but Péter's burgeoning apparatus soon outgrew these premises. It commandeered one neighboring apartment house after another, despite the desperate housing shortage in ruined postwar Budapest. It became a virtual citadel within the city, into which thousands disappeared forever.

Péter personally spearheaded the ruthless purges which reached their peak during the 1949–1952 clash between Tito and the Kremlin. He personally arrested József Cardinal Mindszenty at Christmastime in 1948. By 1952, after the worst of the mass purges, he jailed his right-hand man, Colonel Ernö Szücs, one of the two deputy chiefs of the AVH, who knew too much. Szücs did not even get a secret trial. One night Péter visited him in his cell and shot him with his revolver.

I had some acquaintance with Péter myself. I had seen him at show trials, where he liked to appear with mysterious, dramatic suddenness. He always wore impeccable business suits. Like other AVH officers, he shunned the Russian-style uniforms.

This man, filled with an immense lust for power, was rejected even by his comrades. Only a strange little group remained loyal to him: his wife, Jolán Simon, Professor Babits and his wife, the once beautiful but mediocre actress Ilona Eszterházy, and Hilda Gobbi, one of the country's leading actresses, a woman with a booming voice whose Lesbian inclinations were well known. The police chief and his friends virtually lived together. They occupied three villas in a quiet street of a residential district on the southern slopes of Rózsadomb (Hill of Roses). The street was closed to through traffic and a fourth villa housed Péter's bodyguards. One of them was Colonel István Bálint, a physician and trained psychologist, a robust six-foot-five man with the frightening features of a gorilla. He followed his master like a shadow.

Péter liked to impress people. He once tried to impress me, after a gala night at the opera honoring Stalin's seventieth birthday.

The scene was typical of the Stalin era. Communist functionaries gave long-winded speeches, praising the Soviet dictator to the point of nausea. The audience was supposed to stand and applaud again and again. The small flock of foreign correspondents then residing in Budapest was invited to attend and we sat together in one of the back rows of the parquet. Our group included Wilfred Burchett, the Australian-born newspaperman then working for the London *Daily Express* and now often regarded as the unofficial spokesman of Hanoi, and two Americans with their wives.

Burchett was well liked by everybody, including myself. Reporters, unless they work for a Communist party organ, rarely speak about their political sentiments, and although I sensed that Burchett was sympathetic to the Communist cause, I had no reason to believe that he was a card-carrying Communist himself. Ironically, Burchett was rebuffed by the Hungarian Communists when he wanted to marry a Hungarian woman. She was a pretty little girl working for the press section of the foreign ministry. Why their application for a marriage license was rejected, we never knew.

Two of the four Americans at the opera were Peter Furst, then working for Reuters, and his wife. The couple did not conceal that they were Communists. The others were George May, who worked mostly free-lance, and his wife. Mrs. Furst came to the opera wearing a nice brooch on her dress — small diamonds arranged, as I recall, in the shape of the hammer and sickle. She was wearing it proudly. All four Americans, seated next to us, joined in the revolting but de rigeur rising and applauding every other minute.

Only the Western diplomats in their boxes refused to applaud, though they rose dutifully with the rest. Ilona and I, without having agreed beforehand, did exactly what the American, British, and other Western diplomats did. We rose, but stood in our seats without applauding.

Péter, with Colonel Bálint behind him, sat up in front in a spacious box. He noticed us. The next day Iván Boldizsár, the assistant secretary for public affairs with the foreign ministry, called.

"I have a message for you," he said. "Certain circles did not like your attitude yesterday. Other foreign correspondents were also present but they did not attract attention by not joining the general applause. Would you please keep this in mind for the future?"

There was no need to explain who "certain circles" were. Boldizsár, a brilliant newspaperman, was an old friend. I told him that I would not "behave."

As we know, Péter's career suddenly ended one Sunday afternoon in January 1953. The story of how he was arrested has never been told before, because the few who knew preferred not to talk about it. This, I admit, included myself.

Péter and his usual retinue were together in actress Gobbi's house preparing for a quiet Sunday dinner. His wife, Jolán Simon Péter, was at her office. She was Rákosi's private secretary, an arrangement common among Communist bosses. Rákosi kept her as a hostage to keep his powerful police chief loyal, and Péter hoped she could gain the dictator's confidence.

A telephone call came from Rákosi himself. He wanted to see Péter urgently. He would send his car immediately. Péter, puffed up by this show of importance, proudly stepped into the automobile. He promised to be back for dinner, but he never returned. The same night Rákosi's men arrested Péter's wife, too, as part of a lightning roundup of the top AVH command.

It was not until a year later, after Lavrenti Beria's execution in Moscow, that the Hungarian government disclosed Péter's fate. A one-sentence communiqué said Péter and his accomplices were convicted for "anti-peoples" crimes. Péter was sentenced to life imprisonment. The others, including his wife, got shorter terms.

Only when I was an inmate of Fö utca myself did I learn the real reason for Péter's downfall. One can learn a great deal in prison, despite the complete isolation and the closemouthed guards.

The relationship between the prisoner and his interrogator is a strange one. They are closeted together, almost live together, for six to ten hours a day, for six days a week, for many months, sometimes a year. The prisoner is a pariah, already condemned without a trial — the trial itself, whether public or secret, is a prearranged comedy — although he may speak openly, something he could not afford as a "free man," because, as Aleksandr Solzhenitsyn aptly wrote in *The First Circle:* "Freedom was quite often lacking in freedom."

The interrogator has only one ambition: to produce the confession as prescribed by some higher authority for a given target date. In 1949, for instance, when the AVH prepared the greatest show trial of the anti-Titoist purges, the trial of the former Hungarian foreign minister László Rajk and his so-called accomplices, the interrogators received brief written instructions from General Péter every morning: by ten o'clock the same night they had to deliver a signed confession of some sort in which Rajk, or one or the other of his accomplices, admitted to having sold his soul to Allen Dulles, the French Deuxième Bureau, or to Tito himself.

The technique of obtaining such a confession has not changed much since the darkest Middle Ages. As George Kennan, the diplomat-scholar, wrote in a book review in 1968: "The annals of brutality tend to suffer, like any persistent pornography, from monotony and repetitiousness. When you have seen a few of the details, you have seen them all."

Primitive torture is one of the methods of obtaining a confession, but there are sophisticated refinements: long questioning, replacing the tough interrogator with a sympathetic one, vague promises linked with threats to the wretched pariah's wife or family. But this strange cohabitation of two men facing each other across a desk has a curious by-product. Even the "bad guy," the tough interrogator, must relax and sometimes even he feels the need to talk.

The explanation is manifold. First, the secret police officer in a Communist country lives a sad and isolated life. He is hated, or at least feared. People living in the same apartment house might greet him politely, but avoid, if they can, social contact with him. Who can he talk to? Certainly to his prisoner, whom he can summon whenever he wishes.

The AVH man believes he may talk freely to the man on the other end of the desk because there is no risk. When the interrogation is over, the prisoner will be returned to his cell, and then one day he will be hanged or sent to prison for many years. There is no danger in telling him the truth, the truth the policeman would not tell even to his wife.

And lastly, the AVH man is not different from any other human being at least in one respect: he wants to learn. He is almost without exception of simple background with little schooling and knows very well that his victim is in most cases better educated and more intelligent than he. This, I believe, explains why and how I learned so many things in prison and also why, in turn, I could tell my interrogators, even my tormentors, things I would not have dared to tell a Communist before my arrest.

One day I told the man on the other side of the desk that he did not seem to know that the Communist party had lost even the little popularity it had enjoyed after Hungary's "liberation." The man, Captain Babics, recalled that the Communists received seventeen percent of the vote in 1945, the first and only time the Russians and their Hungarian protégés made the unbelievable mistake of permitting free elections in the country. He asked how many I thought they would get now, in 1955.

Five percent at most, I replied. Babics pondered, then said: "You know, maybe even less . . ."

In 1953 Péter was tried secretly and the charge was Zionism, though the official announcement used the catchall phrase "anti-peoples" crimes. After his conviction he was removed from the Fö utca prison and transferred to an isolated cell in a regular prison for convicts. In the summer of 1955 Péter and several of his former codefendants were brought back to Fö utca, and then he was issued my cell.

It happened frequently that convicts were brought back to the Fö utca prison, always for specific reasons. Some were needed as prospective "witnesses" in the case of a newly arrested man; others, like Noel Field, because their case was to be reopened; again others to act as stool pigeons and spy on a new inmate. Sándor Szalai, a university professor and a Social-Democrat, sent to prison with so many other socialists when in the late 1940's their party was forced to merge with the Communists, was brought back to translate from English to Hungarian everything I had filed for the Associated Press. In the mid-1960's, on a lecture tour in the United States, Szalai jokingly complained to me about how many months he had spent in an isolated cell at work on the thousands of dispatches the AVH had confiscated when I was arrested.

Péter's return to Fö utca followed another shift in the Kremlin. In 1953 Rákosi discarded him to satisfy Stalin's violent anti-Semitism, but in 1955 Khrushchev pushed for reconciliation with Tito and Rákosi read the handwriting clearly. He had to clear himself of the purges of Titoists, so he brought Péter back to "confess" again, not to Zionism this time, but to having extorted confessions from Rajk and the other Hungarian "Titoists," without the consent and knowledge of Rákosi, of course.

Péter kept up his shouting regularly for five months. I could hear him usually in the morning and evening hours. His special guards kept him under watch round the clock. He would start off by banging his iron cell door with his fists and kicking it with his boots. He kept on banging and kicking until his jailers opened the door. Then he would stand in the doorway and yell for all to hear.

"Fascists! Murderers!" he screamed at his guards. Apparently, the guards had orders not to use force but to report immediately to a superior. I could hear scurrying feet, then someone talking in low tones, trying to calm the raving man. One morning Péter responded to the reassurances by shouting: "Rákosi is lying . . . Rákosi is lying . . ."

Sometimes he pleaded with his captors. "I didn't treat the Fascists the way you treat me," he would say. He was lucky that this was true.

One of Péter's harangues confirmed a rumor I had heard before: that in 1953, when Beria was arrested, he was taken to Moscow to testify against the fallen MVD head.

"If the Soviet comrades ever find out. . . . That was not what the Soviet ambassador promised when I was brought back from Moscow," Péter screamed one day. He did not reveal what the Russian diplomat had promised, but it was easy to guess: an early release from prison as a reward for his cooperation in providing evidence against Beria.

At some point Péter learned that his wife was held in one of the nearby cells. After that he shouted only one refrain: "Justice for Jolán Simon . . . Justice for Jolán Simon . . ." But his voice grew weaker and weaker. Once I heard him throw out the aluminum messtin with his meal. I knew he must have started a hunger strike.

The climax finally came on November 18, 1955, the date of my own trial. I was due in court at 9 A.M., but I kept the judge waiting for about thirty minutes.

Péter was banging on his door again. "Open it, open it," he

gasped in his weakened voice. When his jailers finally complied, I heard the thud of things being thrown out.

"Keep your food. I don't need it," he snarled.

After the guards shoved Péter back to his cell, I was hurriedly escorted to the courtroom, but I could see the apples, oranges, and sweets lying around in front of his cell like a picturesque still life, all unheard-of goodies that had been supplied to tempt him into submission.

When I returned at noon, the litter in the corridor was gone, and so was the special guard. Péter had been taken to a hospital to be fed internally. Three weeks later he was brought back. From then on he was a silent man.

The revolutionaries did not free Péter when they opened the gates of political prisons during the few days of freedom in October 1956. But today he is a free man again — as free as someone can be in a Communist country. In 1959 the Kádár regime released all Communists who had been purged and jailed for whatever reason before the revolution. Many of them were hard-core Stalinists and one of them was Péter. Since 1959 every morning a modest but chauffeur-driven Russian Popjeda car brings a short and thickset middle-aged man to a state-owned workshop which manufactures ready-made men's suits. Péter became the manager of the workshop, and in accordance with the strict rules of Communist hierarchy, he rode in a small, four-passenger car, not one of the shiny limousines he once used.

Few people recognize Péter in the car, the man who started as a tailor and reached the end of his career as the boss of a handful of tailors. Only those who once stood trembling in his luxuriously furnished office remember that for eight years this inconspicuous little man was the dreaded chief of the secret police.

But those, like me, who heard him raving and screaming, cursing and pleading, wonder what was behind the façade of calmness on this man's face. He must be haunted by the shadows of three men, all three once omnipotent heads of the Soviet secret police, and all three mercilessly liquidated when there was no longer any need for them. Yagoda, Yezhov, and Beria were executed, and a shroud of secrecy veils the fate of Dzerzhinski, the founding father of what was known in the early 1920's as the Cheka. General Ivan Serov became Beria's successor, but after his sinister role in the crushing of the 1956 revolt in Hungary, Khrushchev no longer needed him. Today Yuri Andropov is Moscow's secret police chief. He was the Soviet ambassador to Budapest in 1956.

4

On Easy Street

It was May 1955 when Kretsmer took over my case and Babics disappeared from my life. Rákosi was at the peak of his power and Nagy lived in exile in his villa in a residential district of Buda. I did not know about these changes, nor did I know, of course, what a significant year 1955 turned out to be: the year of the Austrian State Treaty ending occupation of that country, of the Geneva meeting between President Eisenhower and Russia's Khrushchev-Bulganin team, and of Khrushchev's pilgrimage to Tito in Belgrade.

Not having known about these developments, I could not speculate about the reason for the change in my treatment. Did I care? Not then. Would a man dying of thirst in the Sahara ask questions if he found a bottle of water? I only wanted to enjoy the new situation, the relaxed, almost friendly atmosphere in the same dreaded room where I had gone through so many agonizing hours since the night of my arrest. Certainly later, when I became accustomed to the new situation, I raised the question to myself: why did it happen? But it was obvious that I could not find the answer myself and I could not expect

Kretsmer to enlighten me. The question remained unanswered until the revolution came.

During the weeks of the revolt a newspaperman had little time to think about his own affairs. Yet these were the times when Communists volunteered to bring information to the Western reporter and the revolution opened not only the gates of prisons but also some of the most secret files. These were not only historic, but feverish times. Men whom I did not know personally called me, secret documents were shown to me to make me understand better what had happened during those eighteen months I was kept incommunicado. I was told why my wife and I were arrested, why I was grilled and driven to desperation, and why finally the change came.

The story was too fantastic and my informant knew I would be a doubting Thomas. He showed me one document, the blueprint of our public show trial that never took place. I had to believe him.

In the Communist world nothing happens without a good reason. People are tools to be used and discarded after use, because, however strange it sounds, the Communists revived the motto of the Sacred Inquisition: the end justifies the means. It was and still is Western naiveté to believe that Rajk in Hungary, Kostov in Bulgaria, or Slansky in Czechoslovakia were killed because they were in the way of somebody. Top-ranking Communists were needed to prove with their deaths what otherwise nobody would have believed: that heretical Tito and the Western intelligence agencies had deeply penetrated the highest hierarchy of the satellite Communist parties. They were picked carefully, with a cool head, but without personal animosity.

So were the Martons picked in Moscow. Why we? Because by then we were the only people in Budapest working for American newspapers. We were selected in early 1955 when Moscow already knew, though Washington did not, that in the summer Khrushchev would agree to a summit meeting with President Eisenhower. Before the meeting there would be a show trial, Ilona and I would confess publicly that we were American spies, then I would be hanged and Ilona sent to prison for life.

And why all this trouble? Simply to permit Khrushchev to embarrass the honest, straightforward American President by telling him at their first encounter something like this: "Now really, General, you must admit it is not easy for us to patch up our differences. You Americans are incorrigible. Just now our comrades in Budapest unmasked two of your spies disguised as journalists . . ."

Was this a childish monstrosity? Definitely yes by Western standards. For the Russian type of Communist and for the Moscowites in the satellite countries it was just a tactical move, a feint, the sacrifice of two pawns in this international chess game.

These were Colonel Ivancov's instructions when he came to Budapest with the blueprints of our show trial. I never knew that the Russian intelligence officer was there all the time while Ilona and I were being grilled in Fö utca. I did not know that he was the silent observer sitting in the dark corner in Colonel Balázsi's office one night. That was the reason for Babics's impatience, his dark hints about a deadline in May when he was supposed to deliver me well prepared and ready for a public trial. The Geneva summit was in July, so by then the whole affair must have come to its prescribed conclusion.

Then in May somebody in Moscow thought otherwise. Ivancov was withdrawn and the AVH was told that the Kremlin was no longer interested in the Martons. The AVH was in an embarrassing situation. No show trial was needed; there was no need for confessions either. But obviously they could not say: "We are sorry, it was a mistake. You may go now." We had to be held and disposed of quietly, to be tucked away in prison for many years until forgotten by everyone. There was no need for Babics's rough methods. The terror chapter, as far as Moscow was concerned, could be closed.

It was remarkable, I thought in retrospect, how the ups and downs of our prison life paralleled the course of world events. When the Geneva summit in July 1955 was successfully concluded, we were treated with unusual consideration and were given some privileges. In October, when the second Geneva conference on the foreign ministers' level was a failure, we were tried, though secretly and without fanfare. Two months later, in December 1955, Hungary was admitted to the United Nations and the Supreme Court halved our sentences. In February 1956 Khrushchev dethroned Stalin and soon afterwards Ilona was set free. Finally in July Rákosi was dismissed and three weeks later I was free, too.

The first thing Major Kretsmer did was to throw out all my "confessions" and we started from the beginning. It was a lengthy process. Kretsmer was in no hurry, but the folders slowly began to grow again. The terror gang which assisted Babics disappeared too, including Colonel Balázsi whom I never saw again. There were no more sinister threats about a "deadline" and I would have almost enjoyed the change but for the knowledge that they had also arrested my wife and that my little daughters remained without parents.

Gradually I was granted some "privileges," such as the daily ration of ten cigarettes. These were distributed after breakfast, but without matches, for fear of suicides. Whenever the prisoner wished to smoke, he had to rap gently on the door and wait for the jailer to come and give him a light through the little window in the door. If the jailer was mean, and many were, the prisoner could wait a long time for his light. The added privilege of having matches was most exceptional and it was given to me only in the last third of my stay at Fö utca. By then, obviously considered a Very Important Person, I was permitted to have a pipe in my cell.

Another, and for me more important privilege, was the use of the library. Ever since my early childhood I had been a voracious reader, and in prison a book, almost any book, was the only refuge from torment and misery. "Use of the library" must not be taken literally. It did not mean, of course, that one could leave the cell, go some place, and select a book. It meant that about twice a week the jailer went around, opened the little window in the door and tossed in a book, whether you wanted it or not, provided you were not deprived of this privilege, which I was for many months.

The prison library contained a remarkable assortment of books confiscated from people who were sentenced to lose their property in addition to a term in prison. This was the usual case and it explained the great variety of books in the prison library. Private libraries in central Europe, like Ilona's and mine, were founded generations earlier with hundreds of volumes being added by grandfathers and fathers; so it was not at all unusual for a so-called middle-class family to have an enormous collection of books. Also our verdict contained the confiscation-of-property clause and I dreaded the moment when the jailer would throw in a book which once belonged to me. The moment never came. For some reason the AVH sealed our apartment, having removed only our files.

It was a strange mélange of books I was given, but because they came from the private libraries of intellectuals, I was sometimes lucky enough to get a book I really enjoyed. What a pleasure it was when I got a thick volume of a thousand pages or more, and what a disappointment when I had to be satisfied with the third volume of the history of the Communist party of the Soviet Union. It was a red-letter day when I got a beautiful edition of Virgil's *Aeneid* with the original Latin and the Hungarian translation side by side. I read books in English with which I was not familiar: Hervey Allen's *Anthony Adverse* and Edna Ferber's *Saratoga Trunk*. My wife got *Anthony Adverse* too and she thought it was not only exciting reading but also a perfect substitute for an iron to press a blouse which she had washed — when and how I do not know. Even later, when the jailers also had come to recognize that I was a strange bird — a man kept in the secret police prison long after his trial and conviction — an unofficial privilege was added. When the jailers received a fresh supply of books, some of the more friendly ones opened my cell and let me out to browse among the fifty-odd volumes stacked up on a table in the corridor; I could make my own choice, taking occasionally more than one book. This was a twofold feast. Not only could I select a book, but for brief moments I could walk "free," without being escorted.

One of the books I received was a textbook of mathematics, used by what would be the equivalent of eighth or ninth graders in the United States. I was never good at mathematics and had forgotten most of what I had learned so many years earlier. But this was a treasure and I kept it for months, contrary to all regulations. By then I had a pencil, an unheard-of luxury, and used toilet paper to solve one problem after another. How much I struggled with what was obviously no problem to a fourteen-year-old child, and how proud and happy I was when I succeeded in solving some of the more difficult ones. By then I had time, more time than ever before. Kretsmer was slow in proceeding with my interrogation, doubtless because the AVH had still not decided what to do with us after Moscow's expressed disinterest in our case.

One day there was new distraction in the monotony of prison life. I was escorted to Kretsmer's office and found there another man who, to my amazement, got up from his chair when I entered. The major said the man was from the ministry of the interior — the AVH, in theory, belonged to the ministry, though in fact it was completely independent — and he had a request. My surprise became greater when the man started to talk and said that the ministry urgently needed a translation from English into Hungarian; it was an important document and "we know that nobody could do it better than you." Would I please do it? Nobody had talked to me like that since I became a prisoner and Kretsmer, standing behind his desk, smiled under his nose. I was baffled and flattered, but careful not to show it. Instead I put on airs, spoke to the man almost condescendingly, and said that of course I would do it. How long would it take? the man asked anxiously, handing me what appeared to be several pages from some magazine. Could they have it in two days? In two hours, I replied nonchalantly, provided I got a table, a chair, and my portable typewriter. The man was overjoyed and said that the major would doubtless see to it that I got everything I needed.

It goes without saying that the small, simple wooden table, the chair, and my portable typewriter were in no time delivered to my cell by a jailer who was no less surprised than I was. After all, not every day could a prisoner sit on a chair instead of squatting on his bunk. Meanwhile I studied the pages with intense curiosity. The "vigilance" of the ministry or the AVH or both was bordering on the ridiculous. The title and the name of the author had been carefully cut out, as had the name of the publication at the bottom of each page. It was a wonderful new pastime for me to translate the article, obviously written by an atomic physicist, discussing in philosophical terms the morality of using nuclear weapons in the light of what happened at Nagasaki and Hiroshima. To prepare the translation was interesting from a professional point of view, too. The structure and logic of the Hungarian language is so different from English that only on that day did I recognize the immense difficulty of translating something of importance.

When I was through I knocked on the door with unmistakable authority and told, no, ordered the still perplexed jailer to report to the major at once that I was ready. All right, he would take it, was the morose answer. Out of the question, I

replied, it was "top secret," I was to deliver it personally —
which was a slight exaggeration. The jailer shrugged and disappeared. A few hours later he brought me to Kretsmer's
office. The man from the ministry was there again. He thanked
me profusely and asked whether I would do similar translations
again. Showing no undue interest, I graciously agreed. That
evening I ate my dinner sitting on a chair, with my tin bowl on
a table, turning my back to the Judas, which must have confused the jailers even more, but they did not dare to object.

Several weeks later the same man came with another request.
He had brought similar pages, obviously from the same magazine; again everything that might give me a clue to their origin
had been carefully cut out. But this time vigilance did not help.
The article was an answer to the previous one and whoever
wrote it referred in the text to Leo Szilárd and to the *Bulletin
of Atomic Scientists*. So now I knew that Szilárd, the world-
famous American-Hungarian, wrote the first piece I had been
asked to translate. I could not resist the temptation to tell
Kretsmer how ineffective their vigilance was and that they
could have saved themselves the trouble of mutilating the
pages.

Unfortunately I only received two other similar assign-
ments; both were, however, longer than the articles in the *Bulletin of Atomic Scientists*. One was a bill submitted in the British House of Commons on the peaceful use of nuclear energy,
the other a report on an international conference on the population explosion, held somewhere in India. After my second
trial, when the days passed at a snail's pace, I was hoping in vain
for more work. But the typewriter, the chair, and the table
remained, providing me not only with some luxury, but also
with some curious respect from the jailers.

Slowly, with the days creeping by, Kretsmer and I concluded the review of my case and, it appeared, I was ready for
trial. The first sign that the day was approaching was when a
young man came to Kretsmer's office and told me haughtily

that his name was István Sarkadi and that he was the prosecutor. I disliked this character immediately and did not conceal my feelings, especially when he said he assumed I had recognized the monstrosity of my crimes and would testify at the trial accordingly. By then I was no longer the bewildered, humiliated man of the Babics era. I was composed and calm when I replied that of course I was neither a traitor nor a spy, whatever he thought about me. The prosecutor's next question was whether I had been treated humanely, adding that he had no doubts about it since "legality" had been restored and nobody had reason to complain. I was probably less calm when I told him that this was an error, too, that during the first three months I had been treated as a dog, but I acknowledged that since Kretsmer had taken over my case my treatment was adequate, as it should be. With that the prosecutor withdrew, seemingly dissatisfied with the interview.

When we were left alone, I turned to Kretsmer and told him that I would like to discuss something which I thought was a more serious matter than the pompous visit of the prosecutor. Before the trial, I said, I had to see Ilona. Kretsmer laughed and answered that this was out of the question. We would be together in the dock and maybe we could get permission to talk for a short time after we were convicted and sentenced, but definitely not before. I knew that he would refuse my request so I was ready with my argument. All right, I said, but I must warn him about the consequences. If we were to see each other only on the bench before the judge, we would transform the trial into a comedy. We would ignore the proceedings and talk and talk to each other. I did not ask to see her alone, I argued. He could be there and her interrogator, Major Gerö, too. We had no secrets, but we had been separated for nine months and I wanted to know everything about her and about our children. If, on the other hand, they would grant us a brief meeting, I could guarantee the orderly behavior of both of us.

Kretsmer pondered, shaking his head in disbelief, but finally promised to discuss my request with his superiors. The answer came two days later: the request was granted.

It is strange, indeed, that Ilona requested the same thing from her Major Gerö, and used the same arguments and the same mild blackmail to persuade the interrogator. Gerö's initial reaction was the same as Kretsmer's: out of the question.

Kretsmer had certain conditions: we were not to discuss our case or the forthcoming trial. Nor were we supposed to talk about politics. Of course I agreed.

I did not know when I would see Ilona. But she was told one day earlier and so she was able to "pretty" herself for the great confrontation, meaning that she used the bottom of her messtin for a mirror more carefully than on other days. I was hoping that for the great day they would give me an extra shave, a once-a-week luxury in prison, but I had a four-day stubble when they took me to meet my wife.

I only knew the day had arrived when my jailer-escort passed Major Kretsmer's office and halted before another door. Then, inside, there she was, smiling, with arms outstretched, but with tears in her eyes. We were not alone. Major Gerö was there, usually a cynical man, but on that day apparently moved. Despite Ilona's smiles I knew that she saw on my face what I had gone through in the nine months that we had not seen each other.

Gerö did not permit our embrace to last too long and ordered us to sit down in two comfortable leather armchairs, another sensation neither of us had enjoyed for quite some time. I flooded Ilona with questions, about herself and about the children, where and with whom they were staying and what school they attended. While she tried to answer my questions, Gerö mumbled something which sounded like "Excuse me . . ." and left the room, leaving us alone, though he left the door leading to the neighboring room wide open.

Ilona immediately began to speak in English, as we so often did, and whispered: "Listen to me. The Americans will free us." I looked at her in disbelief, and she took my hand and repeated, stressing every whispered word: "Believe me, I know what I'm talking about. The Americans will free us."

I do not know what I could have asked her in explanation under these circumstances, but there was no opportunity for questions. The major returned and Ilona continued her report about the children. There was one more thing I wanted to tell her before the thirty minutes allotted to us were over. I tried to be casual when I told her I believed she would be free soon, at least many years before I would, and that I wanted her to divorce me. I would be an old man by the time the Communists let me go, no longer of much use to her and the children. She laughed me off and Gerö smiled too, but made no comment. Then the thirty minutes were over, and escorted back to my cell, I could have cursed myself for not having used the time more cleverly — and especially for not having asked her to explain what she meant by the mysterious message.

I had neither doubts nor illusions about the degree of interest the United States took in us, but knew very well how little could be done for someone in the claws of the secret police of a hostile Communist country. Ilona and I were Hungarian citizens and the mere fact that we were working for American wire services was hardly justification to intervene on our behalf. Of course I remembered that no protests had helped when an American citizen like Robert Vogeler, the ITT executive, had been arrested, tried, and convicted. How, then, could I expect any effective help?

I had no doubts about my American friends at the legation in Budapest, nor about my colleagues. But what could they do? I asked myself. I never really believed Captain Babics's clumsy tactics, assuring me every other day that I was a forgotten man as were all spies who were caught and who had lived out their usefulness. But again, what could anybody do for us?

It was characteristic that nobody told me how wrong I was even after my release from prison. Only by coincidence and piecemeal did I learn about the many actions taken on behalf of the Martons. It was a coincidence that when I was searching in old documents at the State Department, I found the blistering American note to the Hungarian government of February 3, 1956, delivered after the Communist regime had announced that Ilona and I had been tried and convicted. "The protracted detention incommunicado and subsequent imprisonment of the Martons . . . have seriously prejudiced free access to news sources within Hungary and must therefore be regarded as an abridgment of freedom of the press," John Foster Dulles wrote.

The Eisenhower administration was not satisfied with the verbal condemnation of the Rákosi regime. Talks about trade were interrupted and an American delegation in Budapest was ordered to return to Washington. The requirement of passport validation for American citizens who wished to travel to Hungary was reinstituted.

Only much later, and again by coincidence, did I learn that the British National Union of Journalists, an organization with which I had nothing to do, protested in writing against our imprisonment. And only now, paging through old newspapers, did I find a *New York Times* editorial of January 16, 1956, which said that in a Communist country "a foreign reporter does not know from day to day how long the policy of leniency toward truth-telling will last and where a reporter who is also a citizen of the country may find himself in jail. This last is what has happened to Endre Marton, an AP correspondent in Budapest. . . . This is what happened to his wife, Ilona Marton, a Budapest correspondent for UP. . . . Espionage in such a country as today's Hungary is what the government says it is. When used as a trap for journalists it may cover the kind of information any good journalist gets and publishes simply because he is a good journalist."

The most insistent in inquiring about us was a great friend with whom in 1956 I covered so many tragic events of the revolution: the late John McCormack of the *New York Times*. Jack, as he was known to his friends, lived in Vienna and from there made regular tours to countries behind the Iron Curtain. The Communists grudgingly respected Jack and feared his sharply critical reports. Whenever he came to Budapest while we were in prison, he always started and ended his interviews with Communist leaders: "And how long do you intend to keep the Martons?"

It was McCormack who told Ilona in August 1956 in his typically thoughtful, cautious way that he had an inkling that I might be released soon. When I asked him in Vienna in 1957 what had made him think so, he told me that he had visited Ernö Gerö, the number one Communist after Rákosi's final ouster, and again raised the same question: when would they release me? Instead of dismissing his question, as had happened so often earlier, Gerö asked McCormack why it was so important to him that a convicted Hungarian spy should be freed. McCormack saw an opening and explained that my imprisonment was a constant memento for every Western newsman of what he might face in Hungary, as was the imprisonment of my colleague, William Oatis, in Prague. Gerö did not reply, but made some notes, and the interview was ended.

After Ilona and I saw each other for those fleeting thirty minutes, the day of our trial rapidly approached. There are routine steps leading to such a trial. First, a preliminary hearing by the judge who will preside at the trial; then "selection" of a defense counsel. Judge Jonás was a notorious man who had presided over many of the purge trials I had witnessed as a reporter. He, like everyone else connected with political cases, had his office in Fö utca. Jonás received me icily and gave me the indictment to read. I was permitted to read only once the long and boring document which accused me of being a spy and a traitor, but offered remarkably little evidence. I could not make notes and was really not too interested in the whole farce. By then I was convinced that I was a burden to the secret police and the only thing they could do with me was to let me "rot" in prison for many years, to use one of the AVH men's favorite expressions.

The selection of the defense counsel was another comedy in a Communist country. I knew very well that the defendant cannot pick a lawyer freely and also that the counsel is a non-entity, a man on the same payroll of the AVH as the judge and the prosecutor. Yet I played stupid and when Jonás routinely asked me whom I wanted as my counsel, I gave him the name of a once famous criminal lawyer. The judge looked at me with suspicious, cold eyes. "You can select a lawyer from this list," he said, handing me a sheet of paper with about a dozen names. The names did not mean anything to me, I said, and in that case I would defend myself. Jonás became angry. "You know perfectly well that according to the law you must have a lawyer," he said. All right, I answered, but I do not know any of those on the list, and he should pick one. Red in his otherwise ashen face, Jonás chose one and dismissed me quickly.

I knew that all this was childish but such little games gave me some small satisfaction. I also knew that Jonás could not revenge himself at the trial for my recalcitrance, no more than he could reward me with leniency had I behaved meekly. The fact that a day had been set for our trial meant that the verdict had been written by a much higher authority, somewhere in the Communist party headquarters.

A few days later I met my lawyer, a timid, middle-aged man who obviously knew little about my case. The meeting was brief and I saw no reason to prolong it. He made vague references to the importance of showing repentance. I cut him short by saying that I had no intention of pleading guilty, but would admit every "crime" I was accused of. I told him that I was interested only in defending Ilona and would use the opportunity of the "last word" to ask the court to acquit her. The little gray man — I was almost sorry for him — had no objections.

We agreed that he should come and see me again to read what I was to prepare for my last plea.

It is strange that the Communists did not eliminate this remnant of bourgeois jurisdiction. According to the law, the defendant has the last word in court; he can say whatever he wants to and without a time limit. In the staged show trials the "right of the last word" becomes a tragicomedy, used by the defendants to heap further abuse on themselves, to overbid the prosecutor in accusing themselves beyond the indictment. I have watched many such performances. The most shocking of them was that of András Szalay, one of Rajk's codefendants in 1949. This man, who was in charge of the Communist party's important cadre bureau before his arrest, was accused of having been an agent of Noel Field and on the payroll of Allen Dulles, head of American counterintelligence in Switzerland during World War II. Szalay could hardly wait to outbid the prosecutor by admitting everything and much more. He said he betrayed "the workers' class" as a police informer before the war. Listening to the torrent of self-abuse Szalay produced at the trial, I could not resist remarking to Joseph Kingsbury-Smith, who covered the trial for the International News Service, "I wonder when he will volunteer to admit that he also killed his mother . . ."

But our trial was held in camera and I could say whatever I wanted; it made no difference anyway. So I prepared my "last words" and tried to be dignified and eloquent, dignified in rejecting the charge that I was a traitor and a spy, and eloquent in asking the court's mercy for Ilona.

At the second meeting with the lawyer he did not object to my draft but remarked that he would have liked to see at least some sign of repentance on my part. Yet he said something which later made me think. He asked, casually and meekly, whether I would pay a fee for his services. I must have looked at him with curious eyes because he added hastily that he would, as a court-appointed lawyer, of course perform his duties without a fee, yet if I could pay him he would appreciate it. I told him that I had nothing except the old suit I was wearing, that everything had been taken away from us — which he surely must have known — and that obviously the sentence, whatever it would be, would include the usual confiscation clause. Yes, he replied, he knew that, but I might be freed some time, and would I then pay a fee? I do not remember what I answered, if anything. The whole suggestion appeared ludicrous under those circumstances.

The trial itself was an uninteresting affair except for one thing: I saw Ilona, and again we sat side by side, on two chairs, without even a jailer between us. Fö utca has everything, from prison cells to courtrooms, a convenient arrangement because the defendant does not have to leave the building for his trial. Even though the trial was to be held in camera, the barber came that morning to shave me properly, my underwear was returned to me, and I wore a necktie.

The large courtroom was almost empty: the judge, the two lawyers, Kretsmer, Gerö, and a sprinkling of secret police officers interested in the case — that was all. There were no witnesses, no evidence was offered. The prosecutor presented the state's case and repeated the trite charges I had read in the indictment. Then the counsels spoke briefly in a feeble effort to bring up some alleviating circumstances, and finally it was my turn to speak.

I was calm and almost enjoyed the little speech I delivered without notes. After all, I was sitting close to my wife for about two hours, I could see the little reassuring smile in her eyes, as if she were repeating the message: "The Americans will free us." Could a man in my position ask for more?

The sentence was ready: we were both to go to prison, Ilona for six years, I for thirteen. With the spectacle over, there was one pleasant surprise. Ilona and I were permitted to take the long walk back to our cells together, with only one well-disposed jailer, who went in front of us and let us talk, in low tones, all the way. Of all the walks we took together, in the tree-covered hills of Buda or among the azaleas of Chevy Chase, this one through the dark, deserted corridors of Fö utca I will always remember.

Our lawyers, as was their duty, appealed the verdicts to the Supreme Court. Back in my cell I tried to prepare myself for the expected transfer to a prison, probably the one at the other end of Budapest where most political prisoners were kept. It would have meant the end of isolation, but the prospect of co-habitation with many other convicts did not make me happy. But days and weeks went by and I was left alone. Did my law-yer know something I did not when he mentioned the fee to be paid after my release?

A couple of weeks later I was summoned to Kretsmer, for no apparent reason. His role in my case was concluded and we had a casual chat; before sending me back to my cell he mentioned, again casually, that Ilona and I might stay in Fö utca until our trial before the Supreme Court. The day, I was told, would be in December.

If evidence is needed to prove that so-called trials in Com-munist countries are prearranged, I can offer some. On the day before the Supreme Court trial I was escorted to Fö utca's new boss, who had replaced Colonel Balázsi and whose name I did not know. I wondered what this high-ranking officer wanted from me. While Balázsi was a butcher, a rude terrorist, his suc-cessor seemed to be an intellectual, a reserved man with good manners. He asked me to sit down and began to speak about the next day's great event.

The Supreme Court, which before the Communist take-over occupied a magnificent building opposite the Parliament, was transferred to a modest, old office building when the Commu-nist party needed the original one for its institute and museum of party history. The evicted high court moved to Fö utca, about ten blocks from the prison.

I was told that if I promised to observe the rules, I would be transported to the Supreme Court in an unmarked AVH car, together with Major Kretsmer and one plainclothesman. There would be no handcuffs, or armed jailer. The Supreme Court building had no entrance for cars, which meant that we would have to step out of the car in front of it. They did not want to attract attention, so the passersby would only see three civilians leaving a car and entering a building. The same would apply to Ilona, who would be transported in another car with Major Gerö and a plainclothesman. Would I agree? I did.

The colonel was apparently relieved. He continued to talk and asked what I expected from the trial. I shrugged and said I hoped for a lighter sentence for me and acquittal for my wife. "Let's talk about you only. What do you expect?" the colonel asked. Ten years, I suggested. He shook his head. "Lower," he said. Eight? I asked with disbelief. Still lower, came the reply. Six? Yes, six, the colonel answered, and dismissed me.

Back in my cell I was pacing up and down. Six instead of thirteen. Might they let Ilona go? No, that would be too good. And six years meant actually four, as it was customary to free the well-behaved prisoner after he had served two-thirds of his term.

Next day our transportation to the Supreme Court took place according to our gentlemen's agreement. What a sensation it was to see people walking on the street. And how I enjoyed stepping casually from the car, turning back to Kretsmer to make some remark about the weather, as if there were nothing more natural than we two, the convict and the secret police officer, strolling on Fö utca together, with the plainclothesman, his hand in his pocket, following us at some distance. The weird scene continued inside. The court was hearing another case, so we had to wait. Had anybody observed the group of four, Ilona in her still elegant camel-hair coat — who would have guessed that she used it as a blanket? — I in my dark blue overcoat, the two majors in mufti, standing in a group and chatting and laughing, he would not have believed that two of the four were "American spies" already sentenced to long prison terms. In fact, when the two lawyers arrived a little later, Ilona's counsel, a witty man, could not resist telling us he was ready to turn back because obviously he was too late and the Supreme Court had already set us free.

Well, it did not, but there was one more surprise waiting for us. Sarkadi, the pompous, arrogant prosecutor at our first trial had disappeared and his place had been taken by a young, good-looking man we had never seen before. When he rose to talk, I pricked up my ears. Instead of repeating the charges against us, the prosecutor delivered a speech which almost sounded as our defense. Summing up, he said the prosecution now believed the lower court was too severe and the state would have no objection if the court lowered the sentences. Then the two counsels, encouraged by the prosecutor, delivered their usual pleas, and I again made my speech asking that Ilona be permitted to return to our children. The verdict: six years for me, three for Ilona.

The rest was uninteresting. Neither of us was transferred to an ordinary prison. Ilona, after nine months in Fö utca, was paroled on April 4, 1956, the Communist holiday commemorating the country's "liberation" by the Red Army. I was not told about it, but one day I was summoned to Kretsmer's office — a large room, since he had become deputy chief of the investigating branch of the secret police — and there she was, elegantly dressed and, I thought, more radiant than ever.

That was the only occasion, early in the summer of 1956, when they permitted her to visit me, but she could write me once in a while and I could answer. There was, of course, nothing in her letters that would have indicated to me the ferment which was going on outside the walls of Fö utca, nor could she tell me anything about it during our one personal meeting. Yet I sensed something in her gay mood, in her reassuring smile and words — and by the unexplainable fact that, against all rules, I was not transferred but kept in the secret police prison.

In one of the few letters I was permitted to receive, Ilona enclosed half a dozen photographs of my daughters, now reunited with her. How bittersweet it was to look at the pictures, one by one, every day, and what a poor substitute for being with them. And then, once, she was able to send me fruit. It was early summer, and I got strawberries and peaches, an unprecedented feast. I also received one of my pipes, some tobacco and a pair of comfortable loafers, a real relief after having worn my more formal shoes for more than a year, without socks or laces.

But the real joy came when Ilona sent me a copy of Webster's dictionary. I had ordered the Webster's several weeks before my arrest, but it arrived only after that day in February 1955. I wonder if there is anybody who has read the unabridged Webster's word for word three times, as I did during those long months. I also got a notebook which I still possess. On its cover, in a sentimental mood which can be forgiven a prisoner, I wrote, using the Greek alphabet, the words of Heraclitus: πάντα ρεῖ. Some vigilant jailer must have found it during a search of my cell and Kretsmer, when I was taken to him, asked me with an almost apologetic smile what these hieroglyphs meant. The free translation would be, I explained, that everything comes to an end, perhaps even my involuntary stay in prison.

It did. On August 16, 1956, I was a free man again.

Eighteen months were taken away from my life and during the first three months I had been "tormented in body and soul," the words Cardinal Mindszenty used when I met him in October 1956, the day he was released. Yet I could consider myself extremely lucky. Had they arrested me during the Stalinist era, I would have been executed. Without the changes of 1956, I would have been kept in prison for many years.

The eighteen months left no scar on my mind; I have no

nightmares and seek no revenge. Ilona is even more magnanimous. She thinks it was an experience which made our lives richer and made us more appreciative of what life offers. She may be right.

5

Rákosi, Rajk, and Nagy

I ask the reader to pause briefly with me and become acquainted with three of the four men who directly or indirectly played dominant roles before, during, and after the 1956 uprising. They were Mátyás Rákosi, László Rajk, and Imre Nagy.

Rajk's role was posthumous; he was hanged in 1949. Nagy was executed two years after the revolt. Rákosi is still alive, a forgotten old man, living somewhere in the Soviet Union.

The fourth man is, of course, János Kádár. But because he still is in power, I propose to appraise this controversial man in the concluding part of this book, when I attempt to draw up the balance sheet of the revolution.

Rákosi was by far the best known of the three. He belonged to the small group of Communist leaders whose names occupy a prominent place in the history of post-Lenin Communism. Some others of this select group were Italy's Togliatti, France's Thorez, Spain's Dolores Ibarruri, better known as La Pasionaria, Germany's Ulbricht, Bulgaria's Dimitrov, and Romania's Ana Pauker.

Born in a small town in southern Hungary, the son of a businessman, Rákosi was an excellent student and ultimately a graduate of Vienna's Consular Akademie, a renowned institution of the Austro-Hungarian monarchy. He served as a young officer in World War I, was captured by the Russians, and became a Communist. After the war, during the short-lived Communist rule of Béla Kun, Rákosi was a deputy minister. He fled the country when Kun's army was defeated and when, for a short time, White terror replaced the Red one. Moscow, however, soon sent Rákosi back to Hungary to organize the illegal Communist party. He was arrested, tried, and sent to prison for life.

Rákosi spent sixteen years in prison. I am convinced that nobody who is kept behind bars for such a long time should be permitted to play a leading role in a nation's life, in whatever political system. Sixteen years is an enormous time and nobody, however self-disciplined, can return to normal life unscathed after such an experience.

Rákosi was freed in a curious deal with the Soviets in the brief period when Admiral Horthy, the regent (head of state) of Hungary, a kingless kingdom between the two wars, came to terms with Moscow in the wake of the Stalin-Hitler pact of 1939. The Russians offered to return to Hungary the flags the czarist armies had captured in 1849 when they helped the Hapsburgs to defeat the Hungarians fighting for their independence. The price Moscow asked for the flags was Rákosi. The Hungarian newspapers, on the government's orders, did not mention the swap. There were colorful reports describing the ceremony on the Soviet border when the century-old flags were returned, but no mention was made about the man who was simultaneously and unceremoniously sneaked over the border, to be feted in the Russian capital as one of the true heroes of international Communism.

Rákosi did not return with the Red Army in 1944, when the lesser Moscowites, including Nagy, reentered Hungary. A man keenly aware of theatrical effects, he had his lieutenants prepare the ground for him first. There were posters with his portrait everywhere, saying only: "Rákosi is coming." Many of the younger generation asked, "Who is Rákosi?" They and everyone else learned the answer soon after Rákosi showed up in the spring of 1945.

Right at the outset, in the fall of 1945, Rákosi made probably the greatest mistake of his career. He persuaded the Soviets that it was safe to hold free elections in Hungary because the Hungarians were grateful for their liberation from the Nazis and voting for the Communists would express their gratitude. His mistake and the fact that Moscow agreed to his proposal prove first that a man who has spent sixteen years in prison cannot judge the situation correctly, and secondly that Rákosi was highly esteemed by Stalin.

Rákosi never recovered from his bitter disappointment when the Communists obtained only seventeen percent of the seats in Parliament against almost sixty percent obtained by the Smallholders, a political party with a fine record in the opposition between the two wars. This was the first and only time the Soviets agreed to have free elections in any of their satellites.

But misjudging the political situation in 1945 was one of the few mistakes Rákosi made during the eleven years he was Stalin's proconsul in Hungary. This ruthless, cold operator invented the "salami-slicing tactics" by first amputating the non-Communist parties, then liquidating them one after the other. The whole process was completed by May 1949, when Hungarians gave 95.6 percent of all votes to the single list of candidates for Parliament. That was the end of the multiparty system. The monolithic dictatorship of the Communist party was accomplished.

Rákosi, of course, used the secret police and, whenever it was necessary, the Russian occupation forces in "amputating" his fragmented and bewildered opposition by eliminating its leaders one by one. Some were jailed, a few were kidnapped by the Russians, many were forced to flee the country. Looking back at the years 1945–1949, József Révai, the top theorist of the Hungarian Communists, said in the party's theoretical organ *Társadalmi Szemle* in the spring of 1949: "We were a minority in Parliament and in the government, but at the same time we represented the leading force. We had decisive control over the police forces. Our force, the force of the party and the working class, was multiplied by the fact that the Soviet Union and the Soviet army were always there to support us with their assistance."

Rákosi used strange and, in retrospect, sometimes childish ruses to impress everyone. During the coalition period in Hungary, when ministers from four parties participated in the government, he was always a few minutes late at cabinet meetings, arriving when everyone else was already seated. He did not waste time apologizing but sat down and took from his pocket a penknife with a long and sharp blade. He cut a sheet of paper into small pieces and having scribbled on each of them what was believed were instructions, handed them silently to his fellow Communists around the table. They acknowledged the instructions with a silent nod.

A veteran Communist, too old to be active after World War II but respected by his comrades for having spent a long life in the party, once asked for an audience with Rákosi when the latter was at the peak of his power as Stalin's trusted lieutenant in the ideological battle against Titoist heresy. (The veteran Communist told me this story many years later as we watched together how the young workers of a factory where he had been a foreman before he retired, fought Russian tanks in a Budapest square.)

Rákosi received the old man one evening in his office at party headquarters, and asked the question every politician would ask on such an occasion: what do people think of me? He got a frank answer.

"They don't like you, comrade. They are afraid of you."
Rákosi pondered for a minute. "They are afraid, you said.
. . . That's good," he answered.

Rákosi obviously learned one lesson from his prison years,
and I, together with all other political prisoners, paid the price.
He himself told the story of how he continued to organize even
in prison, teaching young convicts the Communist dogma and
enlisting them as future party members. He even had a small
radio receiver built in a drawer of the desk in his cell, and he
got Hungarian and foreign newspapers. Once in the late 1940's,
when he held his only press conference for the then sizable
flock of foreign newsmen, the correspondent of the *Manchester Guardian* asked him a question, identifying himself and his
paper, as was required. Rákosi, who dazzled the international
gathering by answering questions in faultless English, German,
and French — of course he spoke Russian and reportedly several other languages — reminisced a little and said he used to
read the *Guardian* in prison. All these luxuries, of course, were
nonexistent for us, Rákosi's prisoners. We had no radio and no
drawer to build it in, not even a Hungarian newspaper — let
alone the *Manchester Guardian* — and we could not "organize" anything because we were alone and isolated. Rákosi obviously would not risk giving us the privileges he had enjoyed
under a regime which otherwise was not liberal at all.

Though Rajk died on the gallows many years before the
1956 revolt, his tragic case should be recalled because of his
postmortem role in the revolution. In 1948 Stalin blackballed
Tito, and Rákosi's Hungary was given a role of dubious dis-
tinction: to spearhead the smear campaign against the Yugoslav
heretic. There was more to it, however, than inventing such
colorful epithets as calling Tito "the chained dog of imperialists." It had to be proved that the marshal was actually an agent
of the West, that he had always been a Western spy smuggled
into the midst of the millions of honest Communists. Tito, of

course, could not be touched in his stronghold in Belgrade. But there were top-ranking Communists in every country in Eastern Europe in whose past there was one suspicious element: they were exposed to the West during one time or another, most of them while fighting in the Spanish Civil War against Francisco Franco. In Hungary it was Rajk; in Czechoslovakia, Rudolf Slansky; in Bulgaria, Traicho Kostov.

I first met Rajk for a few brief minutes one night in 1944 on a dark corner of a quiet street in Budapest during the resistance period against the Nazis. We knew him only as "Kirghiz," an alias which suited him well: he was a tall, dark-haired, slender man, with the ruggedly handsome face of a Mongol. Rajk was a French teacher, a Communist since his early youth, and a commissar of the International Brigade in the Spanish Civil War. When it was over, he was interned in France. When World War II broke out, Moscow ordered him to return to Budapest to organize the underground Communist party.

After the war, in 1946, Rajk became minister of the interior, a post of immense importance in every Communist country because it controls all security organs, including the secret police and the frontier guards. In 1948, however, he was relieved of this post and named foreign minister, a job of little weight as the foreign policy of the satellites was shaped in Moscow.

Rajk did not last long as foreign minister: his involvement in the Spanish Civil War and his subsequent internment in France earmarked him for the principal role in an anti-Tito trial. Another, secondary factor in picking Rajk to be sacrificed was that Rákosi and his closest aides had spent many years between the two wars and during World War II in Moscow and they looked with suspicion on all those who had not (they were called red-white-green Communists after the colors of the Hungarian tricolor), including Rajk.

When plans had been completed for the big anti-Tito show trial, János Kádár, Rajk's friend and the godfather of his son, was instructed to help General Péter, the secret police chief, to arrest him. The scheme was simple. Rajk and Kádár would play chess at the party headquarters and Kádár would see to it that Rajk sat with his back to the door. Then, through the door would come Péter with his men to arrest Rajk. That is what happened, and Rajk's wife, Julia, then president of the powerful Communist-led Federation of Women, was arrested simultaneously.

This was not the end of Kádár's role. Once again he was to be used by Rákosi. Those who remember Koestler's *Darkness at Noon* know how reluctant Communists are persuaded to sacrifice themselves for the sake of the party, and it was Kádár's task to do the persuading. He visited Rajk in his cell and pleaded with him to make the ultimate sacrifice and confess at the trial because the party needed his confession. He brought greetings from Rákosi and the promise that after the trial, in the course of which he would have to be sentenced to death, he would be spirited away to live in peace under an assumed name in the Soviet Union.

Rajk, a man with iron nerves, finally gave in. What neither of them knew was that Rákosi, who did not trust Kádár either, recorded every word that was spoken in the cell, and the tape played a major role in the summer of 1956 when Rákosi was finally ousted.

I covered the trial of László Rajk in 1949. By then I had read *Darkness at Noon,* and to me the parallels were astounding. But *Darkness at Noon* was written by a great writer, and Rajk's trial was overdone by amateur stage managers like Péter, the former tailor, and by the several nameless Soviet secret police officers who wrote the scenario. Everybody performed a role — the judge, the prosecutor, the so-called defense lawyers, the defendants. They all recited their parts after endless rehearsals. But some of them, I suspected, went beyond the prescribed text. The excessive zeal of some of the defendants was almost unreal. They accused themselves, overbidding the prosecutor, of unheard-of crimes bordering on the ridiculous. At times I thought this was their secret message to the world, saying in effect that nobody with a sane mind should believe the nonsense they were confessing to. Many years later when I was "persuaded" to confess and it seemed that I would be the next star of a show trial, I remembered Rajk's trial and thought of doing the same.

Despite the assurances given to him, Rajk was executed in the prison yard and Julia, his wife, was forced to witness the hanging. Rajk believed the promises and when he was led to the gallows he wanted to cry out, to protest, but was quickly gagged and hanged. His rehabilitation and subsequent reburial on October 6, 1956, was the dress rehearsal of the revolution.

There is disappointingly little worth reporting about Imre Nagy's place in Hungary's postwar history prior to his sudden and unexpected emergence as prime minister in 1953. Before that he was a minor star on the firmament of Hungarian Communism, yet he will be remembered as the first man in the entire Communist orbit who made an honest effort to introduce "socialism with a human face." When he was swept back to power in 1956, he accepted the role of the revolutionary leader, first with considerable hesitation, but without reservations when the hour of truth came.

Nagy, like Rákosi, became a Communist as a prisoner of war in Russia during World War I. We know practically nothing about his activities during the short-lived Communist regime of Béla Kun in 1919, but it is safe to assume that he was in Hungary during most of the 1920's, working with the underground Communist movement. In the 1930's he was in the Soviet Union, but cleverly, or luckily, he stayed out of politics and escaped the Stalinist purges, during which so many non-Russian Communist leaders were executed, including Béla Kun. What he did during this time is not clear, but farming was always his main interest and according to one version he worked in a scientific institute of agriculture.

Accordingly it was no surprise that Nagy became minister of agriculture after World War II in the first, provisional Hungarian government and as such was responsible for the land reform, distributing the land of big estates among landless peasants, the former agrarian proletariat.

In November 1945, after the crushing Communist defeat in the parliamentary elections, Nagy became minister of the interior, a post he held for six months only, as he was replaced by Rajk in March 1946. Why he was chosen it is hard to explain: the job of controlling police forces was obviously not suited to this man with the characteristic traits of a peasant.

Between 1949 and 1952 Nagy was absent from the Hungarian political scene. He was never close to Rákosi, not even during the war years in Moscow, and relations between the two became worse when Rákosi pushed the collectivization of farmers, forcing them to give up their newly acquired land and join cooperatives. In 1952 Nagy was brought back into the Rákosi cabinet as one of three deputy premiers.

The reader will learn much more about Nagy in subsequent chapters, about the miraculous metamorphosis during which this unassertive, philosophically minded man became a revolutionary leader who chose death rather than compromise.

6

The Ferment

All my life I will regret that my arrest in February 1955 prevented me from witnessing the gradually increasing ferment inside the Hungarian Communist party that reached its bloody climax on October 23, 1956, the day the revolt broke out. Those eighteen months while I was kept isolated in prison must have been extremely exciting for someone to report from behind the Iron Curtain.

Because of my involuntary absence from the scene, everything I know about this ferment I learned during the few weeks between my release on August 16, 1956, and the outbreak of the revolution. In addition to my wife, my instructors were the rebels themselves and some non-Communist intellectuals. The latter watched the unfolding drama from the sidelines. Whether their active participation in the growing resistance against Rákosi would have helped is questionable. The whole affair remained a strictly intraparty issue at least until the late spring of 1956, and the non-Communists, timid and frightened by the years of Stalinist terror, would have had no opportunity to participate anyway. Also they were understandably suspicious, watching this strange quarrel between Communists but not against Communism.

Malenkov's ouster as Soviet premier in February 1955 sealed Nagy's fate: on March 9 the Central Committee of the Hungarian party censured Nagy for "rightist deviations," and on April 14 he was deposed as premier and dropped from the Politbureau.

It is safe to assume that Rákosi would have jailed Nagy had Moscow permitted him to do so, but he remained free. Khrushchev was in a magnanimous mood. The new Soviet premier had dispensed with Malenkov, his top rival; he had patched up differences with Tito, and fraternized with Eisenhower. Why bother with an aging idealist in Hungary? Nagy's imprisonment would have soured the improving climate of relations with the West and with Belgrade.

Nagy's popularity began to rise almost immediately. He was considered a martyr, Rákosi's victim, and gradually his house became the rallying point of disgruntled Communists, mostly men released from prison and "rehabilitated." And so, slowly, the revolt against Rákosi began, as a strictly domestic affair of the Communist party.

Nagy's ouster and Rákosi's return to full power did not bring about dramatic changes affecting the life of the man in the street. Rákosi was again making bellicose speeches calling for "discipline" and "vigilance," the same trite demands Magyars had grown used to hearing for almost ten years. Rákosi had not changed, nor could he adapt himself to the changed atmosphere in Moscow. He was, in a curious way, an honest politician who remained faithful to Stalinism, the only system he knew, even after it became unfashionable in the Soviet Union. But without the support and direction of Stalinists in the Soviet Union this skilled politician's actions became inconsistent and confused. It was obvious that his inclination was to continue to lean on the secret police, but he did not dare to because Khrushchev, with all his rivals eliminated, was already preparing the ground for his famous Twentieth Congress speech in which he denounced Stalin and everything the dead dictator represented.

Immediately after resuming full power in 1955, Rákosi shelved Nagy's "return to socialist legality," a euphemism for restricting the power of the secret police, but he did not dare to kill it completely. As Miklós Gimes, the Communist journalist who was executed in 1958 together with Nagy, told me in 1956 with unconcealed glee, Rákosi must have had sleepless nights when he remembered the hundreds of rehabilitated Communists who had been his victims in the 1940's, good Communists who had been tortured and kept in prison on his orders. Though powerless, these men and women were at large in 1955, and they were talking about the ruthless terror of the former Rákosi era. Rákosi saw the handwriting on the wall. Yet he did not dare to act, to have these men rearrested. The year was 1955 and anything that had the feel of Stalinist terror, whether in the Soviet Union or in one of the satellites, could have scuttled Khrushchev's reconciliatory efforts.

The indictment of Rákosi by these men who were talking freely all over the country was probably the most important factor in the conversion of Communist writers and journalists, who could now see what they had stubbornly declined to see earlier: that the system in which they lived and which called itself a "people's democracy" was based on terror. They claimed that only the narratives of their comrades opened their eyes, but I could never fully accept this feeble explanation for their ten-year acceptance of the Stalinist regime. There was a time in Hungary, as in other European countries and elsewhere, when it was fashionable for a young intellectual to be a Communist or at least a sympathizer. This, perhaps, was understandable. The oppression of the semifeudal system in Hungary and in most of central Europe, the misery of the depression era of the 1930's, the rise of Hitler and the concurrent impotence of the West, and the shame almost everybody felt during the Spanish Civil War, pushed these young men in Moscow's direction. The trouble was that most of them did not know what they were doing, because they understood little of the hopelessly outmoded Marxist doctrine and its subsequent distortions by Lenin and Stalin.

Their initial ignorance might be forgiven because in Hungary between the two wars the Soviet Union was taboo; one did not speak about it. The classic truism that one should know one's enemy was completely ignored; the myopic and mediocre Hungarian leaders believed the ostrich was right.

What cannot be forgiven was that these extremely capable young men remained blind when Communism moved into their own country and they could observe it at first hand. They were in the courtroom, as I was, when Rajk was tried in 1949. I refuse to believe that they could not see through the clumsy effort to portray their comrades in the dock as traitors, spies, and informers of the prewar police. I cannot believe that only in 1955, when the rehabilitated talked, did the others learn about the terror which reigned in Hungary for so many years. If schoolchildren knew, why didn't the writers and journalists?

But in fact I can offer no plausible explanation for the 1955 volte-face of these intellectuals. When I came out of prison in August 1956, one of them called and asked to see me. At one time I had liked him, and I was curious to hear what he had to say, so I invited him for dinner.

"What brings you to me?" I asked him. There was no need to remind him that he had avoided me for so many years.

"I want to apologize, and I am sure I speak for many of us. I apologize for what we were, through so many years," he said.

I asked him what caused the change.

"Don't ask me, I don't know the answer. The answer I would give you is no good, and perhaps not true either. Maybe once, when we have had time to reflect, we'll come up with an honest answer. Until then be patient with us," he said.

I did not press the issue then and cannot press it now, because the journalist, now middle-aged, stayed in Hungary and I did not. I will probably never know the explanation for the blindness of these men, most of them eloquent apologists for ten years of a regime of terror.

A few of those who chose to leave Hungary when the revolution was crushed made pitiful efforts to whitewash themselves, to explain why they were Communists when it was dangerous to be anything else, and later when it was also dangerous to be a Communist. There is, I believe, no need for them to explain, to clear themselves, to insist on what nobody would believe: that they did not know about the monstrosities of the Stalin-Rákosi era. Everyone who participated in the period of ferment preceding the revolt and everyone who remained faithful to the revolution during the period of passive resistance — and the great majority of Communist writers did — has purged himself. The bungling efforts to explain were worthless and unnecessary.

When judging the writers and journalists who turned against Rákosi in 1955, one should not forget that their role was highly dangerous, and they knew it. When I came out of prison, I found on my desk a neat collection, prepared by my wife, of articles published in newspapers and magazines, together with a memorandum the writers submitted to the Communist party protesting against Rákosi's efforts to take away the few freedoms they had gained since July 4, 1953. The list of signatories was a Who's Who of contemporary Hungarian literature, which included the names of veteran Communist writers and journalists who had spent the years between the two wars in exile along with the names of the younger generation. The memorandum was not made public, of course, but in no time copies circulated in Budapest, and fortunately one of them was kept by foresighted friends for me.

Somebody not familiar with circumstances behind the Iron Curtain might not understand why it was so important that poems and writings openly critical of the Rákosi regime could be published in 1955 and 1956. There are no independent newspapers and magazines in a Communist country. All of them, without exception, including the smallest country paper, belong to the Communist state, to the Communist party, or to one of its organs. There had been no need for censorship: all editors and most of the reporters were party members, or what was worse, timid fellow travelers who knew too well what the party expected from them. In Hungary during this prerevolution period *Irodalmi Ujság* (Literary Gazette), the weekly of the Association of Writers, spearheaded the revolt against self-censorship and invited Rákosi's wrath.

There was nothing to indicate in 1955 that Nagy, deprived of any role in public life, and finally even of his party membership, was active in this growing and ever louder opposition against the man who ousted him, nor, indeed, that he encouraged this trend in any way. As a matter of fact, a number of Nagy's adherents were frustrated by his cautious, conservative approach to the burning problems their party was facing. Géza Losonczy, a non-Moscowite Communist and one of the rehabilitated, told me later, a few days before the revolution, how disappointed he and some of his friends were by Nagy's hesitance. Losonczy, a minister in Nagy's cabinet during the revolt, died in prison before he could be tried.

Having pieced together the events of this period after my release, I must give all the credit for at least the beginning of the ferment to the Communist and fellow-traveling writers, journalists, and a sprinkling of other intellectuals. This must have been a painful fact for many non-Communists in Hungary, and especially for many émigrés outside Hungary, to digest. The latter group in particular, having lived for too long in a vacuum, was reluctant to understand that an anti-Communist revolt of such magnitude could have been prepared almost exclusively by Communists or Communist sympathizers. Many years later in the United States, I had to listen to fantastic theories about the alleged role of non-Communists in the events of

1955 and 1956, and in most cases it was futile to argue with the perpetrators of such wild notions.

Yet the cautious passivity of non-Communists in the ferment period should be understood. They were, first of all, suspicious. It was, after all, hard to believe that men who for years had been writing nauseating tributes to Rákosi should be now out to fell him. They suspected that this was nothing but a Communist house quarrel and, whatever the outcome, Communism was here to stay. Secondly, the non-Communists had no outlet and no place to gather. A non-Communist writer or newspaperman could go nowhere with whatever he intended to write. The same situation applied to verbal criticism of the Rákosi regime. The Communist writers, journalists, and other intellectuals, in addition to their newspapers, had their clubs. The wave of censure spread gradually to the local party organizations, and reached its peak with the debates in the Petöfi Circle, of which I will tell more later. Only then, in the summer of 1956, could the non-Communists participate, mainly as passive listeners, when the Petöfi Circle debates were opened to everyone.

The Rákosi of that period was definitely not the ruthless dictator who previously had crushed far lesser opposition. Not that he had mellowed, but, being the shrewd old fox he was, he knew that the tune to be played must be in rhythm with the conductor in Moscow and that even a minor difference in interpretation of the oeuvre was a dangerous game. Rákosi played the game dangerously: he tried to satisfy Khrushchev by paying lip service to the new trend without really implementing the changes, and he paid the price on July 18, 1956.

This restraint must have been painful for Rákosi. First, he was aware that his former victims, whom Nagy had rehabilitated, were now ready to stab him in the back. There was Tito, whom Rákosi had adorned with all the abusive epithets he could find in the colorful Hungarian language ever since the Yugoslav marshal had been booted out of the Cominform in

1948. It must have been frightening for Rákosi to watch Khrushchev's pilgrimage of reconciliation to Belgrade in May 1955. It was easy for Khrushchev to blame Stalin for the 1948 rift — although whether Tito believed him is questionable — but there was nobody behind whom Rákosi could hide. And then, also in May 1955, the Soviets agreed to withdraw from Austria under the condition that Hungary's Western neighbor would become a neutral country. Nobody knew better than Rákosi the many intangible links between the two neighbors, tied together for centuries under the Austro-Hungarian monarchy in a curious love-hate marriage. He must have known that Austria's neutrality would some day arouse longings among Magyars to follow suit, which indeed became the case in 1956. And finally, 1955 was the year of the Geneva summit meeting between President Eisenhower and the team of Khrushchev and Bulganin, a historic event which determined my imprisonment and release, and my wife's as well.

Opposition to Rákosi within the Communist party was not organized and consisted of several factions. It had no leader because Nagy was not a real leader; he shied from the more extremist rebellious party elements who fought not only Rákosi and whatever he represented, but, perhaps unwittingly, Communism itself. These were mostly the rehabilitated Communists and their friends. Most of them remained party members, but they felt sure — some of them consciously — that Marxism had become bankrupt in Hungary, as Géza Losonczy told me a few weeks before the revolt.

Rákosi stubbornly clung to his job and tried to put on the brakes without resorting to methods of terror. It was a special Hungarian tragedy that he stayed on too long and that steps taken to satisfy the nation's desire for greater freedom were too little and too late. This explains the basic difference between the bloody revolt in Hungary and the bloodless, almost peaceful change in Poland. In Poland Boleslaw Bierut, the Polish

Rákosi, died in March 1956 and was replaced first by Edward Ochab, a middle-of-the-road Communist, and later by Wladyslaw Gomulka, a "nationalist Communist." In Hungary Rákosi had to be ejected with Moscow's help almost by force, but he was replaced by his alter ego, Ernö Gerö (no kin of Major Gerö, my wife's interrogator in prison), no less a Stalinist than Rákosi himself, and Nagy had to be literally forced to take over. But it was too late to prevent what by then was inevitable. Also, to use the same comparison, in Poland Stefan Cardinal Wyszynski, a priest who combined great courage with political skill, was the active leader of his Church, while in Hungary József Cardinal Mindszenty, also a man of courage but an incompetent politician, was kept isolated. This was a considerable difference which should not be ignored in two such strongly Catholic countries as Poland and Hungary.

Rákosi had an added disadvantage: Tito. The Yugoslav marshal was quite willing to be reconciled with Russia's post-Stalin leaders, but certainly not with Rákosi, who for years had heaped abuse on him. Characteristically, when Tito visited the Soviet Union the first time after he and Khrushchev buried the hatchet, he ostentatiously avoided the direct route through Hungary and ordered his special train to proceed through Romania.

Yet until the spring of 1956 it appeared that Rákosi could weather the subdued rebellion of the writers and journalists. After the Twentieth Party Congress in the Soviet Union, his situation became untenable and it was only a question of time until he would be forced out. Rákosi attended the Congress and heard Khrushchev denounce Stalin and everything the late dictator had stood for. When he returned to Budapest he continued to dance on top of the volcano, hoping that Khrushchev's then still secret speech would not become known to his comrades in Hungary. He was, of course, wrong.

Again Rákosi tried the old trick, paying cautious lip service to the new Khrushchev line, but doing as little as possible. Yet he had to do something, so a few weeks after the Congress he himself announced that the Supreme Court had rehabilitated László Rajk who, he said, was the victim of General Péter and his AVH henchmen. Rákosi never stopped scheming. I have already described how he tried to "persuade" Péter, then a prisoner for more than three years, to accept the blame for Rajk's execution, a plan which obviously backfired when Péter refused to play ball.

Rákosi made one grave error when he permitted public debates in the Petöfi Circle, a debating club established for party members in 1955. Petöfi was one of the world's greatest lyric poets, who would have achieved worldwide renown had he not written in Hungarian. This genius was only twenty-five when he died in 1849. He disappeared in a battle against the czarist armies in Hungary's War of Independence and it was assumed that he was killed and buried in a mass grave.

The turning point in the ferment came in the spring of 1956, when the Petöfi Circle debates were thrown open to the public, something unprecedented in a Communist country. Hundreds attended in the beginning, but after a few weeks thousands and thousands wanted to participate and Budapesters packed the streets around the building where the debating sessions were held. They stood for long hours and listened to the vitriolic denunciations through hastily set up amateurish loudspeakers. It was — so everybody who attended told me — a most intoxicating experience to listen to speaker after speaker censuring the regime, many openly suggesting that Rákosi resign. Instead of doing so, he still made halfhearted efforts to save his neck. The Petöfi Circle was reprimanded by the party at Rákosi's request; newspapers which ignored party directives and reported what was going on at these nightly debates were confiscated, but usually only after they had been on sale already for hours. The result was that people were willing to pay exorbitant black-market prices — sometimes a hundred forints for a one-forint paper — for *Irodalmi Ujság,* while other copies were circulated freely among friends and neighbors.

The significance of the Petöfi Circle debates was that they removed the issues from the ivory tower of writers and journalists and presented them to everybody — even to the man in the street, who neither had his own ax to grind, like the rehabilitated Communists, nor was bound by some romantic loyalty to the Communist party, as Nagy himself was. Much later, after my release from prison, I talked to various people who attended some of these meetings, most of them only indirectly affected by the grievances aired at the debates. They said they went even if they had to stand on the street for hours, even if they understood only half of what was said. But all went to enjoy this unheard-of sensation, to watch this manifestation of never-before freedom and to listen to speakers, known and unknown, denouncing what the listener hated. It apparently made no difference to them that the Petöfi Circle debates were organized by Communists and that most of the speakers came from their ranks.

In the late spring and early summer of 1956 the rebellion spread from the Petöfi Circle debates to the party organizations. One episode stands out in my memory. It happened at a meeting of party "activists" and other functionaries of Budapest's thirteenth district, a vast industrial area where, after his rehabilitation, Kádár became party secretary. Rákosi attended the session, another clear indication of his uneasiness. In earlier years the boss of all Hungarian Communists attended only important mass rallies, but in 1956, in a desperate attempt to regain the confidence of rank-and-file Communists, Rákosi came to obscure events arranged by local party organizations, such as the meeting in the thirteenth district.

It was an uneventful evening until, without advance warning, a young man stood up and asked the blunt question: "Comrade Rákosi, why don't you relinquish your post? Can't you see that nobody wants you? Please go, but immediately." Rákosi was taken aback; he ranted about the "voice of the enemy," threatened and cajoled, but the party hacks watched his strange performance in cool silence.

I did not meet the young man until September 1956 when on a lovely Indian summer day, in one of the public swimming pools frequented by journalists, he was pointed out to me with admiration. György Litván — described as a teacher by someone, as a writer by someone else, though he could have been both — was not a born hero, my companions said. He was a timid, quiet man, deathly afraid when he rose at the meeting, but ready to go to jail for his bold action.

Meanwhile Imre Nagy appeared more and more often in public. With no official status, Nagy had no car, so he took the bus to town from his villa in one of the residential districts, and walked around the fashionable downtown streets. He was recognized by virtually everyone and basked in the sensation of being popular, a sensation few Communist leaders know. He was greeted by unknown men and women who stopped to shake his hand, inquire about his health and — at least some of them — to urge him to be ready to return to power. One day he met Ilona.

It happened on the bus which both of them took. Ilona by then was already free but she had no car because the AVH had confiscated our Studebaker, without waiting for the court's decision. The car and my expensive German camera were never returned to us, not even for money; the rest of our confiscated belongings we were graciously permitted to buy back for hard cash from the regime. I was later told that the AVH had repainted the white car black and used it to transport high-ranking officers.

On the bus Ilona was startled at first when Nagy sat down on the seat next to her. The former prime minister immediately recognized the woman reporter who had been so enthusiastic three years earlier when he had delivered his speech on the unforgettable July 4 in the Hungarian Parliament. While they traveled, Ilona told Nagy our story, how the two little girls were left alone, and what ridiculous charges were raised against us. Nagy was visibly shocked and shook his head. "This should never have happened. Never, never," he said.

Although we did not know it, Nagy had finished writing his "dissertation" in defense of his "new course." It was available to a few of his intimate friends who received mimeographed copies. The originals were sent to the Communist party leadership and to Andropov, the Soviet ambassador. Much later, in 1957 when Nagy was prepared for trial and execution, it was published clandestinely in Hungary and a copy, sent by some anonymous benefactor, reached me here in America.

Nagy's book shows him exactly as he was until the last days of the revolution, when events swept him away: an idealistic Communist, a man who believed in what is apparently impossible, a kind of humanistic Communism in which the party is the gathering of noble-minded disciples of Marx, ready to let the state wither away.

"Dictatorship of the proletariat in the people's democracy is replaced by party dictatorship," Nagy complained in his book. "It relies on personal dictatorship . . . and makes the party apparatus and party membership tools of this dictatorship. . . . The AVH, raised above society and the party, became the principal organ of power. . . . The leaders made virtues of self-abasement, cowardice, hypocrisy, lack of principles, and lies. . . . Instead of humanism, cold inhumanity dominates public life."

"The oppressive inheritance of the Stalin era must be radically liquidated," Nagy wrote. Could he foresee that two years later he himself would be liquidated in a wave of neo-Stalinism?

Despite Rákosi's efforts to conceal the truth about the Twentieth Party Congress in the Soviet Union, or at least to interpret this milestone in Communist history to his own taste, his situation became gradually more and more untenable once translations of Khrushchev's speech began to circulate among Hungarian Communists. That copies of this speech reached Budapest, and doubtless other Communist capitals, would have been something unthinkable in the Stalin period, but times had changed, though Rákosi was still reluctant to understand the changes. This may explain his behavior in the spring and summer of 1956. We still do not know whether he was ordered by Moscow to forget about the iron fist of yesteryear, or whether, being a good politician, he knew without orders that he could not resort to terror, however much he wanted to do so. One day he did something to please the people, the other he played the desperate game of procrastination, hoping perhaps that Khrushchev would change his mind, or that Molotov and his old guard would oust the new Kremlin leader, or that Tito would acquiesce to his continued rule in Hungary.

Tito did not. It was apparently impossible for the proud marshal to make peace with two men: Rákosi and Bulgaria's Vulko Chervenkov. The Kremlin had to make the choice either to have full reconciliation with Belgrade or to keep in power these two remnants of the Stalinist past. Obviously both had to go, and in dismissing them Tito was the chief consideration in Khrushchev's mind, not the ever growing and louder dissatisfaction with Rákosi in Hungary.

Yet it took several months until the final decision was made and meanwhile Rákosi, then called the "bald murderer," kept trying. One day he ordered the dismantling of "defense installations," meaning the minefields and barbed wire fence on Hungary's western border with Austria, a step which would have been immensely popular a few years earlier; the next day he proposed the arrest of Nagy and of four hundred writers and journalists. One day he criticized himself in the true Communist fashion, admitting publicly that grave crimes had been committed while he was the omnipotent master of the country; the next day copies of *Pravda*, the Soviet party organ, mysteriously disappeared from the newsstands because they contained an article which Rákosi thought should not be read by Russian-speaking party members.

It was a desperate game and it did not work. The climax came at a Central Committee meeting of the party when Rákosi tried to discredit Kádár in the eyes of his comrades. Kádár was by no means one of the extremists. He did not join those around Nagy and did not belong to the embittered gang of rehabilitated Communists who wanted one thing: revenge. Yet Rákosi must have thought that Kádár could be dangerous, a rallying point for the opposition within the hierarchy, especially as Kádár spoke about the necessity of fully rehabilitating Rajk. On that day, at the Central Committee meeting, Rákosi produced the secret tape recording of the conversation between Kádár and Rajk in the latter's prison cell, when Kádár persuaded his friend to accept the role assigned to him and to admit his guilt in open trial.

The tape was played by one of Rákosi's cronies and those present immediately recognized the two voices. Kádár had to listen to his own voice telling Rajk that it was his duty to sacrifice himself because only through such a sacrifice would "the masses" believe that Tito was the archenemy. Of course everybody knew that Rajk was innocent, Kádár assured the tormented man, and everything had been arranged: after the trial he would be spirited away to recuperate in the Soviet Union, reunited with his wife and son, and then start a new life under an assumed name in a new job, serving international Communism.

According to the version of the event I heard, it was Erik Molnár, a puritanistic veteran Communist, a historian by profession and former minister of justice, who became suspicious and requested that the tape be replayed, right from the beginning, because he observed that Rákosi's man who handled the machine did not play the first few feet of the tape. Despite Rákosi's weak resistance, the committee ordered a replay. The beginning of the tape unmasked the plot and Rákosi's cheap scheming. The tape started with Kádár's words: "I have come at the request of Comrade Rákosi. He asked me to explain to you the situation. He believes you will understand . . ."

This was the beginning of the end for Rákosi. It is still hard to understand why this extremely clever man made the fatal mistake of not erasing the first sentences on the tape which incriminated him. He was like the burglar who leaves his fingerprints all over the place, and this must have been the mistake the bosses in Moscow could not forgive. If a Communist leader resorts to Orwellian tactics to make something an "unfact," he must do it completely. Rákosi forgot this rule and he had to pay the price. The incident in the Central Committee meeting became known nationwide in days, and the report on what had happened must have reached Moscow, too.

The end came on July 18, 1956. Khrushchev sent Mikoyan, his trusted troubleshooter, to Budapest. The Armenian, attending the Central Committee meeting, told Rákosi matter-of-factly that he must go. Rákosi would not believe him. He requested to hear the verdict from the boss himself. Mikoyan had no objections, so Rákosi, still ranting, called Khrushchev from the meeting, and was told that he was through. A day later a Soviet airplane flew Rákosi to Moscow, and the luxury villa on the Svábhegy, the Hill of the Svabians, became vacant.

When the revolution was crushed in November 1956, Rákosi thought the time had come for his return. He was a daily visitor to the Hungarian embassy in Moscow from where he made numerous telephone calls to Communists in Budapest who, he thought, remained loyal to him. This went on until one day *Népszabadság*, Kádár's party organ, protested indignantly against this abuse of the embassy and Rákosi was told that he was an unwelcome guest.

For many years after his ouster Rákosi firmly believed that he was the victim of a "revisionist" plot and that the Hungarian proletariat was expecting him back. In 1970 only Kádár's skillful maneuvering prevented his return to Hungary.

The Soviets apparently got fed up with the seventy-eight-year-old Hungarian and put pressure on Kádár to permit his return. Kádár, who knows that one does not say *nyet* to Moscow, reluctantly agreed and Communist party organizations throughout Hungary were informed accordingly. There was no effort made by the government, however, to keep the issue secret and in no time virtually everybody in Hungary knew about the Soviet request.

This, one must assume, was Kádár's plot. The government and its newspapers were flooded with letters from outraged citizens, and Julia Rajk, widow of the executed László Rajk, threatened to charge Rákosi publicly with murder, should he return.

Though Kádár faithfully reported all this to Moscow, the Soviets did not yield immediately. Rákosi's return, the Kremlin argued, would prove how firm Kádár's rule was.

It was Rákosi himself who overplayed the game. He was told that he could return and live in a luxurious villa on Lake Balaton, where he could enjoy his remaining years. The old Communist would not buy this. He said he would choose the place to live and warned that he wanted complete freedom of movement in the country.

This gave Kádár the opportunity to tell Moscow that under such circumstances he would need a legion of bodyguards to save Rákosi from his countrymen. Then, finally, Moscow gave in and Rákosi was informed that he would have to continue to live in Russia (where he remained until his death in February 1971).

7

Prelude to October 23

August 16, 1956, was a lovely summer day, and I was free, at home, reunited with my wife and daughters. Nothing else mattered that day, not even the shock I felt when I saw myself in the mirror for the first time in eighteen months. What mattered were the tears and the smiles on the faces around me.

Yet from the minute I was outside the prison gate I knew that the strange and unnatural duality, when Life (capital *L*) and my life in prison (very small *l*) moved on parallel tracks which never met, had ended. The two tracks had merged and I had again become a part of the whole, sharing the few joys and the many despairs of others.

It is easy to make a rule that the reporter should be an unemotional, nonpartisan observer whose task is to register and to report whatever he sees. The theory is a noble one, the praxis is different. The war correspondent who was wounded, the reporter who was clubbed covering a riot, knows the difference between theory and praxis.

Few if any "impartial, objective" observers, newspapermen, or diplomats who witnessed what happened in Hungary in the historic fall of 1956, could remain detached and cool. I had dinner with an experienced diplomat on the night of October 25, the day of the "massacre on Parliament Square," and watched him bury his face in his hands and cry. And I saw the tears rolling down the cheeks of a veteran American newspaperman when we talked on the street with an old and fragile man, a retired university professor, who explained to us in beautiful, scholarly English, ignoring the shooting only a few hundred feet away, that this was the great chance of what he called the Anglo-Saxon world to help Hungary and for all Eastern Europe to rejoin the West, to which it had always belonged.

But that was much later. On August 16, the day I was set free, I did not think of things to come.

The "great news" of my release had already reached the world. Major Kretsmer, when he called Ilona and told her to come and take me home, also requested that she write a news story and put it on the wire.

To get back to work was not easy. First I had to learn and understand what I had missed during the months of isolation, a period of tremendous changes, and I had to feel for myself the new atmosphere. I decided to take my time and my editors agreed that after a week or so I should write a series of Hungary Revisited stories. I also needed some rest. We spent a week on Lake Balaton, the place we had visited so often since the Communists had built their Iron Curtain and we could not travel outside the country. As a matter of fact we hadn't asked for passports since 1948, so as not to give the Communists the satisfaction of rejecting our applications. During this peaceful week on the lake I was educated by Ilona about the dramatic events of the summer, and was told the many little details about how she lived before her arrest and after her release, and how the children had spent the months when both of us were in prison.

I wanted to know everything about how Juli and Kati, then ten and nine respectively, lived during that period, and especially how people behaved, friends and others, with two innocent children deprived of their parents. I had good reason to be curious. The Communist world is a cruel one and there were cowards who would not dare to help children whose parents were labeled as traitors to the regime. This was the case with my children, too. We had almost no close relatives in Hungary because Ilona's parents were dead, and mine were living in Australia, together with my only brother. The only close relative was my wife's sister, married to a conductor of the Budapest Opera, and they did their best to look after my daughters.

Nothing characterizes living conditions in Communist Hungary better than that my sister-in-law and her husband could not take my children because their home consisted of only one room. Eventually the secret police found them a larger apartment to enable them to take in my daughters; but too late, because by the time their apartment was ready, my wife had been set free. So the only solution was to find for them a place as "paying guests," and the girls found shelter in an old house on the outskirts of Budapest, the home of a retired professor.

We had few Hungarian friends, partly because we did not need many, partly because we understood when some of them stopped seeing us. Friendship, even casual acquaintance, with stigmatized people like Ilona and me, can be highly dangerous in a Communist country. Some of those who were bold enough to remain our friends cared for my daughters, but not all of them, and those who got cold feet after our arrest and did not dare to go near to the children caused one of the greatest disappointments of my life. There was almost no bitterness left in me toward my tormentors after my release. What they did was their duty as they understood it; they were Communists and in their eyes I must have been the enemy of everything they represented — and they were right. But I felt bitterness toward so-called friends who abandoned two little girls when they needed help and I decided that these people simply would not exist for me any more. I kept this pledge.

The AVH, of course, knew about my daughters and Captain Babics chided me frequently, saying: "What kind of friends do you have anyway? They don't care about your children. Do they think we would hold it against them?"

I was deeply touched when Ilona told me about people who were not our intimate friends, but who had the courage to be almost ostentatiously kind to Juli and Kati. There was Mihály Székely, the great basso profundo, the first man in postwar Hungary to own an American-made car. He had bought it when he sang King Marke in Wagner's *Tristan* at the Metropolitan in New York. And Aladár Tóth, director of the Budapest Opera (husband of Annie Fischer, one of the world's greatest female concert pianists), who invited the two little girls to sit in his box at the opera. What really moved me was a scattering of people I did not know who offered help, even money.

Our American and British friends were Ilona's greatest mainstay before her arrest. She continued to work and it was agreed that the best thing for her was to behave as if nothing had happened. Occasionally our friends staged a "showing of the flag" for her, such as in May 1955 at the traditional British legation garden party on the queen's birthday.

Ilona arrived deliberately late. The British minister's residence was a perfect setting for a dramatic entrance. She crossed the big hall out to the spacious terrace from where a majestic flight of stairs led to the one-acre garden teeming with guests. The British envoy, George Labouchere, wearing his cutaway with a rose in his buttonhole, and Chris Ravndal, the American minister, rushed up the stairs to greet her, the wife of a newspaperman who had "disappeared" several months earlier. Ilona, flanked by the two high-ranking diplomats, slowly descended the marble steps. Everybody saw this unrehearsed scene, including Gerö, then Hungary's number two Communist, Endre Sik, deputy foreign minister, and many others. It could have meant only one thing: the West continued to care for the Martons.

Our best friends were Tom and Sarah Rogers, a wonderful couple and our next door neighbors. How often, Ilona told me, one of the Rogers children, little Louise, a blue-eyed blond angel, came to the fence and called up the terrace to her: "Mrs. Marton, where is your husband?" What could she answer?

The Rogers family lined up at the fence on the afternoon I got home to greet me with warm smiles — and with a bottle of champagne. I knew then that I was home, and I kept wondering how it happened that I found everything in the house the way I had left it, except for a few things, like our car and my camera. Ilona explained the mystery, and her story was highly unusual. Normally when "confiscation of property" was part of the sentence, and that was the case in all instances I could recall, it was carried out immediately. It meant that after the contents were confiscated the convict's apartment or house was taken away and usually given to some loyal party hack. What the regime did with such things as worn clothes or jewelry, I never found out. Books, the pride of every intellectual in central Europe, found their way to prison libraries; art treasures and expensive china were sold in government pawnshops to foreigners who could pay in hard currency.

I had a hunch in prison that despite the confiscation clause of our sentence our belongings had not been scattered around. When I asked for my typewriter, for the Webster's, and then later for the comfortable moccasins, I got them almost immediately. Yet I did not dare to ask, just as I did not dare to ask why I was kept in Fö utca after the Supreme Court trial, against all known rules of the game. This reluctance to ask questions is, I believe, understandable. It is in such situations better to be uncertain than to hear bad news.

When my wife was released from prison she went to her

sister's one-room apartment to change into something in which she could appear before the children, who still did not know that their mother was to rejoin them soon. Then Mihály Székely, the opera singer, and his wife came with their big car to take her to the other end of the city where Juli and Kati lived. Their reunion was a tearful affair. Juli was high up in a tree and seeing her mother she got so excited that she could not find her way down and grown-ups had to rescue her.

But then, when the girls asked their mother to take them home, it dawned on Ilona for the first time that there was no such thing as "home" for her. The next morning she called her lawyer and asked for advice. The lawyer said she should see Judge Jónás. The "blood judge," as Jónás was known, was genuinely surprised to see her.

"I did not expect you so soon. They should have told me that you were released," he said. Ilona explained the purpose of her visit. The apartment was still sealed and uninhabited — a most unusual thing in a city with a tremendous housing shortage — and Jónás had the key. "Go in, you have been paroled, you may claim back your belongings. And don't think for a minute that the apartment is vacant by chance. I kept it that way," the judge said. Did he sense the change? The answer was probably yes. When the revolution came, Jónás committed suicide. Sarkadi, the arrogant prosecutor of our first trial, was killed during the street fighting.

This, however, was not the end of the story. Ilona was in the apartment with our daughters, but nothing she found there belonged to us. The authorities quickly told her what she could do: pay two thousand dollars, and everything would be hers again, except for the car and the camera, which must be kept as "evidence." The Associated Press came to her rescue, the money was paid and with the exception of one precious ring which had disappeared, I found everything as I had left it eighteen months earlier.

For days and weeks I learned feverishly, reading old newspapers and listening to people, tasting the new climate of this once glorious city. Before meeting anyone of importance I wanted to meet the man in the street to get a feel of the change. For hours I wandered through the streets, speaking to people I knew and to others I did not. The change, indeed, was tremendous. There was almost nothing left of the permanent fear that characterized life in Hungary for ten years. There was no more looking back over one's shoulder, there was no flinching when I told those who did not know me that I was an American newspaperman. And, first of all, there was no longer fear of being seen with a man who had been convicted as a traitor and a spy. Of course this was new only to me. By then hundreds — some claimed thousands — of political prisoners had been freed, every day others were released, and my old barber, who by then was forced to give up his own shop and join a "cooperative," did not even ask where I had been for eighteen months, instead of visiting him every two or three weeks for a haircut.

"I read in the paper that you were free," the man said, working on my head with angry grunts, cursing the prison barber for what he had done to my hair. "I have been expecting you for some time," he said. The barber's indifferent attitude amused but also annoyed me. People, I thought, should be more surprised to see me alive. I had no better luck when I enjoyed the unheard-of luxury of a manicure after the old man got through with my head. I did not know the young manicurist and I warned her that I needed special attention because for eighteen months I had had to bite off my nails when they became too long. "Prison?" she asked without surprise. "I know what you mean. They all come in with the same problem . . ."

I also telephoned the press office of the foreign ministry and was immediately asked to come and visit them. This office had to look after foreign correspondents, but during the years our contacts were rare and of little if any value, unless the regime wanted something from us.

I still remember one of my visits to this office during the Stalinist era. The woman who was then deputy chief of the press section, a scared offspring of a bourgeois family, obviously thought that she had to prove every minute what a good Communist she was. The ministry was on the Buda side of the Danube and the windows of the woman's office faced the majestic river. On the opposite side, in the northern industrial suburb of Pest, there must have been a big fire as I saw black smoke billowing into the sky. What was burning? I asked innocently. The woman looked out the window with a blank expression on her face. "Burning?" she asked, "I don't see anything . . ."

That was the ridiculously tragic period when according to the Communist masters of the country everybody had to be happy in this people's democratic paradise. There were no obituaries in the newspapers because obviously nobody died. Accidents, crimes, and murders remained unreported; such things just could not happen. When people were forced to buy worthless "peace loans," usually for a month's pay, they did it "voluntarily" and, of course, happily. The papers printed nauseating articles and photos, showing a poor "overjoyed" worker signing away a considerable part of his meager pay. How could I expect that Mrs. Katona would acknowledge that there was a fire?

The atmosphere was decidedly different when I visited the press section on this early autumn day in 1956. There was no need for me to explain why I came; they were expecting me and obviously knew everything. I found new faces in the office and the new head of the section said he wanted me to meet the man in charge of the American desk in the ministry. This again was unprecedented, as earlier we were never supposed to meet anyone outside the press office. I became more surprised when the desk officer entered. The young man looked and talked like someone who had just left Oxford. Mr. Kun spoke impeccable English, and what was far more important, he did not speak at all as a Communist was supposed to speak. The explanation was simple: he was not a Communist, and a couple of weeks later, during the revolt, he called me to say good-bye. Today he is a renowned China expert somewhere in the West.

Slowly, I thought, I understood what I had missed during my involuntary absence. I wrote my Hungary Revisited pieces, summing up as faithfully as I could the changes and their importance. What I did not write was something which kept my thoughts busy all the time: *quo vadis Hungaria?* I asked myself. Where will this lead? How long will the Soviets tolerate this evolution? The same thought emerged, of course, in many minds, including those of my friends at the Western legations. Both Ravndal and Labouchere, the American and British envoys, had left Budapest before I was released. Labouchere was replaced by Minister Frey, a man I did not know, but Washington was in no hurry to send a new minister to Hungary. This delay was unforgivable in my judgment. Those were exciting times and though nobody could predict that it would end in a bloody armed uprising, the day-by-day changes were important enough to justify a first-class man at the U.S. legation.

The French minister to Hungary made possible my first post-prison contact with some of the men around Nagy. I was invited to the envoy's house for lunch and there I met for the first time in many years Géza Losonczy, one of the architects of the ferment. I had known Losonczy during the late 1940's when he was the number two man — the equivalent of under secretary — in the foreign ministry. Losonczy was one of the "red-white-green" Communists. He had spent many years in prison when Rákosi got rid of the non-Moscowite elements in his party, and was rehabilitated when Nagy was prime minister between 1953 and 1955. During the lunch Losonczy explained in cool, un-emotional terms that what we had seen thus far was just the beginning, that a "humanistic phase" of Communism must follow and nothing could stop this trend. After the lunch, sitting alone with him in a corner of the French diplomat's elegant residence, I asked him how this would come about? It is simple, he said. The Russians must know that replacing Rákosi with Gerö was a mistake, and if they did not know it, Tito must have told them several times. There was only one man to replace Gerö: Imre Nagy.

The only trouble with Nagy, Losonczy said, was his passivity. Despite the humiliation he had suffered, Nagy remained deeply devoted to the party and to the Soviets who, he believed, might have been misled by Rákosi but would soon recognize that changes were inevitable. Nagy really did not care to become a leader; he was convinced that he would be readmitted to the party and that was all he wanted for himself. But despite his passivity he had become a popular hero. People did not think of him as a Communist, but as a Magyar who in 1953 tried to introduce Communism with a human face, to create a Communist country without secret police terror and with bread and butter for everyone. He would be swept back to power; how and when, nobody could tell, Losonczy said.

I was convinced, but our conversation did not answer the burning question: what was the limit beyond which the Soviets would not tolerate this liberal trend. Actually what I heard from Losonczy and other Communists on Nagy's side was no longer new. My meetings with faceless little men were far more significant, I thought. One day I made an appointment at DISz, the Hungarian youth federation established by the Communists, who had forced all other youth organizations either to disband or to merge into this body, firmly controlled by the party.

I was received by a young man who acted like a true Communist. There is a certain Communist style which characterizes the official, whether a cabinet minister or someone of lower rank, whenever he talks to a non-Communist. The style is cool, but cocksure; the arguments are submitted in low tones, but with unmistakable authority, as if saying: "There is no need to argue, these are the facts, this is where we stand, take it or leave it." The young man's style was unmistakably that of a Communist official, but what he said in mid-September, more than a month before the revolution, was very much the same as the famous demands of the youth on October 23.

The whole system is bankrupt, the young man declared. Hungary's relationship with Soviet Russia — he used the word Russia, and not the Soviet Union, an unprecedented deviation from the prescribed Communist lingo — must be reconstructed on the basis of equality, and the economic exploitation of the country must be stopped. There is already a certain degree of freedom of speech, and he pointed at the latest issue of *Literary Gazette,* but it is far from being enough. And, of course, Nagy must be returned to the prime ministry. How will all this come about, I asked? The young man shrugged. "It will, don't worry. There is no way back," he said.

The drama started to unfold in September, and my wife and I were literally running all day to keep abreast of events. The Petöfi Circle lectures became even more popular. For the first time factory workers showed interest in these debates and many industrial plants asked the circle to send speakers to the factories. Nagy's popularity steadily rose, though he himself did little to encourage it. His home became the center of what later his prosecutors called the conspiracy against the Communist regime.

In mid-September the Association of Writers' annual congress became the scene of the first open revolt against party dictatorship. The writers not only pledged never to lie again, but in secret ballot ousted all Moscowites and known Stalinists from their leadership and elected middle-of-the-road liberals.

September passed quickly and the country's temperature rose steadily. October 6 used to be a holiday in Hungary, commemorating the thirteen generals whom the Hapsburgs hanged on that day in 1849 after they crushed, with Russian help, the

Magyars' War of Independence. In 1956 that day became the dress rehearsal of the revolution.

Some expressions become so widely accepted that those who use them understandably forget their origin. Only few who speak about the Iron Curtain know that Churchill coined this phrase. It was my wife who first used the "dress rehearsal" description in one of her dispatches on October 6, 1956, and she generously agreed that I could borrow it. In later years it gave us some satisfaction to see that most books we read on the Hungarian revolution had adopted the expression in describing the events of that day.

Julia Rajk, László Rajk's widow, had demanded for months that the unrevenged crime, her husband's murder, should be punished. This once attractive woman had become a modern Fury, her haggard face dominated by two big eyes filled with hatred and bitterness. Her husband's remains, and the remains of those hanged with Rajk, must be found and reburied, she demanded. Gerö's government did its best to procrastinate. First the excuse was that nobody knew where Rajk was buried; then when an obliging AVH officer suddenly remembered where the unmarked graves were, the government tried to persuade Mrs. Rajk to have a quiet private ceremony with only the family and, perhaps, some party dignitaries present. The widow said she was not interested, and finally Gerö gave in.

October 6 was an unpleasantly cold and windy day, yet two hundred thousand people made the pilgrimage to the Kerepesi cemetery. The fantastic crowd overflowing the old cemetery where Hungary's great were buried, presented a menacing picture, but discipline was kept although, as so often in those days, there were no uniformed policemen around.

The government, without Gerö and Kádár who were at that time in the Soviet Union, was a sad lot, a group of uneasy men standing in a row in front of the coffin covered with the Hungarian flag, listening to speakers, many of them Communists who had somehow escaped the gallows but had been kept in prison for years. All the speakers, including Ferenc Münnich, the man who later played a sinister role when the Russians suppressed the revolution, denounced the Rákosi regime.

There was real drama in the air. Mrs. Rajk stood alone. She did not even go close to the pathetic group of cabinet ministers and party dignitaries. She stood erect, almost motionless, her eyes fixed on her husband's coffin, her arms resting on the shoulders of her little son whom she held in front of her. Then, suddenly, there was a murmur in the otherwise silent crowd: Imre Nagy had arrived. Without even casting a glance at his former comrades in the government, he joined Mrs. Rajk, kissed her on both cheeks, and then stood behind her during the endless ceremony, as if saying: "I protect this woman!"

A week later a brief announcement said that Nagy was reinstated in the Communist party. The same day an equally brief announcement disclosed that Mihály and Vladimir Farkas, father and son, were arrested and accused of "grave violations of legality." Mihály was one of the original Moscowite foursome, for many years defense minister. Vladimir was a Russian secret police officer detailed to Hungary and the chief tormentor of both Rajk and Kádár.

Three men who were tried, convicted, and executed together with Rajk were reburied the same day: Lieutenant General György Pálffy, Tibor Szönyi, and András Szalay. *Szabad Nép*, the Communist party organ, lamented the next day about "dark practices of tyranny, lawlessness, slander, and deception of the people. . . . These comrades were executed as enemies of the fatherland. We were led to believe, and we in fact believed, the slanders about you. Please forgive us, Comrades." The following days many other civilian and military victims of the anti-Titoist purges were reinterred.

Gerö was in the Soviet Union, officially on vacation but actually to meet Tito. Khrushchev did his best to dispel the Yugoslav marshal's distrust of Gerö and he arranged the "coincidental" simultaneous presence of both men in the Crimea.

Gerö's repentance apparently impressed Tito and he invited the Hungarian to visit him in Belgrade.

In October there was an extraordinary event in our family as well: we decided to test the regime. The last time Ilona and I had been abroad was in early 1948 when we still possessed passports. During the Rákosi era only trusted party officials could travel on government business, but after his ouster in 1956 the regime became more liberal in this respect, too. More and more Hungarians got passports, so the decision was made that Ilona should apply and, if she could get one, go to London, talk to our different editors, and enjoy life in the West after so many years of isolation.

Hungarians have always been great travelers and have felt at home in the capitals of Western Europe. Obtaining a passport in prewar years was no problem, not even during the semi-Fascist period immediately before the war. After the war Ilona and I made one six-week tour of England, France, Switzerland, and Austria, visiting old friends and simply being happy that we had survived those difficult years when we had both brushed with death more than once. After that we lived on our memories and so did thousands of our compatriots. Forbidden fruit is always more desirable and the Communist clamp on foreign travel had a predictable effect: even people who had never crossed the Hungarian border before were dreaming about Paris or Vienna.

A special branch of the AVH was in charge of passports and we decided to pull no strings. Our names were too well known, the decision on Ilona's application would obviously be a political one, there was a fifty-fifty chance, and it was worth trying. She got her passport in a few days.

This ugly little red book with the Communist coat of arms on its cover, which we thoroughly disliked, was a tangible proof of the change. That someone who only a few months earlier was a convicted traitor should get a passport was almost unbelievable to us. Tom Rogers, our friend and neighbor, had to go to Vienna on legation business and he drove Ilona up. I watched her go with a strange mixture of pride, happiness, and a little envy, and for reasons I could not explain, with some concern. Neither of us realized then that the revolution would shorten her vacation and delay her return.

Nor did anybody else think that Hungary was on the threshold of an uprising. Gerö did not, or he would not have departed on October 14 for Belgrade to seal his reconciliation with Tito. Neither did the United States, or it would have dispatched a diplomat to head the legation in Budapest. And of course nobody could foresee the tremendous changes in Poland in October, and their impact on Hungarians.

There was no love lost between the little nations of central Europe and the Balkans. Magyars have traditionally felt contempt toward Romanians and Slovaks, a healthy respect mixed with dislike toward the Serbs, and friendly mistrust toward Austrians. But somehow, during their thousand-year-old history, Poles and Hungarians have understood and liked each other despite the fact that the Poles were a Slavic people while the Hungarians had no relatives but the Finns in the distant north.

I was often asked to explain why the bloodless Polish revolution of 1956 was a success, whereas the Hungarian uprising was mercilessly crushed. The answer to me was obvious. In Poland it was the Communist party itself which "revolted," purged itself of Stalinist leaders, and installed Wladyslaw Gomulka who, whatever one thinks about him today, then represented nationalist Communism with unconcealed aspirations to loosen the ties with the Soviet Union. In Nagy's person Hungary had its potential Gomulka, but the Hungarian Communist party lagged hopelessly behind in recognizing what the people wanted, and Nagy, a passive man, had to be dragged by his supporters to resume leadership. When he did, it was too late, things got out of hand, and Hungary went much further than Poland, in fact further than Moscow could tolerate.

Gomulka was named first secretary of the Polish Communist party on October 19, 1956, and the story of how he defied Khrushchev by preventing for hours the landing of the Soviet leader's plane in Warsaw, became known in Budapest immediately. It gave the final incentive to Hungarians and during the following three days events in Hungary galloped with a furious crescendo toward October 23.

Students in university cities, the leadership of the Petöfi Circle, and other ad hoc groups were in permanent session and manifestos mushroomed, spelling out what the nation demanded. The Petöfi Circle published its ten points. The students of the Budapest technical university included in their sixteen points the demand that the Soviets withdraw their troops from Hungary, that Nagy be named prime minister, that former defense minister Farkas, Rákosi's most brutal lieutenant, be tried publicly, that the multiparty system be restored and elections be held, that all political prisoners be released, that freedom of speech and of the press be guaranteed, that the monstrous Stalin statue be removed, and that the ugly, Soviet-pattern coat of arms be replaced by the traditional Kossuth coat of arms.

On October 23 *Szabad Nép*, the Communist party organ, welcomed the students' initiative almost enthusiastically. The overwhelming majority of the students, the paper stressed, were offspring of workers and peasants, meaning that they were good proletarians, loyal adherents of the party. *Szabad Nép* was on the streets with its praise in the morning. Twelve hours later the Stalin statue was toppled and dragged through the streets in triumphant procession, the radio building was besieged, and Russian tanks rumbled all over Budapest.

The revolution was on. Leaderless and unplanned, it spread all over the country.

8

The Volcano Erupts

Some chroniclers of 1956 maintain that Hungarian Communist leaders, foreign diplomatic observers, and reporters should have read the signs correctly and anticipated the outbreak of the revolution. In fact nobody did. Gerö followed the example of French kings who traditionally were out hunting on the day they were overthrown: he was on a train returning to Budapest from Belgrade. The Americans did not think it was coming or they would have sent a diplomat in a hurry to head their legation. Nor did Ilona, because on the same day in London she explained jokingly to a group of British newsmen that the Hungarians would revolt only if their soccer team lost the world championship. And neither did I expect it, or I would not have invited guests for dinner on October 23.

John McCormack of the *New York Times* and his wife Molly were in Budapest. I was deeply devoted to Jack for his courageous prodding of the Communists to release us. He was a handsome, tall man, dignified but with a warm smile, and I still feel privileged to have worked with him for days before the mass of foreign correspondents invaded Budapest.

I had asked the McCormacks to dinner, together with Tom

and Sarah Rogers and a Hungarian newspaperman who had played a prominent role in the ferment period. October 23 was a Tuesday, and the two girls were in school, but I could rely on our maid, an experienced cook. The poor woman must have gotten a few white hairs before the evening was over.

I knew that Nagy was vacationing on Lake Balaton and somehow I naively thought that his adherents would respect his absence and wait until his return for the inevitable show-down. But early in the morning I was told that the students, outraged by the state-owned radio's refusal to broadcast their sixteen points, planned a mass demonstration to honor the Polish uprising. At noon interior minister László Piros forbade the demonstrations, but as soon as the radio announced the prohibition a youthful voice informed me by telephone that the students had already gathered and that they would ignore the order. Piros must have gotten the same information because he withdrew the prohibition shortly afterwards.

The voice on the telephone also told me to go to the statue of József Bem which stands on the right bank of the Danube in a small square, flanked by the foreign ministry, a military barracks, and an apartment house. The place seemed to be most appropriate. Bem was a Polish general, a legendary figure who came to help the Hungarians in their 1848–1849 War of Independence against the Hapsburgs and the czar's troops. Petőfi, the poet, was with Bem's army when he disappeared in the battle of Segesvár.

I rushed to Bem Square, cursing the AVH for not returning my car. Taxis were almost nonexistent, so I took the trolley as far as I could and then ran three blocks to reach the square. It was already packed and still more were coming in orderly, peaceful, almost happy procession along the quai. Their ranks were mixed, young and old, men and women, and a sprinkling of factory workers in their overalls — also, to my astonishment, some young soldiers in uniform. Nothing was planned and nothing arranged, there were no loudspeakers and only those close enough to the statue could hear when Péter Veres, probably the most gifted peasant writer, a middle-aged man, read the sixteen points of the students. For me, however, the most significant episode was when a young woman appeared on the balcony of the foreign ministry waving the Hungarian tricolor with a round hole in the middle. This was the first time I had seen the flag with the Russian-type coat of arms cut out. That same day it became the symbol of the revolution.

Flags probably have a greater meaning in Hungary than in the United States. In this country it is customary to fly the flag on public buildings and elsewhere every day. The American flag belongs to the scenery and the consequence is that an American is accustomed to seeing it constantly. The sight loses its significance. In Hungary, however, display of the flag was restricted to national holidays; it was not something which one flew without some specific reason. This is not meant as a criticism of the American custom, yet when I read about the disgusting defilement of the Stars and Stripes in recent years, I cannot fail to think that the Hungarian custom is probably the better one.

In Bem Square I could not see a single policeman and the soldiers were watching the scene from their barracks windows. A similar demonstration was taking place in front of Petőfi's statue on the other side of the Danube and I followed the crowd across Marguerite Bridge to the Parliament, where the thousands from the two demonstrations merged in the enormous square. When I arrived, the throng of at least fifty thousand was chanting that they wanted to hear Nagy, who was known to have returned from Lake Balaton in the afternoon and was believed to be in the building. Then, from somewhere in the crowd, came the cry: *Ruszki haza!*" ("Russian go home"), which immediately became the slogan of the revolt.

Finally Nagy appeared on the balcony. His speech, in which he asked for moderation but disclosed nothing about what he intended to do, did not satisfy the crowd. On Parliament

Square the rumor spread that demonstrators were pulling down Stalin's statue. I got a ride from a Hungarian newspaperman to the square where the giant twenty-six-foot statue stood. An old church had been demolished to make place for it and party bigwigs stood on its pedestal to watch May Day parades.

Luckily I met the photographer who used to work for me. Though it was already dark, I told him to wait as long as he had to but I must have the picture of the falling statue. The poor man stood there for hours but I got the picture. It took hours because nothing was planned and to topple the bronze colossus was not a job that young university students could do with nothing but enthusiasm. But help came from the factories. A truck drove up with workers carrying acetylene torches and other equipment and finally, after hours of work, with the immense crowd roaring, the giant crashed to the earth. Only two enormous boots remained on the pedestal. There was not a single policeman around but a young army officer volunteered to keep order, urging people to stay away from where the statue was expected to fall. When it was down, I suddenly remembered my dinner party and also that it was not enough to observe, it was time to file a story. I rushed home to the other end of the city.

The table in our dining room was nicely prepared, Margit, the cook, was wringing her hands and quietly complaining that the meat was overcooked, Juli and Kati were doing their best to offer drinks, but nobody cared. In one room McCormack was punching his typewriter and calling his Vienna office, a young man who worked for Ilona in her absence occupied her desk and telephone, Tom Rogers talked every five minutes with the watch officer at the legation — and there was nothing I could do as a host but sit down at my telephone and dictate what I then thought was the story of the day. Molly McCormack and Sarah Rogers tried to save the dinner and at least a warm soup was served on our respective desks. There was no time to sample the rest. Tom Rogers went to the legation and I accompanied the McCormacks back to Pest when we learned that there were demonstrations in front of the building which housed the state-controlled radio.

Everything I witnessed earlier that day, the demonstrations before the Bem statue, in front of Parliament and the Stalin statue, happened in squares, open places where even a huge crowd had enough elbow room. But the radio was in one of the narrow side streets in downtown Pest, the oldest part of the city on the left bank of the Danube. It was obvious that we could not get near the place in McCormack's huge American car with the Vienna license plate, so we parked it on a nearby boulevard and proceeded on foot.

We wormed our way through the crowd in the narrow streets around the radio building and found shelter in a doorway just opposite the entrance. The difference in mood was striking: the demonstrators were in a happy, almost festive mood before the Bem statue, and triumphant when Stalin's statue came down, but here they were angry and bitter. The streets reeked of tear gas, and we could see steel-helmeted AVH soldiers in every window of the radio building with their rifles conspicuously pointed at the crowd below. We tried to get some account of what had happened, but everyone we asked had a different story. They boiled down to this.

At eight o'clock Gerö had broadcast a strikingly stupid, arrogant, and provocative speech which he had apparently written on the train en route to Budapest when the news about the afternoon demonstrations reached him. Then the crowd, led by students, requested the radio to broadcast their sixteen points too, but they were refused. A small student delegation was permitted to enter the building to negotiate and when I arrived there with the McCormacks, the student delegates were on a second-floor balcony right above the closed gate, addressing the crowd. I do not think anybody could hear what they were saying as there were no microphones and all we could see were a few obviously excited young men gesticulating in the dark.

I leave it to the historians to decide whether the Hungarian radio building was the Bastille of the 1956 revolt. For me the similarity was striking, though when I was there the throng was still unarmed. The crowd by then packed all the streets around the building; they were "eyeball to eyeball" with the AVH soldiers in the windows, but for several hours neither of them blinked. Then something happened which obviously could have turned the stalemate into a one-sided affair: three Hungarian light tanks moved slowly, but with a menacing rumble, into Sándor utca. The scene was frightening, and slightly ridiculous. Sándor utca is so narrow that two big American cars would have to maneuver with care to pass each other.

The demonstrators showed no sign of fright, and it was immediately clear that they had no reason to be scared. The unhelmeted tank crews rode their machines in the open turrets, some sitting on the side, and when several women began to applaud and cheer them, they returned the greetings with smiles and waved their hands. The tanks stopped right in front of the building, their engines were turned off, and the fraternization began. I looked in vain for someone in command, but did find a young lieutenant who was willing to talk. Yes, he said, they got orders to come to the radio building. No, he did not know why. And no, he certainly would not order his men to fire on the crowd. "These people are Hungarians, aren't they? And they have no weapons — or do they?" he asked me rather pointedly.

McCormack and I thought we could still reach the last editions of the morning papers in America. Jack's car raced through the streets back to my house, and to a great disappointment. I tried every AP bureau in Europe, the long distance operators promised everything but they could not connect us. Then the phone rang; Belgrade was on the line, AP's office in the Yugoslav capital. I started to dictate: "Stalin's giant statue was toppled in Budapest tonight . . ." and then the line went dead.

Then McCormack remembered that there used to be an elderly couple who operated a commercial teletype and telephone service in Prague which was used mainly by Western newsmen. Both Jack and I had used their services many years earlier, immediately after the war, when it proved to be more reliable and much quicker than any other. Were they still alive? and were they still tolerated by the Czech Communists? We did not know but it was worth trying. Somehow we remembered the couple's name and I found their telephone number in my old files. Maybe the blackout was not complete. Prague, after all, was a satellite capital. It was, professionally, the great moment of a long night when I heard the quiet voice of the old Czech. Sure he remembered me, of course he knew McCormack. Yes, they had connection with the West, they could get our stories on tape and relay them to New York.

Half an hour later, around midnight, we were again on our way to Pest. By then what had started some twelve hours earlier as a peaceful demonstration had become an armed revolt. Most of the streets were deserted, but the main arteries were packed with people, and we could hear the quick staccato of firing from everywhere. We could not get near the radio station. We were stopped one block from Sándor utca by soldiers who told us that the building was besieged and would soon fall into the hands of the insurgents. And where does the military stand? I asked. The answer came with a shrug: "I'm a private. I got no orders except to guard this corner." And what about the tanks we saw two hours ago? McCormack inquired. They are still there, was the laconic answer. Soon, however, several civilians joined us and told us what had happened at the station after we left.

The crowd was angry, first because the radio refused to

broadcast the sixteen points, and later because there was fear that the handful of students admitted to the building were being kept as hostages. But anger usually does not last long with Hungarians. The AVH soldiers were obviously frightened and did not know what to do, especially after the tanks had arrived, taking up what appeared to be a neutral position. A few tear gas bombs were thrown, which was admittedly unpleasant, but that was all. Then, shortly after we left to file our stories, the AVH made one fatal blunder. An ambulance appeared in the streets, inching through the crowd toward the radio building. Somebody became suspicious, the vehicle was stopped, and it turned out that it contained automatic weapons and ammunition for the AVH soldiers. Minutes later dozens of insurgents had arms in their hands.

The first victim — many thousands followed — was killed in front of the radio. He was a young man, we were told, and he was shot and killed when the throng seized the ambulance and armed itself. Some claimed that more than one man was killed, but a middle-aged man who seemed to be the most reliable "news source," insisted that there was only one. While we were talking on the street corner, listening to the firing which came mostly from the direction of the radio building, three factory trucks drove up. They too were stopped by the uncommunicative private, but he turned quickly in the other direction when several men leaped from the vehicles, each with a submachine gun in his hand. I talked to one of them, and he was eager to talk. The man who was killed "in cold blood," he said, was a worker, too. He and his comrades broke into the plant's storeroom and brought guns.

"Are you a party member?" I asked him. "Of course I am," he replied without hesitation. What about the soldiers and their tanks around the radio? "What about them? They won't fight us. They hate the AVH more than we do. Maybe they will even join us," the man said.

We said good-bye to the workers and the taciturn private

and walked two blocks up Kossuth Lajos utca where, at the intersection with the boulevard, an unusually large crowd lined the street. It was two o'clock in the morning and the crowd, three lines deep, was silently staring at Russian tanks moving in formation through the boulevard in the direction of Parliament.

It was too late, the day was too long, and we both still had work to do. We did not know then that some five blocks further to the east the modernistic building which housed the editorial offices and printing plant of *Szabad Nép*, the Communist party's official daily, was besieged, again with AVH soldiers inside and armed insurgents outside. Before going home we decided to drive around, carefully, because Molly McCormack was with us. She was a brave woman, a worthy partner of her husband. Jack offered several times to drive her back to the safety of the hotel. She always refused.

Andrássy ut, the majestic thoroughfare, was completely deserted, but we saw the abandoned bronze torso of what remained of Stalin's statue. It had been dragged there by one of the trucks, but when the iron chain snapped, it was left in the middle of a square. McCormack's car was stopped at the mouth of Andrássy ut by two martial-looking insurgents who blockaded the road rather naively with a few overturned benches. They were snappish and ordered us out. It took some talking on my part to make them understand that not only high Communist party officials drove huge foreign cars, but also American newsmen.

No story was filed that night, and none the next day. Our teletype to the West through Prague was cut off, too.

The night, however, was not over for me. I knew I had to write, whether I could file my story immediately or not. There was no rule during the weeks that followed. Sometimes, miraculously, the telephone worked for a few hours. On other days I found a teletype line, and much of the stuff I wrote went out when one of my Western colleagues got tired of fighting the silent telephone and left for Vienna, or when the American legation sent someone to the Austrian capital, and those who left were willing to deliver my stories to AP's Vienna bureau.

October 23 was crammed with dramatic events and I had witnessed many of them, but whatever I saw was only a fragment of the whole. That night I called several people who had been my faithful informants in the preceding weeks, and none of them was in bed. This was the picture I formed:

Immediately after his late afternoon speech to the crowd on Parliament Square, Nagy was driven to party headquarters a block away. There he was completely isolated and Gerö and his Stalinist adherents appeared determined to remain the masters. Several delegations, mostly writers and journalists, went to the party building, which was under heavy guard, and pleaded with whoever they could to make some conciliatory gesture before it was too late. They were rebuffed. Gerö's gravest miscalculation was the army. The neutral attitude of the three tanks at the radio characterized the mood of the army everywhere. Moreover, there were reports about desertions, about soldiers who had joined the insurgents fighting the AVH, and about others who had abandoned their units and gone home to their families. There was a report that a Budapest barracks had opened its gates to the insurgents and armed them with whatever they had.

On November 19, 1956, D. Shepilov, the Soviet foreign minister, read a telegram to the U.N. General Assembly which contained an "invitation" to the Soviets to send troops to Budapest to put down the uprising. The telegram, Shepilov said, came from the Hungarian government and had reached Moscow on October 24.

The fact that McCormack and I saw the Russian tanks at two o'clock in the morning of that day in the heart of Budapest belies this contention. According to the American military attachés in Budapest, the markings on the Russian tanks we saw identified them as coming from Soviet camps in Hungary and the closest of them was about sixty miles from the capital. There was no indication just when the Soviet units were alerted to be ready to intervene, but (according to the military experts) to reach Budapest by two o'clock in the morning they must have gotten their marching orders by five o'clock the previous afternoon. Though I always considered this of secondary importance, I had my serious doubts about this so-called invitation. The same excuse was used twelve years later when Moscow said it was invited by some unidentified Czech Communists to prevent a "counterrevolution." The Russians do not need an invitation to intervene in a satellite country.

The rapid developments of the day caught virtually everyone flat-footed, including Nagy, who was by no means a revolutionary leader, and also those who prepared the ground for the revolt. Later that day, after the speeches that afternoon at the Bem and Petöfi statues, I did not see any of the writers and journalists who were responsible for the ferment and who were expected to lead.

October 24, in comparison, was a strangely quiet day. Russian tanks were everywhere, guarding the bridges and other strategically important points. I set out with my neighbor, Tom Rogers of the American legation, to make a long tour of the city in his car. There was little sign of serious damage other than to the radio station and to the building of *Szabad Nép*, both by then safely in the hands of the insurgents. The lull was probably understandable. The insurgents were not sure what the government and, more importantly, the Russians were up to. The Soviet troops showed no indication of eagerness to fight the invisible "enemy," and the Hungarian party chieftains had other things to do, such as trying to explain what had happened to Moscow's envoys, Mikoyan and Suslov. I knew that Nagy had become prime minister some time during the night, but in the morning I got two telephone calls from men who were close to Nagy, reporting with concern that they were unable to contact the premier, that he must be in the heavily guarded party headquarters where not even his wife could talk to him on the telephone. It was obvious, both said, that Gerö, then still party first secretary, was holding Nagy a virtual prisoner.

On Thursday, October 25, McCormack and I went to the American legation, hoping to get some expert information on Soviet troop movements and also to try to use the legation's teletype facilities (they functioned for six hours that day). While we were there, a massive wave of demonstrators entered Liberty Square and passed in front of us on their way to Parliament, one long block away. Many stopped when they reached the legation and cheered the United States, waving a few flags with the characteristic hole in the center. It was moving to see the many faces turned upward toward the windows of the legation, as if expecting a miracle.

Suddenly, together with another wave of demonstrators, two tanks entered the square and passed us very slowly. We saw the Russian markings on their sides and the unmistakably Russian soldiers sitting in the open turrets, smiling uneasily and driving with obvious care. The soldiers were not alone. Both tanks carried dozens of jubilant young Hungarians and on each there was one youngster with the Hungarian tricolor. McCormack was curious and we joined the crowd to see what was happening.

When we arrived at the enormous square in front of Parliament, about five thousand demonstrators were milling around some two dozen Soviet tanks guarding the huge building. The atmosphere was friendly and the Russians showed no sign of hostility. A serious-looking man in his forties explained to me that they wanted to see Nagy because they were concerned: the word had spread quickly that he was not free to act. They did not even know whether Nagy was in the building or at the party headquarters. The man also said that after a lengthy but friendly palaver a Soviet officer had promised to notify Nagy that the people wanted to see him and advised them to wait.

Nothing happened for about thirty minutes. The Russian tank crews were openly fraternizing with the crowd; some of them left their machines and mingled with the demonstrators. McCormack and I decided to return to the legation where we had unfinished business. We were about to set out toward Liberty Square when, in seconds, the peaceful picture turned into a holocaust.

I heard many versions of what I described later in my dispatches as the "massacre on Parliament Square," but neither Jack McCormack nor I, the only two Western newsmen who witnessed this tragedy, were certain of how it started and what really happened. The reason perhaps was that neither we, nor the demonstrators and, it seems safe to assume, nor the Russians in the square were expecting trouble when the first sudden salvo of submachine guns hit the square.

Jack and I were lucky. A few minutes earlier we had been part of the crowd now under fire. When the shooting started we were in relative safety under the arcades of the agriculture ministry opposite Parliament. We hit the ground immediately and peeked out from behind the thick columns of the arcade, trying to find out what was happening. It was a macabre picture. The demonstrators were running to find shelter; many were clustered around the pedestals of two statues on the square, one of Ferenc Rákóczi, an eighteenth-century nobleman who fought the Hapsburgs, the other of Lajos Kossuth, who did the same in the nineteenth century. Others were just lying prone on the square. I did not know whether they had been hit or were paralyzed with fear. The craziest sight was the behavior of the tanks. Their turrets were revolving rapidly in all directions, as if looking for the enemy, and their guns were firing wildly. Who had started the shooting? Certainly not the demonstrators: they were unarmed. Suddenly McCormack grabbed my arm and pointed at the roof of one of the six-story buildings at the square's southern end. There was a plume of white gray smoke slowly rising from behind the parapet on top of the building. It was impossible to see who was firing from the roof.

The scene was dominated by the tanks and the big boom of their guns which echoed off the buildings, making an almost unbearable noise. How many died then, one can only estimate. When it was all over — the ten minutes which seemed like hours — Jack and I counted about fifty bodies in a small sector of the square.

Walking back to the legation I felt sick to my stomach and Jack, the veteran of World War I, must have felt the same. We pretended to listen when a friend at the legation told us that two Russian tank divisions had entered Hungary from Romania.

Late in the afternoon, back in my apartment, I still could not accept what appeared unalterable, that there was simply no way of getting the story out. I was not in the mood to sit down and write for posterity the story of the drama I had witnessed in Parliament Square. Then, suddenly, I had a ridiculously desperate idea.

I knew that the communications blackout was not total, that the government and organizations controlled by the government maintained some thin lines of communication open to the West. In "normal" times I would have dismissed as childish the idea of using these lines, but times were definitely not normal. I knew the president of one organization which I suspected had its lines open! I decided to try.

He was, as I expected, not in his office, but the switchboard gave me his unlisted home number. I called him. The direct approach, I thought, was the only appropriate one under these circumstances.

"Look," I told him on the telephone, "something tremendous happened today. It's not only the tragedy, the senseless killing of many people, but this, I feel, is the turning point. From now on the guns will speak. Help me to get the story out."

There was a long silence on the other end of the line. "Even if I want to," the reply came haltingly, "what can I do? Curfew is strictly enforced. There is fighting on the streets all over the city. What do you want me to do?"

I felt great. Here was my chance. "Forget about the curfew and the fighting. That is my business," I said, and tried to be as convincing as I could. "All I ask is that you call whoever is guarding the building and tell him I have your permission to enter and use your teletype." Again there was a long silence.

"I'll call you back," the man finally said, and hung up. My telephone rang about five minutes later, though it seemed a much longer time to me. "All right," I heard his voice. "I gave orders that they are to let you in. I don't think you can make it. You will be shot before you get there. It's not worth it."

I thanked him briefly, afraid he would change his mind. And then I ran. I had no car, but anyway it seemed to be safer on foot. It was a dark night, the streets were deserted, and I stopped at every corner, peeking out to see whether it was safe to proceed. I spent all my youth in the area and was familiar with every house. Only once I was forced to make a detour when I saw a group of insurgents building a barricade, with their guns neatly stacked close by in a cone of World War I fashion. Normally I would have gone over to talk to them, but that night I had but one purpose: to get my story out as soon as possible. I heard sporadic bursts of gunfire from many directions, but my impression was that the fighting was far away, on the Pest side of the city.

I reached my destination in about thirty minutes. I stopped at the gate to compose myself, to look like someone who had every right to walk in. Then I entered the dimly lit lobby and gave my name casually to the morose man at the desk. He nodded: "Yes, I know. You may go up, on the third floor, as you know . . ." I nodded, too. I did not want to tell him that I had never been there before.

The big building appeared to be empty, or almost. Walking up the stairs because I did not dare to ask where the elevator was, I could see a lonely man or woman crossing the corridor, coming out from one room and going into another. On the third floor I heard the familiar chatter of teletype machines behind a closed door.

The few people in the building were employees who lived far away and preferred to stay overnight rather than face the hazards of the streets, with no buses or trolleys. In the large room with the machines there were several men and women reading the tickers. They became my friends during the days that followed.

In earlier years of strict Communist "vigilance" every unknown face in a government office would have been suspicious, but that night nobody cared, or if they did, they did not show it. Everyone in the building must have found out sooner or later who I was and what I was doing, and most everyone was a member of the Communist party. Yet no questions were asked and every assistance was offered. And I needed it. I had never worked on a teletype and had no idea how to operate it, but I learned fast.

The first night I had to ask one of the girls to put in the calls for me, giving her the Telex call numbers of several AP offices in Western Europe. She did not show curiosity but merely rang the long distance operator and asked for the numbers. Then she left me alone, explaining what I had to do should any of the called stations come in.

I was sitting there, waiting, knowing that I should have concentrated on what I would write if there were an answer, but I could not. Fatigue comes out in these times of waiting and I felt dead tired. How long I had to wait that first time I do not recall. It must have been several hours. I tried to recall the chronology of events of the last forty-eight hours, but my thoughts kept wandering into the future. What does all this mean? How will it end? My little family, after such a brief reunion, was divided again. Ilona must be in London and she should stay there, I thought.

The nighttime silence of the large room was suddenly broken when my machine sprang to life. I stared at it, waiting to see what would happen. And then, miraculously, the words appeared on the paper: "Associated Press, Vienna."

I sat there, with trembling fingers, and punched back: "AP, Budapest." Back came the message: "Endre . . . Is that really you?"

The next morning the *New York Times* published on its front page all the three thousand words I had punched out that night: "Parliament Square became a battlefield shortly after noon today when a Soviet tank opened fire on a few thousand peaceful demonstrators whose only weapons were Hungarian flags," my lead said.

The *Times* added an editorial remark in parentheses after the lead. It said: "This dispatch, from Endre Marton, the AP correspondent in Budapest, was received in New York in somewhat skeletonized form. It was the first direct word from the AP Bureau in Budapest since Tuesday night."

How right the *Times* was. Anyone using the teletype for the first time in his life will understand my agonies, the many mistakes I made, with my thoughts flying far ahead of my inexperienced fingers.

When I was finally through, I staggered home. I felt drained but triumphant: the story was out, the world would know. I knew that the papers in the West must be filled with stories about Hungary, written by colleagues who listened to the radios in Vienna or somewhere else, who questioned refugees or just speculated. But my story was real and I felt wonderful. Close to my house I again made a detour to avoid the Southern Railway Station from where I could hear sporadic gunfire. I confess that at that hour I was not interested in anything but to see my bed and fall into it. Yet something stopped me in a street close to our house. There was light in one of the basement windows of an apartment house and I smelled the wonderful aroma of freshly baked bread.

The new generation, especially in America, accustomed to the cellophane-wrapped something we find on the supermarket shelves and call bread, does not know what fresh, warm bread really is. I could not resist going down the narrow steps to the basement bakery. One man was working there, dragging out a few dozen loaves with his long, rakelike tool from the single oven in his small shop. He must have understood my desire and laughed.

"What on earth are you doing on the streets at this hour?" he asked. I explained briefly who I was. "Take one," he said. "I have no flour left and who knows when I will get more."

My daughters woke up as I tried to sneak in. Kati was sobbing on her bed. "Why can't you be like all other fathers are," she said. "All of them in the building were at home with their children, only we were alone. . . ."

I hugged them and tried to explain that I had to do it, that this was the life I had chosen. The still-warm loaf did wonders. We sat in the dark, eating the wonderful bread, and Juli and Kati forgot about their tears.

From then on I became a regular visitor to the office building with the working teletype. Rarely could I get a telephone connection with one of our offices in Western Europe, since most of the time there was a complete communications blackout with only a few exempt places, like the one I had so luckily found on October 25. The office was almost deserted during the daytime too, with only a skeleton crew of employees, the same people who had been stranded in the building when the fighting broke out. They had food in their cafeteria and slept on sofas and armchairs. I remember them with warm feelings because they were polite and discreet, pretending not to know what I was doing and helping when I needed help.

During the ten days I used those facilities, the building, like so many others in Budapest, changed hands frequently. Sometimes, such as on the first night, the lobby was deserted with only one man at the reception desk. At other times, however, I found Russian soldiers in the building, and again on others there were armed freedom fighters in the lobby. Neither of them appeared to interfere with the little work done in the upstairs offices and the few employees went about their routine business no matter who "occupied" the lobby.

But for me it was exciting, to say the least, to find Soviet soldiers guarding the building. They did not care about me, and I went up the stairs with deliberately slow steps, after nodding casually to the man at the reception desk as if I were someone who belonged there. It was a strange feeling, though, to punch my stories about Soviet aggression in an upstairs office while the building was guarded by the same Russian soldiers whom I was blasting in my dispatch.

One day when I called our Vienna office on the teletype, I got Ilona on the other end. It was not easy to carry on a "conversation" with someone one loves on the machine, but we managed somehow. A few hours after she had assured the flock of British newsmen that there would be no revolution in Hungary, her office awakened her abruptly in her London hotel room with the news that a revolution had broken out and the request that she return right away. Over the teletype I pleaded with her to stay in Vienna, told her that everything was all right with us, she should not worry, and that Vienna was the best place to be for the moment. She would not listen. Either we come out right away, or she would try to return.

I will not attempt to give a day-by-day replay of what happened between the October 25 massacre on Parliament Square and November 4, when the Soviets besieged Budapest. There was fighting all over the city, indeed all over the country. The demonstrators became insurgents, the insurgents freedom fighters. The enemy was the AVH for the first forty-eight hours, and the Russians after that. The freedom fighters were a strange mixture of students and industrial workers, mostly young men, many teen-agers, including a sprinkling of girls. The kids, they were called fondly, and the way they fought became military history.

The Russians used almost no infantry, only tanks, why I could never explain. However proud one feels that "the kids" disabled hundreds of tanks and virtually licked the mighty Soviet Union, there can be no doubt that Soviet infantry could have pacified the city and the whole country in a few days. The tank is the clumsiest weapon for fighting in an old city with only a few wide streets. The Russians, however, simplified their job. Whenever their tanks were shot at by a single sniper from a rooftop, they blasted the entire block with the big guns of their T-34s.

The Molotov cocktail, the poor man's atomic bomb, was a mighty weapon in the hands of the kids. One day I watched three of them, including a carrot-headed ugly-duckling girl of about fifteen, who seemed to be their leader, destroy a tank on a street leading to Moscow Square in Buda. It was a simple operation and the three performed it almost playfully, but with precision. The square soon became a stronghold of the revolutionaries, who blocked all entrances to it with cobblestone barricades. The Russians sent a tank to break through, which it could have done easily. But the three youngsters destroyed it before it reached the makeshift barricade.

Whether they worked on their own or were "hired" by the freedom fighters who were defending their fortress on the square, I did not know. The three were lurking in a doorway about a hundred yards from the square, with several soda bottles filled with gasoline. I sought refuge in the same doorway when I heard the clatter of an approaching tank. When it passed the house and headed toward the square, the girl gave orders: "Now!" The rag which served as a wick was lit and one of the boys jumped quietly from his hiding place. The rest happened in split seconds. The boy, running in his worn tennis shoes, reminded me of the reliefs on the urns of the Minoan culture: the bull-dancer, approaching his bull gracefully, but with the precision of an athlete who has practiced his movements a thousand times. When he reached the slowly moving tank, I saw his thin arm in the air, placing the bottle on the tread. Then, when the boy was dancing back to us with a happy grin on his face, we heard the explosion. The tank, without its tread, moved crazily in all directions before it came to a sudden halt. Two Russians jumped from the turret and ran fast in the direction they had come from. The boy, meanwhile, was back in the relative safety of the doorway.

"Where did you learn that trick?" I asked them. They shrugged. "That's easy," the girl replied. "Are you a foreigner?" she asked with suspicion in her childish, high-pitched voice, observing that I made notes. I explained who I was and she laughed. "Then you don't know," the boy with the bottle explained. "We learned in the Communist youth movement how to make a Molotov cocktail and how to use it against tanks. We were told that one day we would fight the capitalists who want to destroy our socialist state." The girl prevented me from asking more. "We have to go. I'm hungry and Mother will be angry if we are late," she said, and the three disappeared around the corner.

On one of those days I had another touching experience south of Moscow Square where the streets run steeply up Várhegy toward the castle of Hungary's former kings. From the slopes of one of these, aptly named Ostrom utca (Siege Street) in memory of Hungary's 145-year-long Turkish occupation, I watched a hundred young people defend their "fortress" in Moscow Square against Soviet tanks.

I admit it was not much of a battle, more a probing operation by the tanks. The leader of the freedom fighters was Szabó bácsi (Uncle Szabó), a gentle, soft-spoken middle-aged man, one of the few revolutionary leaders whose name soon became a legend. János Szabó was executed in January 1957.

A small group of curious onlookers watched with me from our convenient lookout post — much like a theater box high above the stage — and saw how Uncle Szabó's young men fired at the tanks, crouching behind the low parapets of their cobblestone barricades and the railroad carts pushed to the square from a nearby railroad junction. For reasons I could not explain the tanks did not come close and did not attempt to overrun the hastily erected barricades but were satisfied with firing a few salvos from their big guns, circling around as if trying to find the weak spots of the "fortress." There were a few casualties, and we could see two young men with Red Cross armbands running with a stretcher, carrying the dead or wounded into one of the apartment houses on the square.

An elderly man watched what was going on below us with intense interest and made some expert remarks, adding that he was a veteran of World War I and knew what he was talking about. He was what one would call a typical Hungarian, short and muscular, with a grayish martial moustache. He liked to talk, too. He was a retired foreman from one of the large industrial plants in the neighborhood and was living with his wife in one of the old apartment houses on Ostrom utca.

Then, unexpectedly, the old man began cursing softly and jumped to his feet, though just a moment earlier he had explained with authority that though we were safe up there, one should properly crouch close to the walls of the buildings, because one never can tell. What was wrong? I asked. "They shot him, the s.o.b.'s," he replied, pointing down to the square. The two medics, if we may call them that, were just carrying off a young man. Who is he? I inquired. "He's Lajos. He was my best apprentice in the factory. And how often I told him he should not stick his head high," the old man said angrily. Then he said a curt good-bye and set out toward the square.

"What on earth are you doing?" I shouted after him. "Somebody must take the kid's place and it had better be someone who knows what to do," the old man said without turning around. A minute later I saw him taking Lajos's place behind the parapet with a rifle in his hand.

9

General Maléter and
the Nameless Heroes

October 25, 1956, remains in my memory as the day of the massacre on Parliament Square, but the day was probably more significant for two other events. One was the ouster of Gerö as party first secretary, the other that Pál Maléter, an unknown army colonel, joined the freedom fighters. In 1958 he was tried for this and executed together with Nagy.

Anastas Mikoyan and Mikhail Suslov were immediately dispatched by Khrushchev to Budapest when the trouble started. They arrived on October 24, and according to an eyewitness, came to the party headquarters from a Soviet-controlled military airport in a Russian tank. What happened during that night in the Akadémia utca building of the party is well known by now. The two Russians accused Gerö of blundering, ordered him to resign, and named Kádár his successor as head of the party. To make things final, Gerö was spirited out of the country immediately in a Soviet plane, together with András Hegedüs, Nagy's predecessor as prime minister. Gerö made a last attempt to persuade Nagy to sign a document which would have shown that Nagy had "invited" the Soviet intervention on October 23, but Nagy refused.

Maléter's decision to join the freedom fighters was of immense significance. He was the first high-ranking officer to do so and this had a great effect on hesitant Hungarian army units. What he did and why, he explained to me in a few simple words when I talked to him on November 1.

When the revolt broke out, Maléter was the commanding officer of a Hungarian tank unit and as such got orders on October 25 to reoccupy the Kilian barracks which had fallen into the hands of insurgents the day before. Kilian barracks, among the oldest in Hungary, were known by everyone as Mária Terézia barracks, named after the eighteenth-century Hapsburg empress and queen. After the Communist take-over they were named for a little-known Communist of the short rule of Béla Kun in 1918.

Arriving at the barracks with his tanks, the colonel thought it was his duty to avoid bloodshed, and before ordering his tanks to attack he began to talk to the leaders of the insurgents.

Maléter told me: "I didn't need much time. Soon it was obvious to me that I had been fed lies at the ministry when I was told that those in the barracks were 'Fascists,' armed by imperialists. They were a bunch of idealists, young university students, young workers, soldiers, and policemen. And their arms? Old rifles used by reservists on guard duty in the barracks."

The palaver between the colonel and the insurgents did not last long. Maléter and his tanks joined the freedom fighters. He promptly sent word by telephone to the ministry that he had accomplished at least part of his orders, because he was in charge of Kilian, but also told his superiors under what circumstances. From that day on Kilian became a symbol. After November 4 it resisted the Soviet attacks for many days, and the Russians, it was said, lost more tanks there than anywhere else in their war against Hungary.

I did not tell Maléter on November 1, when he was appointed minister of defense, that I was one of the few who knew more about his past than just his name. What I knew about him I had learned in prison, as I had so many other things. Major Kretsmer, my interrogator, had been with Maléter in a Soviet prisoner-of-war camp during World War II.

Much was written about this swashbuckling hero of the revolution in 1956 and then again in 1958 when he was executed. But remarkably little was known about his life, in or out of Hungary. The Communists never publicized him because it did not suit their purpose. The "cult of personality" spotlight might shine on a party bigwig, but there was no room in the light for an obscure lieutenant colonel who had to be sandbagged into joining the Communist party in the late 1940's.

Maléter was a career officer, trained at Ludovika Akadémia in Budapest, the Hungarian West Point. When Hungary went to war against Russia in 1941, Maléter was a promising young first lieutenant.

The husky six-foot-five man was a good soldier, who looked like a combination of an All-American football star and a Hungarian hussar. He was taken prisoner when the Russians routed the Germans and their Hungarian allies in the Ukraine. The dullness of Soviet POW camps did not suit him and he was not interested in Soviet politics, but he disliked the arrogance of his erstwhile German comrades-in-arms.

The Russians needed well-trained soldiers, especially men who could harass the Germans behind their lines, so Maléter volunteered to parachute as a partisan on the condition that he was to fight for his country only. He told the Russians that he was not a Communist and was not interested in undergoing indoctrination. The Russians accepted these terms and Maléter was taken to a school of partisans in Kiev. The young Hungarian learned all the tricks because the Russians are masters of guerrilla warfare. He became a first-class parachutist and guerrilla fighter, but he steadfastly rebuffed all attempts at political indoctrination.

After six months he was put in charge of a platoon of tough, well-trained parachutists. They jumped one night behind the German lines onto a clearing in the wooded mountains of Transylvania in western Romania, until 1918 part of Hungary.

The legend about the tall partisan spread like prairie fire. He and his group destroyed communication lines, blew up bridges and roads, and harassed the Germans in many ways. The group became a constant threat to the vital lines between Nazi Germany and the Romanian oil fields.

He was captured once, luckily by a Hungarian unit fighting on the German side. Maléter proved to be not only an exceptionally good soldier but also a skilled propagandist. He talked the whole night with his captors and convinced them that a good Hungarian should fight against the Germans and not with them. The next morning they released him, and the entire unit joined his partisans in the woods.

After World War II Maléter stayed with what remained of the Hungarian army. He was a junior officer, shunned by other prewar officers because he had fought with the Russians, and suspected by the new ones because he belonged to the "old class." In 1949 Maléter joined the Communist party. The terror regime of Rákosi by then had purged almost all officers who had served in the prewar army. Those with higher ranks were executed, a lucky few were exiled to some remote village in the countryside. Maléter, now a Communist party member, was promoted in due course to the rank of major, later to lieutenant colonel. Opinions differ on whether he really became converted to Communism, or thought this was the only way to save his life and career. His wife, who divorced him in 1953 and fled with their three children from Hungary during the 1956 revolt, said in an interview in New York that they had become estranged because Maléter defended Communism and she opposed it.

During his days in the Kilian barracks an entire district, one of the largest in the Hungarian capital, followed Maléter's orders. Every house in the area became a fortress. The street corners were manned by young men and women with obsolete rifles, and the deadly Molotov cocktails.

On October 30 the Russians pulled their troops out of Budapest, and Mikoyan and Suslov agreed to negotiate the withdrawal of Soviet forces from Hungary. The gates of Kilian barracks opened. Maléter became a brigadier general and two days later minister of defense with the rank of major general.

At ten o'clock on the morning of November 3, in accordance with the Mikoyan agreement, three Russian generals, Malinin, Stepanov, and Cherbanin, arrived in the building of the Hungarian Parliament to begin talks on the "technical aspects" of Russian troop withdrawal. Maléter headed the Hungarian contingent consisting of Major General István Kovács and Colonel Miklós Szücs. Minister of State Ferenc Erdei was the civilian member on the Hungarian side. At noon the talks were adjourned and the participants agreed to meet again the same night at the Tököl military airport on Csepel Island, the Russian headquarters in Hungary.

The talks continued in a friendly atmosphere. Around midnight the door of the conference room opened and a Russian entered, wearing a uniform without insignia. The man conferred briefly with the Russian general Malinin, who shrugged and left the room without a word. The newcomer turned to the Hungarians. "You are under arrest," he said in Russian. He was Ivan Serov, head of the Soviet secret police since the liquidation of Beria in 1953.

Two hours later Soviet troops reentered Budapest and the second tragic phase of the revolution began. It was no revolution any more: it was war between Soviet Russia and Hungary.

Maléter was held incommunicado, reportedly in the Fö utca building of the secret police, taken over by the Russians after the revolt. Legends mushroomed around him. For weeks it was rumored that he had escaped and was leading insurgent units fighting guerrilla battles in the countryside as late as December 1956. Then, in June 1958, came the brief announcement that he had been convicted and executed.

After the revolution the Kádár regime tried to restore the façade of legality with typical Communist elephantine grace. The government book issued in Budapest with the title "Counterrevolutionary Conspiracy of Imre Nagy and His Accomplices" simply denied that Maléter had been arrested by Serov. "Contrary to hostile rumors," the book said, "Pál Maléter was arrested by the Hungarian authorities and not by Soviet military units."

Why, one may ask, was this lie necessary? First, nobody had claimed that Maléter had been arrested by Soviet military units. He had not. When General Malinin left the room, according to an eyewitness, he was genuinely distressed by Serov's intervention. Second, it was ridiculous even to suggest that Maléter had been arrested by "Hungarian authorities." There were few Hungarian authorities anywhere, and certainly none in Tököl, a well-guarded Soviet army base. Furthermore, any Hungarian authority which could have been properly named as such was under the orders of the Nagy government, the only Hungarian government which existed that night, and the government Maléter represented.

Goebbels tactics must fail when all details of an event become known to many, and that happened after the Soviet trap was set for Maléter. There was one man in the Maléter group who, though detained briefly, was released soon after: Erdei. In those revolutionary days, as I have said, even died-in-the-wool Communists talked, and every detail of Maléter's "arrest by invitation" became known.

One must assume that Malinin and the other two Russian generals negotiated in good faith. They were soldiers; it was not their task, and neither was it Maléter's, to discuss whether there should be a troop withdrawal. This was a political question, arranged by Mikoyan and Suslov with Nagy and Kádár.

The soldiers were talking about the procedure of the with-drawal, going into such amazingly secondary details as how many Hungarian army units should present arms at ceremonies for the departing Soviets, and how Soviet war memorials, dam-aged or demolished during the revolt, should be restored and maintained after the pullout.

Although between October 25 and the day of his arrest, No-vember 3, Maléter was the undisputed military leader of the revolt, this did not mean that a chain of command was estab-lished leading to every group of freedom fighters in Budapest, much less in the provinces. These groups were pretty much on their own and there was little if any coordination between them either during the October 23–November 4 period, nor during the more bloody period which began at dawn on No-vember 4.

The two periods must be divorced from each other both po-litically and militarily. The difference in the political situation was obvious: before November 4 there was a legal Hungarian government which, as the days passed, gradually sided with the revolution, representing its aims in the negotiations with Miko-yan and Suslov, and when they departed, with Ambassador Andropov. After November 4 there was an interregnum, sev-eral members of the legal government exiled themselves in the Yugoslav embassy, and the new Russian-appointed Kádár gov-ernment was in an unidentified place, first outside the country, later in Szolnok, some sixty miles east of Budapest. Despite the many clashes between freedom fighters and Soviet forces dur-ing the first period, it would be an exaggeration to speak about a war, but war is the correct word to describe the military activities in the period after November 4.

I spent most of the time during the first period on the streets where I thought the real story was, once or twice a day visiting Parliament, where the political activities of the Nagy govern-ment were concentrated. Information was easily available, in dramatic contrast to the prerevolution era, when the foreign correspondent was more or less restricted to his ability to read between the lines in the party newspapers.

Covering the streets I was often alone; at other times I was joined by some of my American and English colleagues whose number swelled to around a hundred as the days passed. It was good to be in their company after the many years during which Ilona and I were the only ones reporting from Budapest.

The Hungarian revolution was unique for a number of reasons, but first of all because of its unprecedented purity and the naive enthusiasm both of those who fought it and of the many others who watched the fight with prayers for success. By purity I mean that suddenly a people which had for years regarded dishonesty as a virtue found its better self again. The example I describe borders, in retrospect, on the ridiculous, but at the time it was heartwarming to me.

On October 26 at midafternoon, on my way home, I passed a government-owned grocery shop with half a dozen garbage cans outside. The streets were almost empty, the shops closed, with their iron shutters down. Two simply dressed men were walking in front of me. They had come from the central telephone office just opposite the shop and, I figured, must have been repairmen.

On top of one of the cans was a head of cabbage, surprisingly crisp to have been thrown away. Oblivious of my presence, the two stopped for a minute; then one of them took the cabbage in his hand, saying, "I'll take it home, Margit will be happy . . ."

"Don't do it," said the other, gently, without anger in his voice. "Let's not stain our revolution . . ."

I admit that after so many years this sounds corny. Then it was part of something beautiful, when a whole nation seemed to be carried away by the purity of their revolution. A head of cabbage thrown into the garbage really can symbolize this purity.

This sudden emergence of honesty was probably the reaction, or as one would say today, the backlash of the almost obligatory dishonesty of many years. Hungarians were neither better nor worse than other central Europeans, but though one can find few things to praise about prewar Hungary, the fact remains that there was remarkably little corruption, the crime rate was low, bank tellers did not embezzle, and industrial workers did not steal. This national honesty changed dramatically when, according to the Communists, everything belonged to the people, including the banks and the factories, the land and the mines. The reason for the change was by no means that the blue- or white-collar worker was in a worse financial situation than before. But the slogan "yours is the land" or "yours is the factory" backfired when it became immediately clear that it was nothing but an empty lie, that no capitalist banker or industrialist could invent such devilish tricks as the Communists did to exploit the worker.

There were additional factors. In capitalist times the worker could freely revile the man who owned the plant or shop. Under Communist rule he was expected to be happy and smiling; if he was not, he was suspected of being the enemy who had wormed his way into the rank and file of the glorious working class. The capitalist was often hated, or at least disliked, but he was also respected because he had a higher education, and usually even the most embittered worker admitted that he knew how to run the factory. The Communists simply elevated another worker and named him director of the plant, usually someone whose only merit was being a reliable party hack, a man whom the party and ministry could trust to carry out instructions blindly. Of course the others asked: who does he think he is? Why is he better than I am? Yesterday he was with me in the workshop and today he is all puffed up in the plush manager's office and a chauffeur-driven car brings him to the factory every morning.

The silly "the factory is yours" slogan helped to change the morality. If it is mine, I take it home, many said, and they did, whatever they could: tools, raw materials, the end product. Cheating and stealing became a national pastime. But during the revolt, a nation suddenly found its basic honesty.

During the fighting many shop windows were shattered. Walking the streets I saw some empty ones; in many of them there was a handwritten note: "I took the displayed goods to the janitor," and some added carefully a list of the things. They were neatly signed.

When all was over, in the second half of November, wooden boxes appeared on many street corners of downtown Budapest with a little note asking for donations for the families of those who were killed during the fighting. Passersby gave generously and I saw many a box filled with paper money. Yet nobody guarded the boxes. There were no kind ladies or elegantly dressed children around, the usual helpers in charity drives in prewar times. Once I stood with some of my curious colleagues for half an hour to see whether anyone would take a bank note instead of adding one. Nobody did.

I know that there were brutal excesses — luckily I did not witness any of them — when AVH men were summarily executed by the angry mob. These lynchings were of course exploited by the postrevolutionary regime to support the contention that the revolt was a fascist counterrevolution. Many Hungarians excused the killings by explaining that their anger against the "strong arm of the regime" was understandable. I will not join either side; after all, it was no less an authority than Lenin who said that "revolutions always attract the best and worst in society." But I also know about cases of magnanimity when AVH men were involved.

Strangely, Colonel Balázsi and Captain Babics, my two tormentors in prison, were the lucky "heroes" of one incident. The AVH, believed to have been a perfectly organized institution, made the fatal mistake of not furnishing its members with false documents. The reason was probably superconfidence that nothing could happen to them, and frankly, before the revolution I shared this belief. Many AVH men wearing civilian clothes were captured when they could show nothing but their real identification cards.

Balázsi and Babics escaped from Budapest and were headed north toward the Czechoslovak border some time between October 23 and November 4, when the party and its organs disintegrated. AVH men got last-minute orders: you are on your own, try to escape to Czechoslovakia, where the AVH will be reorganized into fighting groups, and wait for the signal to return. Somehow, in a village between Budapest and the border, Balázsi and Babics were recognized by a farmer who had been an inmate of Fö utca several years earlier. Their identification cards confirmed that the farmer was right. Some in the village suggested that they be executed summarily, but the village elders decided otherwise. There was a lawful government in Budapest, they argued; the two should be returned to stand trial. An escort was formed and Balázsi and Babics were sent back to prison for a few days. On November 4 they were freed.

One night, walking home from my daily excursion to the "clandestine" teletype, two men passed me in front of my house. Both were middle-aged, but one had a rifle and the other was obviously his prisoner. I stopped them and explained who I was. The prisoner, the guard said, was an AVH man found hiding in an attic. He was small fry, detailed to the office of the AVH in the district where I lived, but he should be interrogated. The prisoner, without handcuffs, busily nodded that his guard was right. He could have been shot right there, and there would have been one more corpse on the streets, but he was not. I was curious and the next day visited the police to find out what happened. The prisoner had been questioned and set free.

On Sunday, October 28, I visited one of Budapest's surgical clinics on Üllöi ut, some two hundred yards from Kilian barracks. The street was a shambles and the clinic itself had gaping holes in its walls. Most of the wards facing the street had had to be evacuated and patients had been taken to neighboring clinics through the gardens. Doctors led me through the wards whose beds were occupied by men, mostly young, wounded during the fighting. On the second floor was the ward for children. Here I met Lajos, the twelve-year-old freedom fighter, whose arm had been shot through when he and his gang tried to blow up a tank. He was playing with a toy airplane in his bed.

"What did you fight with, Lajos?" I asked him.

"Oh, I had only an old army rifle," he answered. "You know, I got a submachine gun from the soldiers, but Mihály took it away from me."

"Who is Mihály?" I asked.

"He's the boy living next door. He's sixteen, so he is stronger and he had only the old rifle. . . . But it was a good rifle, I liked it. A Tommy gun is of course different," he sighed.

The life of a war correspondent — we thought we deserved this name — was not without risks. On Monday, October 29, I toured the area of the Kilian barracks with two Swiss reporters in their Volkswagen. The sector was firmly in the hands of the insurgents, and the barracks themselves and the adjacent old apartment houses were under almost constant fire from Russian tanks. We hoped to get into Kilian somehow. It was rumored that there was a hidden entrance from the narrow street behind the barracks but we never got there. A two-man patrol stopped us some three blocks from the barracks. A martial-looking woman who reminded me of a stallkeeper in one of Budapest's open markets was the leader. She was an extremely big woman with a kerchief on her head and a booming voice, and she gesticulated menacingly with the submachine gun in her hand. The man with her was quite obviously her subordinate. We were ordered to get out of the car but firmly refused to comply when she wanted us to stand facing the wall, with our hands above our heads. My companions spoke no Hungarian and were immediately suspected of being Russian spies. It did not help much that I spoke Hungarian, because that meant to her that I was the guide of the "Russians," consequently an AVH man. It took some forceful arguing to persuade the woman to take a look at the Volkswagen's Swiss license plate, to inspect our press credentials — luckily she could read — and instead of shooting us, to help us find General Maléter. Finally she burst out laughing and let us go.

Returning from our adventurous but unsuccessful excursion, I invited the two Swiss reporters to my house to have a bite and to work on their stories in Ilona's abandoned office. We had hardly settled down when the door opened: my wife was back from what was supposed to be her first peaceful vacation in Western Europe.

"Of course I'm back. It is, after all, your birthday. We were in different cells on your birthday last year — I just could not miss this one," she said.

Ilona came with Russell Jones, a roving reporter of United Press. For days they had been working together in their Vienna office as Ilona monitored the Budapest radio. Then, despite my pleas on the teletype, she decided to come back. They rented a car in Vienna, supplied themselves with food, a bottle of Scotch, and a box of tranquilizers. The journey by road from Vienna to Budapest normally takes about five hours. They were en route for a whole day.

The border was wide open; nobody bothered to check their passports. But then the adventure started. One town was in the hands of the Russians; in the next the insurgents were the masters. Ilona and Russ swallowed a few of the pills, listened to the advice of friendly peasants, made detours to avoid places where roadblocks had been set up, and finally they arrived to celebrate the birthday I had completely forgotten about.

Late in the evening of November 3, only a few hours before the Soviet onslaught on the city, Ilona and I were in the general neighborhood of the Kilian barracks. November 3 was the second day that not one shot was fired in Budapest. General Malé-

ter's men in the defense ministry and the reorganized police
restored order in almost perfect coordination with the insurgents and even the sporadic excesses ceased. But we wanted to
find out for sure that this quiet extended to Kilian, where fighting had been almost uninterrupted since the revolt had broken
out ten days earlier.

Luckily AP sent me a Volkswagen from Vienna which
probably saved our lives, or at least our freedom at dawn the
next day.

Close to Kilian a few young freedom fighters, members of
Maléter's "army," guarded an intersection with an antitank
gun captured from the Russians. The Soviet tanks had disappeared two days earlier, but the "kids" were still lingering
around. Their rifles and the army belt around the waist of the
shabby coats they wore gave them a childishly martial look.

When we stopped the car, two of them approached with
their rifles ready. A friendly smile came to their faces when
we identified ourselves. One of them was a girl. An American
cigarette made many of the young people happy those days
and it was easy to persuade her to sit with us in the car.

As journalists, Ilona and I have had many exciting experiences: the war, the horrors of Nazism and of Russian occupation, the months in prison, and then the revolt. The girl's slow
narrative is one we will never forget.

Her hands were dirty and so was her face. The matted blond
hair hung from her clumsy soldier's cap. Yet she had an angelic
face with innocent blue eyes looking out wearily through the
car window. Julia was a textile worker in one of the big factories in Ujpest, the northern industrial suburb of Budapest. She
lived with her parents, both factory workers themselves. She
was their only child.

"I was a member of DISz. We all were." She was fidgeting
with her gun. It sounded like a farce. DISz was the monolithic
Communist youth organization, one of the Communist party's
most powerful organs, supposed to train future party members.

Julia was born just before World War II broke out, and she had been brought up under Communist rule. She had to work, as her parents did.

"I knew nothing else but work, but till 1953 I thought this was life," she said. In 1953, after Stalin's death, the Communists committed the gravest blunder: they destroyed a god in Moscow and the demigods in the satellites. I always had the feeling that this was their most serious mistake, but only on that night, talking to Julia, could I clearly see the link between events in and after 1953 and the revolt of the Hungarian youth. They had been brought up to worship Stalin and his imitations, and then, suddenly, were told that the god was just a man with many sins.

"We were cheated, we knew then we were cheated," Julia said, and her fingers grabbed the gun excitedly. Then, she recalled, Nagy replaced Rákosi and life for her became free for a year, at least much freer than ever before.

"When Rákosi came back in 1955 and Nagy was removed, we knew this hour would come. We exercised daily with our submachine guns and we were taught how to make a Molotov cocktail using an empty bottle and gasoline. We were told we would need it against the Americans."

Julia looked at her cheap wristwatch. "Maléter is going to the Russians tonight. You think they will pull out?" she asked. I had no answer.

"Maléter is a hero. We respect and trust him. But Nagy is our father. He is one of us, a good and kind man."

What did she expect from the future? Ilona asked her. She smiled and her face became beautiful.

"A long, pink evening dress. I saw one in the movie . . ." and she looked down at her legs, in a man's trousers, and her feet, in clumsy boots too big for her. She thrust back her long hair. I saw a red scar on her forehead.

"Nothing . . . a bullet. It came pretty near, though," she said. There was no trace of bragging in her voice.

"Yes, and I want to dance in my pink dress. I never had the chance to dance. There was always too much work, in the factory and at home. And my old people were always depressed and sad," she said.

It was time for us to go. Ilona stroked the girl's head. "You'll get your pink dress, Julia," she said. When we drove away I asked my wife whether she believed what she said. She did not answer.

About a month later, when the Russians and Kádár were firmly in control and mail again began to arrive from abroad, Ilona got a letter with an Irish stamp on the crumpled envelope. We knew nobody in Ireland.

"I read your article on Julia in the paper. I am nineteen and live with my parents. We all think she should get her pink dress," the letter said. "And maybe she would like to come and live with us. We would be happy. Would you tell her? I am very excited. She must be a good and kind girl. I trust your description was true. Do find her, please . . ."

I found in my notes the name of the factory where Julia said she worked. I drove out. The general strike was still on. Workers guarded the factories but Western newsmen were welcomed guests. I was led to the chairman of the workers' council and inquired about Julia.

"How do you know her?" he asked. There was a long silence after I explained. "She died, the poor thing," the elderly worker said. His graying head hung deep on his chest. Julia died defending the Kilian barracks, the Alamo of the Hungarian revolution. General Maléter was no longer with them because the night before he had walked into General Serov's trap. Kilian fought desperately without its leader. The whole area was shot to rubble but its defenders did not capitulate. Most of them died in the barracks and the surrounding narrow streets.

Julia's parents found her bullet-torn body in one of the hundreds of open coffins in the cemetery. Workers of the textile plant covered it with the Hungarian tricolor.

My wife did not answer the boy from Ireland. The drama was not over and she had no time to write the carefully worded reply the young man deserved. Then, when we had to leave Hungary, we destroyed this letter with so many other things dear to us.

10

The Revolution Succeeds
—the Russians Return

I have intentionally devoted more space to Ilona's and my personal experiences during those twelve days between October 23 and November 4 than to the description of the course of political events. Right or wrong, the small fragments of remembrance, the poignantly ridiculous story of the head of cabbage in the trash can, Julia's dream about the pink dress, and all the vignettes remain in my memory more clearly than the speeches, the changes in government, and troop movements. I know I will never forget them.

But the reporter obviously cannot ignore the enormous changes which occurred during this brief span of time, changes which transformed Nagy from a conservative Communist into a revolutionary leader and which must have stirred the thinking of the Moscow leadership. Here briefly is the day-by-day history of the twelve-day period.

The first two and a half days of the revolt, between noon of October 23 and the night of October 25, were characterized by two decisive factors: Gerö's desperate efforts to remain in power and suppress the uprising, and Nagy's virtual imprisonment at party headquarters. The turning point came late on

October 25, when Mikoyan and Suslov forced Gerö to resign and leave the country. Though Nagy was freed and moved immediately to the Parliament building, according to all accounts from his close associates he remained the loyal party man, the Moscow-trained Communist, the opponent of everything that would weaken the Communist party's role as the country's sole leader. Budapest radio, mouthing the trite party line, still talked about "counterrevolutionaries," threatening them with dire consequences in the name of the government unless they surrendered.

The first tangible evidence of a change came on October 26 when the Communist party's Central Committee, led by Nagy, issued a lengthy statement recognizing publicly for the first time that some of the revolutionaries' demands were justified. The "mistakes and crimes" of the past were acknowledged and the promise was made that Soviet troops would return to their bases — after order had been restored. A new government was promised, based on a "broad national foundation," a vague phrase nobody cared to explain.

The explanation came the next day, on October 27, when two long-forgotten men joined the Nagy government: Zoltán Tildy and Béla Kovács. Tildy's reputation was not the best. A Protestant clergyman, he was a prominent member of the opposition Smallholder party in the prewar Hungarian Parliament. After the war, when the Smallholders won the 1945 elections, he became the country's first president, a man who apparently believed that he could work with Rákosi and was accordingly an appeaser to the bitter end in 1948, when he was forced to resign. Tildy was kept for years under house arrest in a villa on the Buda side of the capital. Béla Kovács, a respected peasant politician and secretary general of the Smallholder party, refused to compromise and was removed from the political scene by the Russians. In February 1947, they simply kidnapped him when Parliament, defying Rákosi's request, declined to suspend his parliamentary immunity. Kovács was held in Russia for seven years and then he returned, after Stalin's death, almost unnoticed, to live quietly in a village near Pécs in southern Hungary.

On October 27, the fourth day of the revolt, Tildy became deputy prime minister and Kovács minister of agriculture. Characteristically, however, as Kovács told me on an unforgettable night on November 4 in the refuge of the American legation, he had not even been asked whether he would accept the cabinet post; in fact, there had been no way to ask him, since communications with the countryside were more or less nonexistent.

The other members of the Nagy cabinet were Communists; they were hard-core Rákosi followers, with the possible exception of two. Professor Babits was a mild-mannered veteran believer in Marx, who became minister of health. (Strangely, Babits was also a former friend of AVH chief General Péter.) The second was György Lukács, the maverick philosopher who got into trouble with every Communist regime, although he was probably the greatest philosopher Marxism has produced. Two other non-Communist members of the cabinet were József Bognár, a Smallholder party member, and Ferenc Erdei, a member of the Peasant party, who were both frank fellow travelers during all of the years when their parties were oppressed by Rákosi.

In Washington on the same day, October 27, Robert Murphy, then deputy under secretary of state, called in Tibor Zádor, the Hungarian chargé d'affaires. According to Lincoln White, the State Department spokesman, Zádor told Murphy that he was informed by the Hungarian legation in London, which was in radio communication with Budapest, about what was happening in Hungary. Zádor admitted that the students who started the demonstrations on October 23 voiced justified demands, but added that the October 23 intervention of Soviet troops was "quite legal" under the Warsaw Pact.

October 28, the first Sunday after the outbreak of the revolt, brought further developments. For the first time Budapest radio admitted that the rebels had won. Nagy spoke on the radio and announced that he had ordered an immediate cease-fire and that Soviet troops had begun their withdrawal from Budapest. Nagy also proclaimed the dissolution of the AVH and the reinstatement of Hungary's traditional coat of arms to replace the despised Soviet emblem. But probably the most significant event of the day was an editorial in the Communist party organ *Szabad Nép* which protested vehemently against Soviet charges that what happened in Hungary was a "counterrevolutionary fascist attempt at a coup d'état." To the contrary, *Szabad Nép* argued, the revolt was "a great national democratic movement which unites the whole people, suppressed by the despotism of the past years."

On Monday, October 29, Budapesters finally began to believe that Nagy had kept his promise: the Russians had disappeared from the city. It was a quiet day, but many also sensed it was the quietness before the storm.

Tuesday, October 30, brought another leap forward. Nagy announced the end of the one-party system and called for new elections with all the political parties of 1945 participating. Also Tildy, Erdei, and finally Kádár spoke on the radio and the latter was emphatic in saying that he, the new first secretary of the Communist party, agreed wholeheartedly with Nagy, Tildy, and Erdei. Kádár also announced the formation of the new Hungarian Socialist Workers' party to replace the totally discredited Communist party. The preparatory committee of the new party was formed without a single Stalinist among its members. They were Nagy, Kádár, Ferenc Donát, Géza Losonczy, Sándor Kopácsi, Professor Lukács, and Zoltán Szántó.

But the day also produced two important announcements in two Communist capitals, Moscow and Peking. The Chinese Communists said that "the demands of the Hungarian and Polish peoples were justified" and accused the Soviets both of "bourgeois chauvinism" and of having disregarded the "principles of equal rights." The Chinese declaration was especially noteworthy because later Mao Tse-tung became the harshest critic of the Hungarian uprising. Of far greater importance, however, was the Soviet declaration on relations between socialist states, as reported in *Pravda* on October 31.

Saying that "the countries of the great community of socialist nations can base their relations only on the principles of complete equality of rights, of respect for territorial integrity, political independence and sovereignty, and of noninterference in the internal affairs of one state by the other," the Moscow declaration admitted that this "Leninist principle" had been violated in the past.

"The Soviet government is prepared," the declaration continued, "to review with the other socialist countries, signatories of the Warsaw Pact, the question of Soviet troops stationed on the territory of the abovementioned countries."

The following was the key paragraph in the Moscow declaration: "Being of the opinion that the continued presence of Soviet units in Hungary could be used as a pretext for further aggravating the situation, the Soviet government has now given instruction to its military commanders to withdraw their troops from the city of Budapest as soon as the Hungarian government feels that they can be dispensed with. At the same time the Soviet government is prepared to engage in negotiations with the Hungarian government and the other signatories of the Warsaw Pact regarding the question of Soviet troops elsewhere on the territory of Hungary."

October 30 was probably one of the busiest days of the revolt. In the afternoon I was told that Cardinal Mindszenty had been freed by an army unit and was on his way from Felsöpetény, where he had been kept under house arrest, to Budapest. Esztergom, a city on the Danube some forty-five miles north of the capital, was the cardinal's official residence as he was also archbishop of Esztergom, but in addition he had a small mansion on the hill in Buda where the royal castle stood.

When I arrived at the mansion, the winding, narrow streets of the historic hill were packed with people hoping to see the cardinal, who was already inside his house. A Hungarian army tank guarded the prelate's house and soldiers were posted on the roofs of adjacent houses.

I had met the cardinal before, when I interviewed him in his majestic residence in Esztergom on two occasions and when I covered his trial in 1949. When I stood with him in the small anteroom of his Budapest house, I was touched and impressed because the cardinal had not changed; he was the same haggard, slow-speaking man I had known before. He said he remembered me.

"I was tortured in body and soul," he replied to my question. "It is God's miracle that I am here and that I am as I am. What I went through is unspeakable and would defy the imagination of any normal man." He asked me to come and see him later because, he said, he needed time to acquaint himself with the events which had freed him. Neither of us knew then that our next meeting would take place in the shelter of the American legation.

Because of Mindszenty's arrival I missed another event of the day, and I was glad I did. How it started and why is still obscure, but a group of revolutionaries besieged a building which housed the Budapest organization of the Communist party and was occupied by AVH soldiers. The battle lasted for hours and when the defenders of the building capitulated, several of them were mercilessly shot down when they emerged from the building with their hands raised above their heads. One of them was Imre Mezö, a party functionary known to have been a loyal follower of Imre Nagy.

There was, I am convinced, no justification for this senseless killing on October 30, when the revolution appeared to be victorious. Moreover, I feel sure that this disgusting event greatly influenced the thinking of many Communists, including Kádár, who until then had sided with Nagy.

The next day, on October 31, Mikoyan and Suslov were again in Budapest, and according to information from Nagy's aides, presented the premier with a copy of the Moscow declaration. The two Russian envoys spent the whole day with Nagy, Kádár, and Tildy, but other party and government figures were occasionally invited to attend the negotiations. According to one version given to newsmen, Mikoyan and Suslov offered the immediate withdrawal of those Soviet troops which had been sent into Hungary after October 23 to reinforce the units already in the country, and promised to negotiate the withdrawal of all troops at a later, quieter time. During these talks Tildy was the principal spokesman for the Hungarian side. He turned down the Soviet offer, requested the withdrawal of all troops and, one informant insisted, he told Mikoyan and Suslov that Hungary would renounce the Warsaw Pact.

I recorded at least five versions of what went on in the forty-eight-hour talks with Khrushchev's two emissaries. Whichever interpretation was correct, I am convinced that the talks were crucial and formed the basis of the decision in Moscow to return to Budapest in force and to crush the revolt. Though all versions differed, all of them agreed on one point: Mikoyan and, to a somewhat lesser degree, Suslov were understanding and sympathetic. One source who was present at the negotiations said that the two Russians in effect agreed to the Hungarian demands to reintroduce the multiparty system, to avoid interference in domestic developments in Hungary, and to withdraw Soviet troops from the entire country. Another source who had, in my judgment, a more analytical mind and greater familiarity with the Russian way of thinking, was more cautious when he told me that Mikoyan and Suslov "took notice" of the Hungarian position, as explained to them by Tildy, but did not commit themselves.

Late that evening, when I dropped into an armchair to relax after another exhausting day, I turned on the radio and listened to someone — who he was, I never learned — confessing in an emotion-choked voice: "For many a long year we were lying, the radio lied day and night on all wavelengths. . . . In the future we shall tell the truth, the whole truth, and nothing but the truth . . ."

How well I knew, and who did not, that the radio, completely controlled by the state and the party, had been lying along with the newspapers, the periodicals, and every book printed in that period. I believed the man's dramatic confession. It was part of the renascence of a nation forced to lie and to listen to lies for so many years.

However relaxed I was then, my day was not entirely over. A high-ranking army officer, a professional soldier who during those days regularly briefed me on the military situation, called that night and his voice, usually calm and to the point, was troubled. He said he was perplexed by the conflicting and contradictory reports on Soviet troop movements. But surely they are leaving, or have already left Budapest, I said. "Never mind Budapest," he answered impatiently. The reports from the countryside and from the border areas were confusing. Some units appeared to be moving in circles, some had departed or were approaching the border to depart. Many others, fresh units, were entering. One city in the countryside had been evacuated by the Russians under almost festive circumstances, with the newly elected mayor wishing the Soviets Godspeed, but a few hours later another Russian regiment, which was obviously new in the country, entered the city and occupied the barracks evacuated by the departing troops. I asked my friend what he made of all this.

"They will never give up Hungary. Suez presented them

with the perfect excuse on a silver platter. I'm ready to leave and join whichever fighting unit can use an old staff officer," he said, and hung up. Weeks later I was told he had been killed while commanding a motley group of soldiers and young freedom fighters in the mountains around Pécs.

In mentioning Suez, my soldier friend referred, of course, to the British-French-Israeli adventure which many Hungarians believed was a catastrophe because it diverted Western attention away from Hungary and gave the Russians the opportunity to act as they pleased.

On Thursday, November 1, the military attaché at the American legation confirmed the alarming news about strange Russian troop movements. There were other disturbing reports. The Soviet troops which had supposedly left Budapest had surrounded Ferihegy, the city's main airport. Optimists were ready with an explanation which they claimed came from Andropov, the Soviet ambassador. The families of the Russian "advisers," thousands of them, were to be evacuated in a major operation which required the exclusive use of the airport.

Mikoyan and Suslov had left the night before and Andropov took over as the Soviet spokesman. He had four, possibly five appointments with Nagy on November 1 to discuss the increasing number of reports pouring into Budapest on new Soviet troop arrivals. First Nagy received the diplomat alone, later together with members of his cabinet. The premier vehemently protested the entrance of new troops and finally, at their last meeting late in the afternoon, informed the Russian that he had dispatched a telegram to Dag Hammarskjöld, secretary general of the United Nations, requesting that he put the Hungarian question on the agenda of the Security Council. Hungary, the message to Hammarskjöld said, had renounced the Warsaw Pact and was a neutral country.

Kádár provided the drama at this last meeting, I was told by a high-ranking Nagy aide who was present. This rather introverted man appeared to lose his patience when Andropov insisted that Russian troop movements were not inconsistent with the October 30 Moscow declaration. "I will come down to the streets and fight your tanks with my bare hands," Kádár shouted, gesticulating with his fists and standing close to the unperturbed diplomat. Nobody, I was told, used such harsh language in the meetings with Andropov, yet Kádár defected and sided with the Russians the same night.

I spent most of the day in Parliament, where late in the afternoon I listened to Nagy's radio speech in which he informed his people that from that day on, Hungary was a neutral country and that he had asked the great powers, the victors of World War II, to recognize and to defend the country's neutrality. When I left the building, little candles were flickering on the sidewalks close to the walls of Parliament. It was All Saints' Day and Hungarians remembered those who died in the square on October 25.

On Friday, November 2, our personal lives again became entangled in the national tragedy. After a careful assessment of the situation, the U.S. legation decided to evacuate the American women and children to Vienna. A convoy was to leave during the day and Sarah Rogers, our friend and neighbor, urged Ilona and the two girls to join it. It was a heartbreaking decision for Ilona to make — as a wife and mother on the one hand, and a newspaperwoman on the other. Sarah Rogers had to leave right away with her four daughters and she tried to persuade Ilona to follow her. She would drive slowly, she said, so that Ilona could catch up with the convoy. My wife promised to consider. She did not leave.

Andropov again entered the huge Gothic building on the Danube to tell Nagy the Soviets were ready to start talks about the withdrawal of their troops the next day, November 3. But the number of reports about new Soviet troop movements across the border increased and Nagy dispatched a second message to Hammarskjöld repeating his request that the Hungarian question be put on the agenda.

Even in more relaxed times Budapest was a city of rumors, but in those days, understandably, it was more so. Early in the afternoon there was great excitement in the corridors of Parliament because it was said that a United Nations delegation was on its way to Budapest. Some had even maintained that it was already circling above Ferihegy airport but had no permission from the Russians to land. Some lesser officials of the Nagy government said matter-of-factly that this was what they expected, that the airplane would land somewhere, if not at Ferihegy then at one of the smaller airports, and that the U.N. delegates, whoever they were, would see to it that the Russians kept their promises and withdrew in orderly fashion. How the rumor started, nobody could find out. It was, alas, a rumor without substance.

Lingering in the vast building I bumped into one of Nagy's trusted aides, a newspaperman and "red-white-green" Communist. He spoke with unusual candor about the future, with only a modicum of bitterness in his voice.

"We Communists are aware that we have lost, that the next elections will complete our defeat," he said. "But we deserve it, with all the mistakes we made during the ten years of our rule."

In the afternoon a group of Hungarian newsmen and photographers invited me to join them and visit the compound where Gerö, Révai, and other top party members of the Rákosi era once lived. The guards had disappeared, the compound was wide open, ready for inspection, I was told. We drove up Svábhegy, the mountain on the Buda side which I knew so intimately in winter, having crisscrossed it for years on skis. From the street one could see nothing but trees in the many acres of the fenced-in compound. Inside there were villas, standing separately in the dense woods. We visited the one which belonged to Gerö.

It was an unexciting experience wandering through the empty rooms of a dull house, with every piece of furniture left there, but no personal belongings, not even a piece of paper or a pair of old tennis shoes forgotten in a closet. Everything was tasteless, almost cheap, the home of a modest bureaucrat who did not care about the luxuries of life. Books, not too many, on the shelves, mostly the mass editions of party literature ranging from Marx to the volumes of Rákosi's speeches. And telephones everywhere with direct lines to party headquarters, to the homes of others in the compound, the guardhouse of the AVH, and to Rákosi's villa, also on Svábhegy but standing alone about a mile from the others. I have always disliked intrusion in the private lives of others and Gerö was no exception. The whole thing was more depressing than interesting, and I left quickly.

The first encouraging news of the day was waiting for me when I got home. The workers of Budapest factories had passed a unanimous vote of confidence in Nagy and pledged to end the strike and resume work on Monday, November 5. Probably none of them could imagine that on Monday the city would turn into a battlefield.

Meanwhile in Washington, also on November 2, spokesman White told reporters at the State Department that Nagy had informed the United States about his protest against new Soviet troops entering Hungary, that his country repudiated the Warsaw Pact and had proclaimed neutrality. What was the American response? a reporter asked. "I know of none," White replied. Will there be an answer? was the next question. "I just can't answer that," White said.

On Saturday, November 3, Parliament was again the place to be. Before noon I caught a glimpse of the golden shoulder straps of Russian generals:- finally the talks about the pullout started. General Mikhail Malinin headed the Soviet group; the two others, as I have already mentioned, were Generals Stepanov and Cherbanin. The Hungarian contingent was led by General Maléter. Hungarian aides kept us informed about the state of negotiations and their reports were optimistic. Since withdrawal was unquestionable, the talks centered on questions of detail, and Malinin was in a cordial mood. Midafternoon, the two sides recessed to reconvene for dinner and another round of talks in Tököl on Csepel Island, Malinin's headquarters.

Late in the afternoon, the Nagy government held its first and only press conference and some one hundred and fifty newsmen crowded around a huge oblong table in the "Salle des Gobelins." I could not see a single representative of *Tass* or *Pravda*.

Nagy did not come — "the pressure of business," we were told — but Tildy and Losonczy were there. It gave us a strange feeling to attend the first "free," Western-style press conference since 1947. There was no coffee served and there were no flowers on the table, the usual paraphernalia offered instead of news on the rare occasions of a press conference during the Rákosi era. Though Tildy and Losonczy answered the questions calmly, I sensed that they were worried. Despite the talks with Malinin the reports from the Russian and Romanian borders were coming in with maddening monotony: a regiment entered here, a division there, young combat-ready soldiers, mostly Asians.

There was a silly incident when a colleague from London, a newsman of Hungarian descent, interrupted the conference protesting loudly and rather childishly that Iván Boldizsár was acting as an interpreter, translating Tildy's and Losonczy's answers into English. The newsman accused Boldizsár of having been a fellow traveler (which he was), but with the same reasoning he could have objected to Tildy or Losonczy, who remained a loyal Communist despite his arrest in 1949. I knew that Boldizsár had been one of the four hundred earmarked by Rákosi for arrest in 1955, and in a louder voice than I should have, I told the Britisher to shut up.

Tildy and Losonczy acknowledged that Soviet reinforcements were arriving, but offered no explanation. They let us go, promising to tell us more the next day when Maléter concluded his talks with Malinin.

The next day, Sunday, November 4, never came. I must have slept like a log until around five in the morning, when I awoke suddenly: the air was ringing with the muffled tone of heavy gunfire from afar. The Russians were besieging Budapest.

My little family must have been a pathetic sight, doddering about in pajamas. It was dark outside, the streets around the house were empty and peaceful, but the deep bangs of tank guns came from all directions. I switched on the radio; it played the anthem and then Imre Nagy's familiar voice:

"This is Imre Nagy speaking, president of the council of ministers of the Hungarian People's Republic. Today at daybreak Soviet troops attacked our capital with the obvious intention of overthrowing the legal Hungarian democratic government. Our troops are in combat. The government is at its post. I notify the people of our country and the entire world of this fact." Then the anthem again, and then an announcer reading Nagy's statement in English and French translations.

By then we were not listening. Both Ilona and I furiously dialed the long distance operator in our respective offices. When she answered, I gave her the numbers of half a dozen AP offices in Europe. Can I ever forget the girl's voice, muffled with tears: ". . . It is too late, oh, it is too late . . . I cannot connect you any more . . ."

I was standing in my office and my first thought was how disciplined, how mature my two daughters were, looking at us without tears, without signs of panic, without asking unnecessary questions, like two little soldiers waiting for orders. What should the orders be? I wondered.

The telephone rang, it was McCormack's quiet voice from the Duna Hotel, on the other side of the river. He could not get his story out either, everyone was awake, the international

crowd of newsmen were visiting each other, many were pack-
ing without knowing where to go. There was no point in staying in our apartment; we should join them in the hotel. There,
at least, we would all be together and near the major Western
legations on the Pest side.

We packed a few belongings and were ready to leave. The
three-story house where we lived had two apartments on each
floor. The one neighboring us belonged to a high-ranking
Communist party functionary who had disappeared when the
revolt broke out, leaving his wife and two children behind.
When I closed the door of our apartment behind me, the
woman came out from theirs, unkempt, in a dressing gown,
looking bewildered, and asked, "What is going to happen
now?"

I felt suddenly very bitter. We did not know each other — I
had hardly ever seen her — but the woman's anguish was genuine. At that moment she was not the wife of a party functionary, and likely a party member herself, but a woman left alone,
scared of the gunfire, afraid for her children.

"Madam," I replied, "really! You have no reason to be afraid
any more. They are back, and they are your friends."

Oh, how I cherished the little Volkswagen with the Vienna
license plates standing in front of our house that morning. I
packed the car and put the children in the back seat. When I
started the engine a young man passed us, hurrying down the
hill, with a rifle in his hand.

"Where to?" I asked him, and I immediately knew how silly
my question was. "Can you hear them?" he asked back, as he
disappeared around the corner. We met several more while
driving toward the Chain Bridge, the shortest way to the Duna
Hotel. The approach to the bridge is through a tunnel under
the hill of the royal castle and driving through it I remembered
one day during the short-lived Communist rule of Béla Kun
after World War I when my mother and I had to lie prone in

the tunnel while Communists and anti-Communists were shooting at each other over our heads.

There was no shooting in the tunnel that day, but I put on the brakes as soon as we reached the little square between the mouth of the tunnel and the Chain Bridge, the loveliest of all bridges over the Danube. Two Russian tanks blocked the bridge entrance and I saw no point in arguing with them. One thing struck me immediately. The tanks were not the T-34 type, so well known to me from events of the previous week, but the then new T-54 monsters, not used by the Soviet occupation forces stationed in Hungary before the revolution.

I made a sharp right toward Liberty Bridge, the next one over the Danube. We had luck, the bridge was still open, but our car was the last to pass. Speeding across the bridge, I could see in my mirror several Russian tanks arriving in the square between the Gellért Hotel and the Liberty Bridge on the Buda side.

The lobby of the Duna was teeming with newsmen of all nationalities. Our closest friends were there, but many others had already left for the legations of their respective countries. Those who remained were seasoned veterans who had seen trouble around the world, and there was neither hurry nor panic. One Britisher, an authority on eastern Europe, was skeptical about our story; he simply would not believe that what we had seen were Russian tanks. They might have been Hungarian tank units, he suggested.

I was not in the mood to argue. The hotel was only about half a mile from Chain Bridge. Let's walk there, I proposed. A group of about a dozen of us set out, but hastily retreated when a T-54 turned its gun menacingly in our direction. The colleague from London was quick to apologize.

There were many fewer people in the hotel lobby when we returned from our brief excursion and everybody was ready to leave when the gunfire became heavier and came closer. Suddenly I felt a great emptiness. Would it not have been better to have stayed at home, or turned the Volkswagen westward to find an escape route to Austria? It was so easy to be a foreign correspondent during the previous days, with the immense advantage of knowing the language and knowing the city intimately. But now everyone had discovered that his country had a legation in Budapest and they were entitled to ask admittance in time of peril. What should we do? Going back to Buda was impossible; the bridges were blocked. Staying in the hotel, soon to be abandoned by everyone, seemed to be the only possibility, however ludicrous.

Somebody asked, "And what about you?"

"We stay," I replied in a casual voice. Somehow I felt, and tried to behave accordingly, like the senator of ancient Rome who remained seated in his *sella curulis* on the Forum when the barbarians besieged his city.

Our friends decided otherwise. I saw John McCormack disappear into a telephone booth, with Russ Jones and Sy Freidin listening in. John talked to someone briefly and then came back to us.

"I talked to Tom Wailes," he said. "You are welcome to come with us to the legation."

Ilona and I had met Edward T. Wailes, the new American minister, once before, around November 1, when he and his wife Cornelia arrived in Budapest. We knew that he was a seasoned diplomat, transferred to Budapest from Pretoria, where he had been ambassador to South Africa. When the Waileses arrived, they did not go to their residence, which was in the hills of Buda, a thirty-minute drive from the legation, but stayed in the chancery with several other diplomats whose wives and children had been evacuated to Vienna.

Our first impression of Tom Wailes was excellent. He was delightful to talk to, there was no trace of pomposity about him, and the couple immediately adapted themselves to the austere circumstances of living at the chancery. But most important was that he was there, smiling, self-confident, unperturbed but inquisitive — and suddenly everyone around him became smiling, self-confident, and unperturbed, too. It is a trite platitude that so much, almost everything depends on the man who heads a foreign mission, and this was certainly true of the legation in Budapest. The question which remains unanswered was why had Washington been so late in sending Wailes to Budapest, why had the legation been left for months without a minister? Christian Ravndal, Wailes's predecessor, a good friend of ours, had left before my release from prison. The summer and autumn of 1956 had brought tremendous changes which shook the Kremlin, but the legation in Budapest was left without a head, a blunder which should not have been made.

During the week we spent at the legation I grew to like and respect this remarkable couple. Wailes was sent to present his credentials to Nagy, but it was too late. Then he refused to do so when the Kádár regime took over (he was obviously under instructions from Washington). Finally, in February 1957, Wailes was asked either to get accredited or leave — and he left. For eleven years after that the U.S. legation in Budapest was headed by a chargé d'affaires. How often I was asked: why did the United States punish Hungary and not the aggressor, the Soviet Union?

My fondest personal memory of Tom and Cornelia Wailes dates back to a day late in December 1956 when Ilona and I got word that the Communists might arrest us again. The Waileses knew about the threat and approached us with the suggestion that we sign a letter authorizing them to adopt our daughters. They would use the letter if we were indeed arrested. They had no children and it was generally known that they were wealthy people. While Ilona and I were pondering what to do, the Waileses found formidable competitors in Tom and Sarah Rogers, who insisted that it was their duty to look after our girls for several reasons, one of them being that our friendship dated back many years. I still have to smile recalling the half-serious, half-joking argument between the two couples, quarreling about who should adopt our daughters, forgetting about our presence as if we had already been dragged away by the AVH.

The Waileses argued that they had no children and the Rogerses already had four. Four or six made no difference, the Rogerses maintained, and the Waileses, with due respect for their high rank, did not know what it meant to bring up girls. The argument ended with a tie that day, but two days later Sarah Rogers brought up the issue again and finally Ilona and I gave the Rogerses a letter, which they were to use if we were arrested and in which we consented to their adoption of the girls. On January 16, 1957, when Tom Rogers stopped his car with the four Martons on the Austrian side of the border, he solemnly returned the letter to us.

After Budapest, before he retired to the full life of a financially independent, healthy, and vigorous man, Wailes was ambassador to Iran and later to Czechoslovakia. It is strange indeed that both men whose memory became for me inseparable from Hungary 1956, Jack McCormack and Tom Wailes, later died of a stroke, the most benevolent death a man can pray for. Both proved to be true friends in trying times, and their memory remains dear to me.

It was a motley group in the legation, about fifty "refugees," American newsmen and broadcasters, West German technicians of NBC and CBS television crews, and Ilona the only woman, Juli and Kati the only children. A few steps above the ground floor was a large room where the legation used to show movies; this became our "home," and we tried to make it comfortable. Being what we were, we immediately organized something which resembled a newsroom. Typewriters were placed on a long table, radios blared from some unidentified, faraway, and weak station broadcasting the new Kádár government's desperate pleas to the population to stop fighting the Russians —

and we were busily writing, only we did not know why, or for whom. The legation's teletype machine was cut off, too.

There was no lack of stories. One of the most memorable events of the morning of November 4 was the moral and physical courage of István Bibó, a member of Nagy's cabinet. This professor at Szeged University was a respected member of the National Peasant party, though less well known than many of the writers and other intellectuals who formed the NPP after the war. Bibó had retired from political life when it became apparent that his party was gradually being transformed into a front organization of Rákosi's Communists. He reappeared again during the revolution. Early in the morning of November 4, when the Russians were approaching Parliament from all directions, everybody left in a hurry but Bibó. Nagy and several others, all Communists, found asylum in the Yugoslav embassy; Tildy and other non-Communists went home or somewhere else. But Bibó refused to leave. He locked himself in his office and called the Duna Hotel where most newsmen stayed, inviting them for a news conference. When a group of daring reporters reached Parliament Square, they were turned back by the Russians, who by then had occupied the building.

But Bibó did not give up. When we arrived at the American legation I remembered the news conference which never took place. We called Parliament and got Bibó on the telephone. He was calm. Yes, he said, the Russians were banging on his door but he dismissed them, telling them that he had work to do. He said we should not waste time but take a statement he had drafted. I took down his words:

"Hungary has no intention of pursuing an anti-Soviet policy; in fact she wants to live fully in that community of Eastern European free nations which wish to organize their lives in a society where liberty, justice, and freedom from exploitation exist. I also repudiate before the whole world the slanderous statements that the glorious Hungarian revolution was stained by fascist or anti-Semitic excesses. The Hungarian people turned only against the conquering foreign army and against native hangman units. The popular justice which we experienced for a few days on the streets as well as the unarmed appearance of the old conservative forces could have been stopped by the new government in a very short time, and the assertion that for this purpose a huge foreign army had to be called or rather recalled into the country, is cynical and irresponsible. On the contrary, the presence of a foreign army in the country was the main source of unrest and disturbance. I call on the Hungarian people not to recognize the occupation forces or the puppet government which may be set up by them, and I call upon you to use against them every means of passive resistance."

The Russians, one has to admit, respect courage and integrity. Bibó was left alone. Some time during the day he went home and began to work on a remarkable document, a memorandum which, as he said, presented a realistic solution of the Hungarian problem. The Kádár regime, when it began the merciless oppression of any potential opposition, arrested Bibó early in 1957. He was sentenced to life imprisonment, but years later, when Kádár thought that the time had come to relent, Bibó was released with many others.

Meanwhile our radios in the makeshift newsroom were repeating Kádár's announcement explaining that he and several other former members of Nagy's cabinet had decided on November 1 to desert Nagy because of his reluctance "to fight the counterrevolutionary danger" and defeat "fascism and reaction." Kádár also said he had requested the Soviet Union to suppress "reactionary forces" in Hungary. It was obvious that Kádár's words were broadcast somewhere outside Budapest, maybe outside the country, from a weak, second-rate radio station. None of us knew on that day what happened on November 1, the day Kádár said he divorced himself from Nagy. There were several versions and many explanations. I will dis-

cuss them later when I try to assess Kádár's enigmatic role before, during, and after the revolution.

Shortly after our arrival at the legation we were requested to
go down to the cellar which served as an air-raid shelter in the
old building. The legation had heard that the Russians were
threatening to bomb the city from the air if resistance continued. When we got down, I looked around the dimly lit
cellar. A man in black was sitting alone in a corner, his head
deep on his chest, as if absorbed in prayer. He was József Cardinal Mindszenty, Hungary's prince primate, archbishop of
Esztergom.

II

The Cardinal—
Seven Days in Exile

Diplomats are discreet people and the newsmen were not told that the cardinal had been admitted to the legation some time before. I knew that the United States traditionally frowned at the use of its missions as a refuge, unless the man who asked for asylum was persecuted for his political beliefs and was in mortal danger. Mindszenty was undoubtedly such a man, yet I was astounded to see his motionless figure sitting on a simple wooden chair in the corner of the cavernous cellar.

For a moment I was hesitant: should I join him, or was it appropriate to ask permission as, after all, we both were guests? Then, however, I went over to the cardinal and sat down next to him. He recognized me with a nod and we talked. For how long, I do not remember.

I strongly believe that a book should be written about Mindszenty by a historian whose task would be to find for the cardinal a high place in the postwar history of Catholicism in central Europe. I will write my personal impressions of this man, keeping in mind that he is alive and still the guest of the U.S. embassy in Budapest, the building in which he has spent thus far twice as much time as in prison.

The circumstances under which the cardinal was granted asylum are still shrouded in some mystery. He spent the night at his Buda residence and was awakened when the shelling of the city started; after a brief telephone conversation with some-one in the government, he joined Imre Nagy in the Parliament building, accompanied by his secretary, Monsignor Egon Turchányi.

The two priests found chaos in Parliament. The premier had delivered his radio message and was ready to leave. The Soviets closed in and Mindszenty was advised to leave, too. The American legation was only a block or two away. It was eight o'clock in the morning when the cardinal and his secretary knocked on the door of the legation.

There are strange coincidences associated with this event. At 7:50 in the morning, some ten minutes before Mindszenty's arrival, a coded State Department message reached the legation: should the cardinal ask for asylum, he might be admitted. Minister Wailes had hardly time to read the decoded message when the marine guards reported that Mindszenty had arrived.

It was shortly after midnight, Washington time, when the message reached Wailes. It had been drafted in the late evening hours when at the State Department a handful of Americans anxiously studied intelligence reports predicting imminent trouble in the Hungarian capital. The group included Jacob D. Beam, then deputy assistant secretary dealing with European affairs, now U.S. ambassador to Moscow, and two of his immediate aides: Robert M. McKisson and Henry P. Leverich, both veteran experts of central European affairs.

This group drafted the message in response to an inquiry from the legation in Budapest which mentioned as a theoretical possibility that Mindszenty might need assistance. The draft was sent up to the fifth floor of the old, Twenty-first Street wing of the Department where the offices of the top echelon then were. Robert D. Murphy, then deputy under secretary of state, the highest ranking official keeping vigil that night, made the final decision. There is some evidence that before doing so Murphy conferred by telephone with Herbert Hoover, Jr., who was acting secretary of state (John Foster Dulles was already in the hospital, having been operated on for cancer only a few hours earlier), but nothing indicated that the matter was submitted to President Eisenhower that night. It is unquestionable, however, that the White House was duly informed the next morning — probably *post factum,* when Mindszenty was already safe inside the legation.

As we began to talk, the cardinal was eager to hear what had happened since his arrival, especially what the august body of the United Nations had decided to do. "A man who is drowning needs no message," he told me bitterly. "What we need now is that the secretary general of the United Nations come to Budapest today and not tomorrow. There has been too much voting and oratory. What we need is action now."

Finally, when I thought the time had come to return to the others, I could not resist asking him the question which was on my mind and which must have been on his, too. Why did he come here? Why did he choose to be a refugee?

Mindszenty pondered before he answered. "Somebody must remain alive to tell the world what is happening," he said. Writing down his words they seem pompous and conceited, but then, on that day, they did not sound like that. His head hanging low, he answered my question in low tones, struggling to express himself, like an elderly priest searching for some justification for hiding, instead of accepting martyrdom. I was moved.

But, in fact, there were few times that the cardinal had moved me. When I had visited him in Esztergom with other Western newsmen, Mindszenty, the high-ranking priest who had become a celebrity for his lonely Don Quixote fight against Communism, was a disappointment to all of us. In two interviews, instead of speaking about the broad issues of the Communist menace, of the valiant resistance of Magyars in

general and of his church in particular against Communist
strangulation, he spoke about trifling incidents, complained
about trivial grievances, such as how in a small village a priest
did not receive his pay, or how nuns in another place were
forbidden to teach. It was, to put it frankly, outright boring,
not only what he said but how he said it, in the unctuous slow
delivery of a nineteenth-century village priest, not a cardinal of
Rome.

And that was what Mindszenty really was, a provincial
priest, stubborn, brave, but hopelessly parochial. On my second visit to Esztergom I was accompanied by an American reporter who worked for one of this country's weekly news
magazines. He was a playboy type of journalist and on our way
to Esztergom he spoke with equal enthusiasm about finally
meeting this already-legendary prelate, and about the good
time he had had in a Budapest nightclub the night before. But
after listening for about an hour to Mindszenty's uninteresting
story, the events of the night before proved to be stronger than
the nonstory of the cardinal, and my American colleague dozed
off unashamedly in his armchair.

More important was my disappointment when I covered the
cardinal's trial. He was accused of treason, as were I and thousands of others, low and high, celebrities and nameless little
people, in every Communist country. It would be pointless to
recall now the exact charges — they must have been, and will
always be, ridiculous to everyone everywhere. Of course he
did not commit treason, not even according to Communist
standards. Yet he had to be eliminated because Mindszenty
took the historic political role of the head of the Hungarian
Roman Catholic Church seriously. He was the First Banneret
of the Realm, one of his traditional official titles which made
him number three in the hierarchy of the kingdom, and for
Mindszenty this was not a colorful but empty medieval title, a
remnant of the past.

Mindszenty was singularly unfit to lead a clandestine conspiracy aimed at overthrowing the Communist regime. He was lacking in diplomatic skill and his origin and upbringing seriously limited his ability to be a political churchman, such as Stefan Cardinal Wyszynski still is in Poland.

László Rajk, the veteran Communist, could be persuaded that cooperation and confession at his trial would help the higher interests of his party. But Mindszenty was the priest of a church that had hundreds of martyrs during the almost two thousand years of its history. He was not bound by allegiance to the party, but to Rome. I was deeply disappointed that the cardinal did not choose martyrdom when he was tried for three days in February 1949.

From this point of view the speculation that he was tortured and even drugged is irrelevant. He probably was. Mindszenty himself told me on the day of his release that he was "tortured in body and soul." Having been a prisoner of the Communists myself, I have no doubt that this was true. Yet neither torture nor drugs can explain his behavior in court.

"I voluntarily admit that I have committed the acts I am charged with according to the penal code of the state," Mindszenty wrote in a letter from prison to the minister of justice. The letter was read by Vilmos Olti, the presiding judge, at the outset of the trial and when the cardinal acknowledged that he had written it, the court accepted it as a plea of guilty.

I know from personal experience that the Communist police — and, I have a hunch, the police of every country, whether Communist or not — can break a man, however strong he is, physically and morally. Only a broken man will "confess," produce evidence against himself and against others. "Confessions" repeated during the trial itself can be explained, too. The defendant might have been warned that should he withdraw his pretrial confessions or speak about torture, he would be treated even more harshly afterwards, or that his family would suffer. But one of the advantages of being a Catholic priest is to have no close family — Mindszenty, in fact, had only his aged mother — and an open trial provides the opportunity to stand up and tear apart the ridiculous accusations, unmask the whole system, and denounce the defendant's tormentors. This was what I expected from Mindszenty, and he did no such thing.

There is one fact about which I have no doubt: the cardinal was not drugged when he appeared in court. I had known him before and for three long days I observed him on the defendants' bench. The less than six weeks between his arrest and trial had left no trace on Mindszenty. He was calm, attentive, listening carefully to every unimportant testimony of his codefendants. Why did he not use the unique opportunity of the "right to the last word" to tell the court and in fact the whole world — there were a handful of Western reporters present — that the trial was a cheap comedy, come what may afterwards? Archbishop Stepinac of Yugoslavia was tried two years earlier and he remained silent during his trial, ignoring the whole proceeding, which is one effective way of protest. He spent many years in prison. Bulgaria's Traicho Kostov, a Communist, refused to play ball during the anti-Titoist purge trials, and by repudiating in court his pretrial confessions he made his judges look ridiculous. He was sentenced to death and executed.

Why not Mindszenty? The answer, I assume, is that the cardinal was no hero, and nobody should condemn him for that. To become a prince of the Roman church does not necessarily mean that the man is fit to become a martyr. Becket of Canterbury was murdered but not forced to make a confession, so he became a saint. The Communists have no use for a corpse without a confession, so they got their confession from Mindszenty. But then the Communists gambled and tried the cardinal in public trial. When the moment of truth arrived, Mindszenty let it go. He will not be a saint.

Mindszenty was sentenced to life imprisonment and he was freed on October 30, 1956, after almost eight years in jail. During the four days of his freedom Mindszenty made one speech carried by Budapest radio on November 3, only about twelve hours before he knocked on the door of the U.S. legation in Liberty Square. The speech was neither interesting nor inciting, as the Communists later claimed it was. Certainly the militant conservatives must have been disappointed, because the speech was moderate. It asked for "a society without classes . . . private ownership restricted by the interest of society," and spoke out against "personal revenge." Hungary, Mindszenty said, was neutral and "we do not give a cause to the Russian empire for bloodshed. But," he asked, "has the idea not occurred to the leaders of the Russian empire that we will esteem the Russian people much more if they do not subjugate us?"

It is characteristic of every totalitarian system, whether its color is brown, red, or black, to lie when lying is in its interest. The leaders, whether Nazis or Communists, know very well that there is no press and no individual who will stand up and call them liars. Joseph Goebbels, Hitler's propaganda chief, said that if one repeated a lie often enough, it would be accepted as a fact. That was exactly what the Communists did with Mindszenty's November 3 radio address.

The Latin saying *verba volant, scripta manent* (words fly away, writing remains) is especially true in our time, dominated as it is by radio and television. Had Mindszenty's speech remained in printed form, the Communist smear campaign would have been less effective. But it did not, because the day after the cardinal spoke the Russians attacked and no papers were printed. Only a few remembered his words, and when the Communists kept repeating for years that Mindszenty, this fugitive of justice, demanded the restoration of the Catholic church's big estates, that he in fact urged the restoration of the prewar, semifeudal political system, more and more people believed the lie. Many years later a Communist newspaperman from Eastern Europe (not a Hungarian) discussed with me in Washington the cardinal's case and remarked that Mindszenty was "hopeless," a man who still thinks in nineteenth-century terms. When I asked him whether he had heard the speech or read the text of it anywhere, he admitted that he had not. The next day I gave him the verbatim English translation of the speech and asked him to read it. He returned it with a sour face. "It is boring stuff, but I admit it doesn't contain anything I thought it did," he said.

November 4, 1956, was a Sunday and when we were finally permitted to leave the cellar, the cardinal celebrated mass in Wailes's office, which became his home and still is. I doubt that any American embassy has the elaborate equipment necessary for a Catholic mass; the Budapest legation certainly had not. Yet it was moving in its simplicity, and the television cameras, "imprisoned" in the legation on this historic day, were busy for an hour.

That was my last encounter with the cardinal. He is kept incommunicado, much to the annoyance of every American newsman visiting Budapest, but perfectly understandable under the circumstances. Yet he saw Ilona and our daughters several times during the week we spent at the legation. He knew that my wife was the only Hungarian woman and the girls the only Hungarian children in the legation, and one evening he sent for them. He was on these nights a kind, elderly parish priest, and when he let them go he put his hands on their heads and said, "Through you I bless every Hungarian woman and child."

Although I did not see Mindszenty again, on my last day in Budapest he once more played a role in my life. It was January 15, 1957, and we were ready to leave the country the next day, when I received a telephone call from Colonel Jámbor, the secret police officer who had set me free some five months earlier.

"We know that you are leaving tomorrow. Would you do a last favor to your country?" the AVH man asked. I pricked up my ears. "Take Mindszenty out with you and we will roll out all the red carpets we have to the border."

I told him that I was perplexed and the first question in my mind must be: Is this a trap?

"Look," he said, "I do understand your suspicion, but you should understand me. Mindszenty at the American legation is a nuisance, for us and for the Americans. If he gets out he will be on the front pages of your newspapers for how long? For three days, perhaps. And then? Then he will disappear behind the thick walls of a monastery somewhere in Rome and the world would forget him soon."

I told Jámbor that the only thing I could do was to go to the legation and tell the minister of his suggestion. Half an hour later I was closeted with Wailes and Tom Rogers. We discussed what the AVH man had said and the decision was that Mindszenty should not be told about the offer. Nobody could guarantee that it was not a trap, though no one of us thought it was, and we all knew that there was probably nothing that could induce him to leave his country.

And there has not been anything since, in the many years that have elapsed, that could move this proud and stubborn seventy-seven-year-old priest. The Vatican tried and failed. The pope, *primus inter pares* among the bishops, cannot give orders to a prince of the church, only advice. Mindszenty thanked him for the advice, transmitted by the Holy See's special emissary, Cardinal König of Vienna, but said he would leave only if he were ordered to do so.

And so the aging cardinal has been the guest of the American legation since November 4, 1956. He gets his meals from the cafeteria, takes his daily walk in the tiny cement courtyard, reads, listens to the radio, and prays. By now he speaks fluent English. The Americans take turns in bringing his food to his third-floor room and providing him with company if he so desires. As long as his mother was alive, she occasionally could visit him, and an American doctor comes from outside the country, usually from Belgrade, to check his health at regular intervals. Mindszenty has tuberculosis and now he receives his meals on paper plates which are immediately burned in the embassy's incinerator.

Is he a nuisance, as Colonel Jámbor predicted he would be? He might very well be, for the Communist regime, the United States, and the Vatican. For the Communists he is a nuisance because he is there. AVH men are sitting in their cars day and night watching the embassy, prepared for something they know will never happen: that the cardinal will walk out, or that the embassy will attempt to smuggle him out. But more importantly he is a nuisance because every day dozens of passersby look up to the third floor window and say to themselves with pleasure: here lives the cardinal; he outwitted the Communists, bless his heart.

He is a nuisance for the Vatican because as long as he is in Hungary the pope cannot name anybody to the Esztergom diocese and Hungarian Catholics remain without a supreme spiritual leader.

He is a nuisance for the Americans because he will probably remain there until his death. However modest and unpretentious he is, the old chancery was not built to house a cardinal, and there is always the nightmarish fear that some day he may need hospital care or an operation.

His presence certainly slowed down the "normalization" of relations between Washington and Budapest. When President Kennedy was assassinated, Kádár faced the dilemma of whether to go to the legation and sign the book of condolences, as Communist leaders in other capitals did. He finally decided he could not, because of Mindszenty's presence in the building.

Yet, in a way, for the Communist regime Mindszenty's "imprisonment" in the embassy is the second-best solution. Kádár and his government would be embarrassed if the cardinal emerged one day. What could they do with the old man? Put him back in prison to serve a life sentence imposed by the Rákosi era which Hungary's present masters continue to denounce? So for them it is much better if the cardinal stays where he is.

And, I feel, he will. Whatever his merits and failures, the cardinal is a patriot, in the old-fashioned, nineteenth-century sense of the word. He is first a Hungarian and then a prelate of the church. And as a patriot he believes in the words of his nation's anthem: ". . . here you must live and die."

The international flock of newsmen spent the week of war in the American legation. What started as a peaceful demonstration on October 23, that night became an armed revolt, and soon a war against a foreign aggressor.

I think all who enjoyed the hospitality in Liberty Square must be grateful to our hosts. Ilona, I, and the two girls certainly remember that week as an extraordinary experience, full of frustration for a reporter cut off from any means of communication, but otherwise relaxed and feeling safe as the guest of an invisible host: the United States.

We slept together on the floor of the big room where, in quieter times, the legation used to show movies, and there were enough blankets to make us comfortable. Ilona was the only woman in our crowd, but there were some others in the building: a few diplomatic wives who refused to be evacuated and who prepared wonderful meals, served in the legation's tiny cafeteria. We were lucky, the stocks were apparently adequate despite the great number of additional customers, and there was plenty of everything.

The legation was usually cut off from Washington and the West, but for short periods of time there were mysterious ways of communicating with the State Department and Wailes agreed that on such occasions we could send out a pooled story for the major wire services and newspapers in America. Gathering material was no problem. After two days some of us left the building, though many others preferred the safety of the legation, obviously believing that a good war correspondent can write a perfectly authentic story in the shelter, based on what his more daring colleagues tell him. I myself had my doubts.

The immediate area of the legation was quiet. Parliament and the Communist party headquarters were only a few blocks away and the Russians had firmly held this innermost district right from the beginning. On November 5, our second day at the legation, Wailes came to me and asked for advice. The cardinal, he said, got a telephone call informing him that the Russians had set fire to Parliament and that the huge Gothic building was burning. Mindszenty, Wailes said, wanted to make a declaration to the world through the legation, condemning this vandalism. Wailes gave me the statement to read and asked whether I believed the information was correct. I told him I did not. Though one could not see Parliament from the legation windows, had there been a fire we certainly could have seen smoke from that direction, and there was none. I offered to go out and check; I knew every corner and I could be back in fifteen minutes. Wailes pondered, but then said no, it was not worth the risk. The prelate's statement remained unused, and Parliament did not burn.

The telephone call to Mindszenty was only one of many. Every reporter who established contacts before November 4 received phone calls, and we also called our sources, including the strongest resistance centers, such as the Kilian barracks. I was always surprised that the legation's telephones were not cut off; only long distance calls could not be placed.

The first night, after a pleasant meal in the cafeteria when everybody tried to make himself as comfortable as possible, a junior attaché tiptoed to our corner and asked me to come with him to the ground floor. There, at a table, sat the man whom I considered the most honest political leader of postwar Hungary, Béla Kovács, secretary general of the Smallholder party until the Russians kidnapped him in 1947. We knew each other, not too well, though, and I had not seen him since he was taken to Russia nine years earlier. We sat together for several hours and talked about the mistakes of the past, the drama of the present, and the uncertain future.

After World War II Béla Kovács had been the biggest obstacle in Rákosi's path toward the total annihilation of non-Communist political parties. This man of complete integrity refused to bargain or to make a deal with Rákosi. He had to be crushed. In 1947 the AVH "discovered" what it called a widespread conspiracy and the Communist papers printed fat headlines saying that those who were arrested confessed and implicated Kovács. Rákosi thought he had succeeded, but to everybody's amazement Parliament was firm once more and for the last time, and refused to suspend Kovács's parliamentary immunity. The next day Soviet army units blockaded the street where Kovács lived and when he emerged from his house, he was arrested. Three months later the Russians sent his "confession" to the Hungarian government, in which he admitted to having spied on the Soviet army.

Kovács was released without fanfare seven years after his arrest. He returned to Hungary and lived quietly in the southern part of the country where he was born. He was named to Imre Nagy's cabinet on October 27, 1956, without his consent, and he came to Budapest reluctantly two days later. Kovács had never believed that the Russians would allow the revolution to be victorious, the Communist party to share power with others, or the country to secede from the Warsaw Pact. But he could not remain on the sidelines and be labeled a coward, though he did not trust his former friend Tildy, who in the past had been too ready to come to terms with Rákosi.

Kovács asked the Americans to admit him for the night but not longer. He had no place to live in Budapest and did not want to jeopardize any of his friends by asking them to take him in. The next day he would go back to his village: "If they want to get me, they will know where to look for me." He was the first to tell me that Nagy and many Communists who remained loyal to him went to the Yugoslav embassy after Ambassador Soldatic called Nagy at dawn to say that Khrushchev had informed Tito about his decision to use force to quell the revolt.

This was the last time I saw Kovács. The next morning when we awoke he was gone. How he managed to get out of the city and get back to his village, some two hundred fifty miles from Budapest, I did not know. Later, in December 1956, Kádár tried hard to persuade him to return and to join him. Kovács declined. He was not molested and died quietly several years later.

The next day, on November 6, some of us decided to explore the city. Our goal was the Duna Hotel, about a mile south of the legation. As good soldiers we proceeded two at a time, with about twenty yards between each group. Because I knew every corner I led the convoy, preferring the narrow side streets to the open spaces, yet it was impossible to avoid crossing an occasional street with a tank mounted in its mouth. We skipped through single file, John McCormack, Seymour Freidin, Russ Jones, and a few others. A dead man's body was lying on the sidewalk in front of the hotel and the stench of death hung over the city.

The Duna was empty, but some of its brave employees remained and our small group received a hero's welcome. From the windows facing the Danube we watched the duel of guns, the Soviets on the Gellért Hill, in the citadel, once a fortress built by the Hapsburgs to control the city after the 1848 War of Independence, and the freedom fighters on the Vár Hill, firing from behind the ancient walls surrounding the former royal castle. It was too convenient to be true to watch this spectacle from a hotel room across the river. We withdrew quickly when a Russian tank stopped on the embankment just under our window and turned its gun in our direction. The Soviets, we knew from experience, thoroughly dislike witnesses.

From then on, while we lived at the legation, some of us left our haven every day. We had adequate information about the various fronts, and on several occasions we succeeded in sneaking quite close. It was a curious war: tanks on the one side, small groups of freedom fighters, students and young workers, soldiers and policemen, fighting with small arms or occasionally a machine gun or an antitank gun, on the other. Accordingly, there was little man-to-man fighting and almost no sign of Russian infantry. A tank can do nothing but destroy, and that was what the Soviet tanks did. I witnessed one of these "battles" in a narrow street close to the Kilian barracks. It started with the freedom fighters using their Molotov cocktail tactics against a tank and then opening fire on the Russian crew when it abandoned the disabled vehicle. A few minutes later two other tanks arrived and pounded the entire block, severely damaging every five- and six-story apartment house on the two sides of the street.

Back in the legation we were in telephone contact with other parts of the city. There were many calls informing us how an important resistance center was taken, and how the revolutionaries reoccupied another.

By Saturday, November 10, it was clear that the war, as far as Budapest was concerned, had come slowly to an end. Most of our Western colleagues decided to form a convoy and leave for Vienna; there seemed to be little point in waiting any longer for the restoration of communications. Only Russ Jones of UP and Ronald Farquhar of Reuters stayed, and they went back to the Duna Hotel. Ilona, the children, and I said good-bye to the Waileses and the little Volkswagen took us home.

It was a depressing moment when we shook hands with our colleagues, their cars lined up neatly in front of the foreign ministry. Few words were said — what could they have said to a man who stayed behind with no protective passport? None of us could say au revoir; at that moment it appeared most unlikely that we would see each other again. The Iron Curtain once again descended and cut me off from the free world.

12

Passive Resistance

We were sitting in the dimly lit lobby of the Duna Hotel, the old flea bag on the Danube which had served as headquarters for Western reporters. The lobby was now used as a dining room because some of the huge windows of the real dining room, facing the river, had been blown out on November 4, when the Russians attacked the city.

"We" were a handful of Western reporters, six at most. The others, perhaps a hundred (nobody cared to count them), had left when the fighting stopped in Budapest. Some had been frustrated because there was no way to get the copy out; others were scared of the shooting. The remaining reporters, Russ Jones, Ronny Farquhar, and a few others who arrived after the fighting subsided, lived in the hotel, though my wife and I had returned with our daughters to our apartment since leaving the legation. The only other residents of the hotel were an elderly couple from Holland who had been stranded when the revolt broke out because they had no car.

There are exciting plays and novels about hotels and the Duna would deserve a saga. The few remarkable employees who did not run away kept it going for a few foreigners.

There were well-prepared meals for everyone, good wines and even Scotch, strong coffee, and bread baked on the premises. When the fighting was over, more and more people ventured in for lunch, but in the evenings the place remained eerie.

So it was on that mid-November night when the young Russian came in. We had eaten our dinner and were just sitting around, exhausted physically and mentally, trading rumors about what had happened during the day and speculating on what would happen next.

The Russian was in his early twenties, handsome and drunk. Of all the empty tables he picked the one next to ours, ordered a bottle of wine, and stared at us with glassy eyes. Togetherness is also practiced in the Soviet Union so we were not surprised when he asked permission to join us.

The Russian wore a lieutenant's uniform and spoke passable German. He was from Leningrad — the only Russian city with *kultura*, he explained proudly — and the commander of four tanks guarding Oktogon, a square in the heart of Budapest. He politely murmured something about the chill of November nights, and accepted the chair offered to him. There was silence around the table as we waited for him to start the conversation.

Having introduced himself, the lieutenant asked who we were. He did not seem surprised when my colleagues said they were reporters from the United States and from Britain. I told him briefly that my wife and I were Hungarians, but working for American wire services.

I do not know whether he fully understood me but he looked at us with curious eyes. "Magyars. They aren't afraid of us. . . . What kind of people are they anyway?" he mumbled. Then, turning to my wife, he asked:

"Tell me, where do your people get the guts? I am sitting on my tank the whole day long and people, women and children, walk under the barrel of my big guns without fear, without even turning their heads, just ignoring me. This is unbearable, this is not human. People either should hate me and come and argue with me, or they should welcome me for having saved their country from counterrevolutionary fascists, but they do neither. They just ignore me . . ."

My wife did not answer, nor did I. I always feel uneasy in the company of someone who has had one glass too many, and there was no point in explaining to this young man from Leningrad that he was experiencing the manifestation of the third phase of the revolt: passive resistance.

There can be no argument about two dates in the revolt: October 23, when it started, and November 4, when it grew into a war against a foreign invading army. The transition from the second to the third phase cannot be linked to a certain date because the war period was completed early in Budapest, but many weeks later in some remote areas of the country.

The passive resistance period lasted much longer than the first two phases and, to me, it was more impressive. It was easy to demonstrate, to march with thousands, to carry flags and become intoxicated by your own voice demanding freedom. It was less easy, but still invigorating, to fight tanks with bottles filled with gasoline. However, to continue resisting and sabotaging the might of a modern army of occupation with the bitter recognition that there was to be no help from the outside world and that this was the end of a dream — this, to me, was heroism of the first magnitude.

Writers, journalists, men released from prison — the great majority of them Communists — were responsible for the preliminary phase: the ferment. They were joined by workers and students during the demonstrations, and workers and students did the fighting. But when the fighting was over, the entire nation participated in the passive resistance.

Since the Communist take-over in the late 1940's Hungarians had heard nothing but the glorification of the "dictatorship of the proletariat" and praise of the workers' class which must rule the country. The glorification was nauseating at first, boring later, and ridiculous all the time. There was not one worker in the top ranks of the Communist party hierarchy. The trium-viri — Rákosi, Gerö, and Révai — were the educated offspring of bourgeois families.

The revolution, and especially its third phase, was to prove that there was much truth in the glorification of the workers' class. I owe a deep bow to the Hungarian industrial workers. After so many years it is still heartwarming to remember the many hours I spent with them almost daily during this period.

It is brave to hold a gun in your hand, however ineffective it is in fighting tanks. Hungarian history is filled with wars against invaders, usually superior in numbers and equipment, and it was in this tradition that Magyars fought the Russians in 1956 with whatever they had. But the admiration should go to the "proletarian" in his sixties, sitting at his lathe in one of the unheated workshops in the giant Csepel plant, not caring about the horrors of the coming winter, about no pay and little food. He ignored the Soviet tanks milling in the plant's courtyard as well as the entreaties of the government agents. He simply re-fused to work "for them."

How dignified this old man was and how well he knew what was going on. I talked to him and acted also as an interpreter for Farquhar, the Reuters correspondent. The old man turned to me. "Is he English?" he asked. When I nodded, he said: "I want you to translate every word I'm saying. Would he please convey our thanks to Mr. Eden for having stabbed our revolu-tion in the back."

So the old man knew about Suez. Like so many others, he blamed this "adventure" for having diverted Western attention, thus encouraging the Russians to use force in crushing the re-volt.

Ronny, his freckled face turning red, just nodded while jot-ting down the old man's words. Was he right? I still do not know.

For me these visits to factories had a special meaning. Never since the Communist take-over had a Western correspondent been permitted to visit an industrial plant of any significance, and now I could walk in whenever I pleased. Only twice before had foreign correspondents been invited to a conducted tour: once to see a chocolate factory and another time to Herend, a one-hundred-year-old factory famous for its porcelain. And even then a ridiculous "vigilance" was in force. Two American reporters, one a Communist, thought there was nothing wrong in bringing along their wives to the chocolate factory. How wrong they were. The women were stopped at the gate and no argument helped. Their names were not on the list prepared by the press section of the foreign ministry and they were not admitted.

My almost daily visits to Csepel and other industrial plants were not restricted to talking to the old man at his lathe and the hundreds of other workers. Often I was invited to sit in at the meetings of the local workers' councils where, I was told, "you can watch how democracy is made at the grass roots."

I did watch and my surprise and admiration grew. In hindsight it was perhaps pathetic how grown-up men who had spent a lifetime working with their hands, seemed to ignore the harsh facts of life, that there was no hope, that the Russians were again the masters, that Imre Nagy had exiled himself in the Yugoslav embassy, that the United Nations and the Western democracies could do nothing but utter weak protests. But there was little oratory and no false hopes. The workers were sober, neither depressed nor daydreaming. But they believed that refusal to work was the only weapon which could force the Soviet-installed regime to make concessions. They discussed that pressure on the government, and how they themselves could survive the weeks, perhaps months, of no pay. There was also serious talk about protecting, cleaning, and oiling the precious machines for the day work would be resumed.

"For ten years we were told that all this belongs to us. It was a lie: it belonged to the state and the state was a much harsher exploiter than Baron Weiss ever was," the old man at the lathe said one day. The Csepel industrial empire, Hungary's version of the Krupp works, belonged to the Weiss family and then to the Nazi SS before it was nationalized after the war.

"I really don't care who owns it," the old man said. "But maybe the day will come when it will be worthwhile to put in eight hours of work. And maybe what is happening now will bring that day closer."

There was some help, not much, coming from the farmers. One day I saw a peasant's cart drawn by two horses in the Csepel plant. It was packed with potatoes, vegetables, and a few slabs of bacon. The middle-aged peasant had been sent by a nearby cooperative on Csepel Island in the fertile farmland south of Budapest, and the foodstuff was a present to the workers on strike. It was not much, but the gesture was appreciated, and the peasant himself was moved by his contribution. "We can't do much," he muttered when I asked him. "We have no organization and are scattered around. But we thought we could help this way."

One of my encounters with "democracy at the grass roots" was around the end of November when Russ Jones of United Press and I drove to Dorog, the important coal mining center, thirty-five miles west of Budapest. The mines of Dorog normally employ more than ten thousand miners and have an output of sixty-five hundred tons daily. We came unannounced, on a bitterly cold day, and drove up to the main administration building.

Everything seemed deserted although two Russian tanks were deployed conspicuously close to the main building. We couldn't see their crew and went upstairs, hoping to find somebody. On the second floor we heard voices behind a closed door. I knocked and a man in his thirties came out. I explained who we were and that we had come from Budapest to compare the situation in the countryside with that in the capital. The man nodded. The mine workers' council was in session inside, he said, and he asked us to wait until the meeting was over.

Couldn't we sit in? I asked, and told him that had happened frequently in Budapest factories. The man was skeptical but said he would ask. There must have been some debate inside, but finally he returned and motioned us to enter. Inside, about fifty men sat around a long conference table. We stood in the door for a minute while the man introduced us, mentioning our names and the wire services we worked for. When he finished, the workers around the table rose, turned toward us, and applauded.

It was not a noisy affair, there was no undue enthusiasm, the faces remained serious. But they applauded, all of them, without exception. This was their dignified way of greeting two men who represented a world they thought sympathetic to their desires.

Russ, a sensitive man, turned to me and there was pain on his face. "How do we deserve this?" he whispered. I had no answer.

Then we were seated at the table and the meeting continued. The issues were not "revolutionary." The strike was on and would continue until the Russians left, but coal was needed for the hospitals, so the council carefully listed the institutions which could get it from the mine's vast stocks. It was a serious debate and the decisions were clear: no coal for anything which might facilitate the Kádár government's rule until the workers' demands were met.

One council member, an engineer, raised a question about maintenance of the mines. Again everybody participated, painfully observing parliamentary rules. Yes, the decision was, the pumps must go on working, the mines should be ready to operate again some day. It was ironic that this meeting which lasted for hours took place in an unheated room when hundreds if not thousands of tons of coal must have been lying around unused.

"There is no coal for anybody, and that includes us," a miner replied most seriously when I inquired jokingly about the freezing temperature in the room.

Workers' councils mushroomed all over the country, replacing at least temporarily the trade unions, one of the most hated institutions of Communism. A trade union in a Communist country is, of course, a misnomer. They are tools of the party, concerned only with how to exploit the worker more effectively. The pattern for the workers' councils came from Yugoslavia. It still is a mystery that so many knew about the experiment in Tito's country because there was no word in the Hungarian publications about the Yugoslav version of plant management; and yet, as far as I know, the first workers' council was established on the second day of the revolution in Miskolc, an industrial center in northern Hungary.

Was this evidence of Yugoslav influence? Or, in a broader sense, did Tito have his hand in the Hungarian revolution? The marshal's attitude before the revolt was unequivocal. When Khrushchev begged Tito to forget how Stalin had treated him in 1948, he demanded Rákosi's ouster. Nagy, on the other hand, was acceptable to the marshal. Tito's behavior after the revolt was more ambiguous. First he gave asylum to Nagy in his Budapest embassy, an unheard-of thing in a Communist country. Then he bitterly assailed the Soviet intervention as he did in 1968 after the invasion of Czechoslovakia. But later Tito professed more understanding of Moscow's position and even hinted that the Russians might have had a reason to suppress "counterrevolution." He was willing to forget the real slap: Nagy's abduction when he left his refuge in the embassy, and his execution, despite the safe conduct given to him.

All this, however, does not tell us if Tito played an active role in fomenting the revolt. It is doubtful that we shall ever learn the full truth.

Nagy was invited to seek refuge in the Yugoslav embassy at one o'clock in the morning, November 4, by Dalibor Soldatic, Tito's ambassador to Budapest, who called the premier at his office in Parliament. Nagy did not go home that night. He was still hoping for a miracle, that General Maléter, then already a prisoner of the Soviet secret police, would return from General Malinin's headquarters, and that the Russian troops ringing the city would not attack. Soldatic's telephone call must have shattered all these hopes. That was when the Yugoslav diplomat bluntly told Nagy that Khrushchev had informed Tito of his decision to use force to suppress the "counterrevolution" in Hungary.

At five o'clock in the morning, when the siege began, Nagy sent his car for his wife, his daughter, his son-in-law and confidant Ferenc Jánosi, and his two grandchildren, with the instruction that they should be delivered immediately to the Yugoslav embassy. Having delivered his last dramatic radio appeal to the world, he joined his family, together with Julia Rajk, widow of the executed Communist leader; Zoltán Szántó; Zoltán Vas; György Lukács, the philosopher; Géza Losonczy; Ferenc Donát; Gábor Táncos, president of the Petöfi Circle; and journalists Sándor Haraszti, Miklós Vásárhelyi, and György Fazekas.

Nagy spent nineteen days in his refuge. I tried to see him but Soldatic, correctly, did not permit reporters to visit his ward. Yet my Yugoslav colleagues kept me informed and so I knew how Nagy, whose weakness and indecisiveness so often frustrated his revolutionary friends, grew immensely in stature during those days of isolation, how he remained true to himself and to his dream to reconcile Communism with humanism.

The Yugoslav embassy on Heroes Square was surrounded by Soviet tanks and the MVD kept an around-the-clock watch outside the gates. I visited the embassy twice during those nineteen days but could not see any of the Hungarians. The second time, when I left, two uniformed MVD men grabbed me outside the gate and a third one, obviously an officer but without insignia, rattled something in Russian, a language I do not speak. When I produced my press pass, issued by the Hungarian foreign ministry, which described me both in Hungarian and in Russian as an accredited American correspondent, they let me go without much enthusiasm.

Desperately seeking popular support, Kádár tried to persuade Nagy to join him. On November 15, the Budapest radio quoted him as saying that "Nagy never has been an enemy of our system and I see no reason why he should not resume a position in public life." This happened after the November 12 visit to Budapest of Mikoyan and Suslov and there was some speculation that Khrushchev's envoys had instructed Kádár to attempt a reconciliation with Nagy. But Nagy firmly refused any "deals" with the man who had betrayed him and the revolution.

This he made clear in a handwritten note on a page torn from a notebook sent to me in mid-November. The messenger, whom I cannot identify, was a young girl with no political background who had visited her friend, one of Nagy's companions in the Yugoslav embassy.

The message reached me in the Duna Hotel late one afternoon. "I want the world to know," it said, "that there can be no compromise. The Soviets have to respect the agreement I made with Mikoyan. I trust you will tell this to the world." I did.

I do not believe the Yugoslavs were happy to give refuge to such a large group and Tito, however much he sympathized with the Hungarian revolution and with Nagy, obviously did not want to rock the fragile boat of relations with Moscow unnecessarily. There was hard bargaining between the Yugoslavs, acting as counsel and spokesman of the self-exiled premier, and Kádár. Several proposals were made and rejected, including one that Nagy should seek asylum in Romania, then one of Moscow's most loyal satellites, a suggestion Nagy indignantly ignored. This honest man, too honest perhaps to be a politician, also rejected Kádár's entreaties to emerge from his hideout, to join him, or at least to indulge in some good old-fashioned Communist self-criticism and promise not to work against the new regime. It will be significant for the historian to note that at the same time Kádár made similar overtures in other directions, all aimed at finding a broader basis for his shaky regime. He sent messages to Béla Kovács, negotiated with Zoltán Tildy and with István Bibó. He was rebuffed by all of them. It was obvious that none of them wanted to be linked to the Hungarian Quisling. When Kádár's efforts failed, Tildy and Bibó were arrested; the former was tried together with Nagy, the latter separately. Kovács, however, was spared.

Finally, on or around November 15, the haggling with Kádár over Nagy's future appeared to be settled. It was agreed that Kádár would give the Yugoslavs a written guarantee granting safe conduct to Nagy and his associates to return to their homes unmolested. On November 21, Kádár answered a note from the Yugoslav government as follows:

"In the interest of terminating the matter, the Hungarian government, agreeing to the proposals contained on page 3, section 8 of the letter of November 18, 1956, addressed to me by the Yugoslav government, hereby confirms in writing its verbal declaration that it does not desire to apply sanctions against Imre Nagy and the members of his group for their past activities. We take note that the asylum extended to the group will hereby come to an end and that they themselves will leave the Yugoslav embassy and proceed freely to their homes."

This, Tito and Nagy believed, settled the affair. There is serious reason to assume that Kádár also thought so. The Russians decided otherwise. Forty-eight hours after Kádár issued the *salvus conductus*, the Soviets kidnapped the revolution's prime minister.

I was not there when it happened, but the story of this incredible breach of faith was told to me by a Yugoslav who was himself manhandled by the Russians on this occasion. Late in the afternoon of November 23 an ordinary Budapest bus came to the Yugoslav embassy. It was already dark at six-thirty in

the evening, and the bus was chosen to avoid too much attention. Nagy and the others came out in small groups and took
their seats in the bus. Nobody cared about the Russians who
had been lingering around the embassy for several weeks.

When everybody was seated, a young Yugoslav attaché
whose job was to see that everything went smoothly and that
the Tito-Kádár pact was observed, signaled the driver to pull
out. The minute the driver started the engine an MVD man
jumped up to him, while another boarded the bus from the
rear. The few Yugoslav diplomats who were at the gate — the
majority watched Nagy's departure from the windows, again
so as not to arouse unnecessary attention — tried to intervene
and two young attachés managed to jump on the already moving bus. The trip was short. Instead of taking Nagy home, the
bus stopped a few blocks away from the Yugoslav embassy in
front of the Budapest headquarters of the Russian military
command. There the two Yugoslav attachés were unceremoniously booted out and the bus drove off escorted by several
Russian military vehicles.

Did Kádár know that the Soviets would ignore his safe conduct? Was he an accessory to one of the most shameful political kidnappings of history? I do not think he was. There is, of
course, no proof of Kádár's innocence, but all my sources, including one who was personally very close to Kádár, told me
how desperate Kádár had been when Nagy was abducted, and
when he was executed eighteen months later.

My willingness to believe that Kádár, a simple man always
blindly accepting the orders of his Soviet masters, was just a
tool but not an accessory, is partly based on a strange scene I
witnessed one afternoon. The day was November 25. I was
standing in the dark corridors of Parliament, waiting for a
"source" who had promised some information.

Suddenly a door opened and in the bright light coming from
the room I recognized Kádár on the threshold. He stopped in
the door, like someone who had changed his mind, turned

around, and said in a plaintive, loud voice, almost shouting: "I can't do it. . . . I won't do it!" Then a second man appeared in the door, Ferenc Münnich, who went over to the Russian side with Kádár and who first became minister of the armed forces and of public security and later prime minister in the Kádár regime. "Of course you'll do it," Münnich said in a soothing voice, like a male nurse talking to a stubborn patient in a mental hospital, and the door of the room was closed behind them.

A few hours later that night I thought I knew what Kádár did not want to do and what he obviously had to do: to lie. I remember having broken a pencil in anger when Kádár said in a radio speech that night that Nagy and his associates had asked to be taken to Romania and that "we have already said we have no intention of bringing Nagy to trial. We will keep that promise."

That promise was not kept either. For eighteen months nobody heard where Nagy was. There were strong rumors that first he had been kept in Sinaia in Romania, then in Odessa in the Soviet Union, and finally in the Fö utca prison of the AVH, but always in Russian hands.

The lying continued internationally. The Romanian government sanctimoniously assured the U.N. General Assembly in December 1956 that "the stay of the group of Mr. Nagy in Romania would be marked by all the rules of hospitality and that all necessary steps would be taken to guarantee the personal safety of Mr. Nagy and his friends. Similarly the Romanian government gave the assurance that it would observe the international rules relating to political asylum."

All these "assurances" by Kádár and by the Romanians were empty promises. On June 17, 1958, first Moscow, then Budapest, announced that Nagy and his "accomplices" had been convicted after a secret trial. Neither then nor later was it disclosed where the trial was held, before what court or judge, or who the prosecutor and the defense counsel were. The announcement said that the premier, General Maléter, József Szilágyi (Nagy's secretary), and Miklós Gimes, the journalist, had been sentenced to death, others to long prison terms. "The sentences are final. The death sentences have been executed," the announcement said.

Why did they do it? Albert Camus, the great French writer, probably gave the answer in his *Socialism of the Gallows*. He wrote: "The Hungarian uprising was originally directed against a generalized lie. Hence it was necessary to assassinate the men who were fighting the lie and then try to dishonor them through a reversed lie by calling them Fascists."

Legend has it that when Napoleon kidnapped the prince of Enghien and had him executed, Talleyrand remarked: "It was more than a crime; it was a blunder." The same can be said about the abduction and assassination of Imre Nagy.

Councils were formed everywhere during the first days of the revolt. In nonindustrial enterprises and offices they were called either revolutionary or national councils. They were formed in the ministries and, however ridiculous, even the AVH had its own revolutionary council. The councils gained almost complete control over industrial plants when most of the government-appointed managers were either removed or stayed away from the factories by choice. On November 2, when many thought that the revolution was victorious, the workers agreed to resume work on Monday, November 5. Nothing came of it: the Russians besieged the city on November 4.

During the second, or war phase, the majority of the freedom fighters were young workers. There were of course many students fighting on the streets, some of bourgeois origin, but middle-class families have traditionally held control over their sons and daughters and many of these young people who jubilantly demonstrated during the first phase were forced to stay behind their mothers' aprons when the fighting became serious.

The third phase of passive resistance was the most glorious in the short lives of the councils. The Soviets were helpless against them. With a gun in hand one can force a single man to work, but no army can force tens of thousands of striking workers to return to their workbenches. The councils of Budapest factories — the capital is by far the most important industrial center of Hungary — established a central organ, the Greater Budapest Council, and a young man emerged from nowhere as the leader. His name was Sándor Rácz, and he was in his mid-twenties.

I spent many long nights in the smoke-filled rooms of the Greater Budapest Council in the Akácfa utca building of the Budapest trolley company. There was much coming and going in the shabby rooms because for many weeks workers' delegates had been negotiating with Kádár, usually every afternoon in Parliament.

The Greater Budapest Council was a haphazard organization. Its leaders and members, all delegates of factory councils, were manual workers and not professional trade union men. They had no written statutes and did not care about parliamentary procedures, but they knew their strength and knew that Kádár desperately needed their help to reopen the country's idle industrial plants.

Before the revolution Kádár had been popular among the workers. Traces of this popularity remained even after November 4 and several council members, fiercely loyal to Nagy, grudgingly acknowledged that they still trusted Kádár despite his betrayal of the revolution.

"This son of a bitch is from our ranks, he must think as we do," one of them told me.

Kádár talked openly with the delegates of the Greater Budapest Council in their almost daily meetings. They were workers as he had once been. On one occasion he told them: "Bring back Nagy, bring him out from the Yugoslav embassy, and I will gladly give him back his chair." On another occasion he said that the presence of Soviet troops "offends our national pride" and acknowledged that the revolution, contrary to the official claim of a reactionary conspiracy, had been a "mass movement with noble aims." Nothing illustrates better the chaotic and confused situation in the weeks after November 4 than the fact that these words were duly reported by *Népszabadság,* the new official Communist party organ.

Kádár knew that he could not impress the workers by taking a haughty attitude. In his talks with the council representatives he forgot himself only once to the point of demanding, "Whom do you think you represent?" He immediately backed down when his outburst drew the well-deserved retort: "All right, let's discuss who we represent. Let's begin with you, Comrade Kádár. Whom do you think you represent?"

The workers never hesitated to tell me about these conversations when they returned to their Akácfa utca headquarters. They quickly grew accustomed to my constant presence and filled me in on their visits to Kádár. Only Rácz, their leader, remained aloof. Though he could not fail to notice that I and some of my colleagues were permanent visitors, he did not object, but he rarely spoke to us. Once we discussed the Hungarian language broadcasts of Western radio stations, which had become extremely important sources of information when the short-lived free press of the revolution was suppressed after November 4. Rácz shook his head: "They shouldn't tell us what to do. We don't need their advice. We don't need anybody's advice who is not in Hungary."

Only once was the usual hustling and bustling in the small rooms in Akácfa utca replaced by dead silence, when the workers listened to what Nehru had said in a speech in Delhi. Nehru had been extremely cautious in assessing what had happened in Hungary. For weeks he had refused to join either the West's condemnation of the Russians, or the Communist condemnation of the revolt. Then in November he ordered K. P. S. Menon, India's ambassador to Moscow, to go to Budapest and find out the truth. The diplomat and his aides talked with Kádár's people, with other diplomats — and one night with three Western reporters.

Russell Jones, the UP correspondent who had come to Budapest at the end of October with my wife, knew one of Menon's aides, a young and attractive Indian diplomat. One evening the Indian phoned Jones at the Duna Hotel. The ambassador, he said, would like to see him and the Martons. We drove out in the wintry night to his hotel on Marguerite Island, a wooded island in the Danube in the center of the city. Menon was not feeling well and received us in bed. He had one request: we should tell him our version of what had happened in Hungary and why. Ilona, Russ, and I took turns. We talked for hours.

Menon was a diplomat and an Asian; he did not indicate how much he believed of what he heard, but one of his aides scribbled feverishly while we talked. It would be presumptuous to believe that Menon's report to Nehru was based on what we three told him, yet we felt great when shortly after the diplomat's departure from Budapest Nehru, in a speech to a UNESCO conference in Delhi, finally conceded that there was a "national revolution" in Hungary, that "human dignity and freedom were outraged" by what the Soviets had done, and he charged "cruel suppression of popular desire for a change."

"What happened in Hungary," Nehru explained in another speech on December 13 in the Indian Parliament, "demonstrated that the desire for national freedom is stronger even than an ideology and cannot ultimately be suppressed. What happened in Hungary was not essentially a conflict between Communism and anti-Communism. It represented nationalism striving for freedom from foreign control."

I received the text of the Indian leader's speech at the American legation. The same night my wife asked the workers at Akácfa utca whether they were interested in hearing what Nehru had said.

I still can see the silent crowd sitting on the floor, on

benches, and on a few chairs in the dimly lit, smoke-filled rooms. Connecting doors were opened so that everybody could hear. They listened, smoking their cheap cigarettes, with the serious, tired faces of men who had spent their lives laboring with their hands. They asked my wife to sit on a table so that everybody could see her. And then there was dead silence while she translated Nehru's speech from English into Hungarian, sentence for sentence.

To understand why so much importance was attached to what Nehru said, to his long-awaited, perhaps grudging acknowledgment that there was a revolution in Hungary in the true sense of the word, one must remember the immense prestige of the Indian statesman who was the recognized leader of the nonaligned world.

My wife had another encounter with Menon under much more dramatic circumstances, on December 4, one month after the Soviet onslaught on Budapest. It was a cold but snowless day when women from all parts of the city had started to march. How the word spread nobody knew, but hundreds came, then thousands, and when this sea of women reached the Tomb of the Unknown Soldier on Heroes Square, there were about twenty thousand of them. Heroes Square is at the end of Andrássy ut, the long main thoroughfare of Budapest, named after Stalin by the Communist regime of Rákosi (though everybody disregarded the new name). Women from all walks of life marched, the famous actress with the streetcar conductor, and all of them were carrying flowers. The men who wanted to join them were chased away. "This is our demonstration," the women said. "Go away! You tried and failed. It is our turn." They did not tolerate me either, although I tried to explain that I was a reporter doing my job. The lovely, straight avenue was teeming with women, and women only.

The Russians, of course, were alerted. It was easy to frighten women, they thought, so they dispatched their tanks.

The endless column of women marched undisturbed almost all the way. There was no singing and no flag-waving this time, and the silent thousands offered a menacing picture. About two blocks south of Heroes Square the Russians tried to stop the black column. Two of their tanks drove down from the square, slowly moving toward the women. A Soviet colonel stood on one of the tanks and when his clumsy vehicle reached the column he spoke to the women, shouting at the top of his voice, obviously pleading with them. Nobody understood him. He spoke Russian.

The women ignored him and his tanks. Their lines opened and then closed again behind the monsters, leaving them hopelessly engulfed by the oncoming thousands.

There was some confusion when the women reached the huge square. In seconds the tomb was bedecked with flowers, and more and more flowers. There were half a dozen tanks in the square; the soldiers kept their engines roaring but could not move. They watched the women with curious eyes. The colonel was finally forced to abandon his tank and push his way through the women. He could not stop this mass demonstration but wanted to prevent the world from learning what had happened.

There was not much he could do with the few reporters. We hid behind the massive columns of a museum flanking the square, probably hiding more on account of the women who did not want us than the chubby Russian colonel. But the photographers were an easy prey because they had to move around to get their pictures.

The greatest war booty for the Russians that day was the film crew of the Hungarian government-owned news agency. These brave men, happy that after so many years they could do real journalistic work, were pushing their heavy, old-fashioned camera close to the tomb, apparently thinking that while their leaders were quarreling about whether it was a revolution or a counterrevolution, their duty was to take pictures.

This, in the Russians' book, was bourgeois nonsense: the crew was summarily arrested and their film confiscated.

I had better luck with my photographer whom the Associated Press had sent to Budapest to cover the revolution. He was a young Frenchman, on his first "war" assignment, and he was no hero. I quickly discovered that I only had to remind him of French grandeur whenever he balked. He would run out from the Duna Hotel, proudly swinging his camera — and whistling the Marseillaise.

I was luckier, as I said, than the unhappy Hungarian cameramen, because though the Russians got hold of my Frenchman, he was smart enough to quickly exchange his exposed roll for a new one, and surrender the latter to the Russians.

The only serious incident remains a mystery. One shot was fired and with the thousands of women around it was impossible to ascertain who fired and why. Some said afterwards that one woman was killed; according to another version she was wounded.

The women obviously knew that they had defeated the chubby colonel with all his tanks, and that the city belonged to them all day long. From the Square of Heroes they returned downtown and the demonstration continued in front of the American legation. There my wife met Menon again.

When the women packed Liberty Square where the legation stood at one corner, they were much livelier than on their grim march to the Tomb of the Unknown Soldier. There were no flowers any more, but questions, pleas, sometimes angry faces turned upwards toward the legation windows, and shouts: "Why don't you come and help us?" My wife was there, with pad and pencil, the reporter's tools.

The Russians — what lack of imagination! — again sent in their tanks from neighboring Parliament Square, and the scene became ugly. Parliament Square and the Square of Heroes are wide open spaces, but Liberty Square is a lovely, old-fashioned narrow park with trees, benches, flower beds, and four lanes

for traffic. The tanks, wobbling clumsily, advanced and retreated, feinting attack, but the women did not yield. Yet the
situation became dangerous and my wife, trying to make notes,
was pushed to the wall of the legation building. Then a black
limousine drove up slowly, carefully, through the masses of
women. When it reached the legation, its door opened and
somebody called out of the car: "Ilona!"

It was the young Indian diplomat who had invited us a few
days earlier to brief Ambassador Menon. He asked my wife to
get in, which she gladly did, and to explain what was going on
to the ambassador sitting in the back seat. Menon listened,
watching the swirling mass of women from behind the car's
closed windows.

The demonstrations on December 4 were the only ones in
which women participated exclusively. Dozens of others followed. There was something happening almost every day and
anonymous telephone calls usually advised the handful of foreign reporters what they could expect, and when.

Some of the demonstrations ended in a stalemate without
casualties, like the one on Liberty Square, with neither the
tanks nor the women yielding ground. Others were bloody
affairs in which the Soviets and the reorganized gangs of the
Hungarian secret police chased and beat up demonstrators, ar-
resting whoever they could catch. There were ugly scenes
when people carrying the Hungarian flag with the characteristic hole in the center were caught in narrow side streets. They
were beaten mercilessly by club-swinging AVH men and by
the Russian soldiers who used the butts of their rifles.

One day there was a telephone call to the Duna Hotel. "You
want to see a bonfire?" a youthful voice asked. Then he invited
us to a school only a few blocks away.

On the first day the schools were reopened, some time in
December, the students of a secondary school in the heart of
the city piled their Russian-language textbooks in the middle of
the street and staged a bonfire. It was good fun and an easy

way to get rid of the hated textbooks. Students of other schools came running up with their books and the pile grew, burning fiercely in the dry, wintry air. A few Hungarian policemen came but there was little to do. The youngsters disappeared in the doorways and behind the gates of the school.

The Hungarian police, or whatever remained of it after the first two phases of the revolt, was probably adequate to handle schoolchildren but the dirty jobs were done by the Russians. Occasionally there was some shooting, usually started by some desperate Hungarian sniping on Russians from a rooftop. It was tragicomic to watch the large-scale military maneuver directed by some bemedaled Russian officer to catch a lonely sniper.

Participation in the repression by the Hungarian police was sporadic and without enthusiasm. Whenever there was a major demonstration, they disappeared completely. Whether they were reluctant to participate or were ordered to stay away by the Soviet, nobody knew.

The reorganized secret police was not idle, however. The AVH made sporadic arrests in November and many more in December, though the regime's heavy hand came down really hard only after the end of the year. Kádár's indecision was one of the reasons, probably the primary one, for the late start of retaliations.

Another reason was that in November and December the Kádár government did not know yet in what direction to turn. Kádár himself still talked about revolution and not about counterrevolution, still hoping, one may suspect, to get the twenty million dollars worth of food and medical supplies President Eisenhower had promised to the Hungarian people on November 3 in his first enthusiasm.

A further reason was the complete disintegration of the secret police during the fighting in Budapest. The AVH had to be reorganized before the government could turn against the "counterrevolutionaries."

Another demonstration on November 23, one month after the revolution broke out, was the most impressive of all because it involved the entire city of almost two million people. How it was organized remains a mystery. The answer is probably that it was not organized in the usual sense; instead the leaders had to rely on the most primitive grapevine. For days the order was whispered that on November 23 for one hour, between two and three in the afternoon, Budapest must become a dead city.

And so it happened. The unknown organizers had no help. No newspaper printed their appeal and no radio advocated it. There were handwritten, primitive notes on the walls, some of them hastily removed by the police only to be replaced by others.

We in the Duna Hotel knew about the plans. It would not work, the skeptics said. Half of the people would never know about it, the other half would not care. When the hour came, we divided the city among us. My wife and I drove our Volkswagen to the intersection of Rákóczi ut and the main boulevard where the National Theatre then stood, and parked the car at the curb.

Ten minutes before two the normally crowded street rapidly became empty. Some people stood in the doorways, motioning the few who were still on the streets to join them. And when the clock of the nearby church struck two, life stood still everywhere.

Sitting in the car I remembered the hours of air raids during the war. There was more life then on those streets than during this hour. We felt subdued and talked in low tones, afraid to disturb the almost painful silence. Then suddenly we heard the rumbling of an approaching vehicle. It was a Soviet armored car packed with soldiers, with their rifles at the ready. They wore combat fatigues and steel helmets, and when they slowly passed our car I could see the tension on the young faces looking around in disbelief. I suddenly remembered the young Russian officer in the Duna Hotel: "What kind of people are you, anyway?"

Two more armored cars passed us during that hour but, again, there were no Hungarian policemen or troops visible. And exactly sixty minutes after it started, life returned to the city's arteries.

Back in the hotel we compared notes with our colleagues. The situation had been the same everywhere, in the residential districts of Buda and in the industrial suburbs: deserted streets, complete silence, and the tense, perplexed faces of the Russian soldiers patrolling in their armored cars.

The problem that day, and every other day, was to get the story out. Though telephone connection with the West had been restored after the armed resistance had been crushed, it was painfully slow, when it worked at all.

The Duna was an old, second-rate hotel which became "famous" only after it was spared by some miracle during the 1945 siege of Budapest. The Red Army had carefully burned out all its more luxurious competitors on the Korzó, between Chain Bridge and Elisabeth Bridge on the bank of the Danube. The hotel had an outmoded switchboard operated by two middle-aged ladies. They were magnificent.

The little room with the switchboard and the two women was in fact a windowless closet. It was on the same floor where my colleagues lived and where, in one room or another, my wife and I worked during the day. We usually placed our calls at the same time, and then waited and waited, sometimes for hours, sometimes in vain. When a reporter became impatient, he just walked over to the little room to plead with the two operators, as if this would speed things up. They did their best, argued with the long-distance operator, begged and threatened, did all the tricks to connect us with London, Paris, Vienna, and they usually succeeded.

They were always cheerful, those two, and how grateful they were when we shared with them the canned food or chocolate, coffee or oranges that were shipped to us from Vienna.

The two operators were not the only females in the Duna helping newsmen. There were two others, much younger, and obviously dedicated to what is believed to be the oldest profession in the world. Yet, strangely, they did not practice their profession in those days, at least if one can believe our male colleagues who stayed in the hotel. But they helped, almost inconspicuously, by washing shirts and socks and sewing buttons. Their reward was not much — a glass of whiskey, a tin of coffee, a box of cigarettes.

On December 9 the foreign correspondents witnessed the *Götterdämmerung* of the Greater Budapest Workers' Council, and played a major role in it. This is how it happened.

Sándor Rácz, the council's young president, elected by five hundred workers' delegates on November 13, was no great friend of reporters, nor of the West in general. But he tolerated us and did not object when others provided us with our daily story. Most interesting were the reports about their regular bickerings with Kádár.

Relations between Kádár and the workers deteriorated rapidly until the end of November, when Kádár told the delegates that there was no point in continuing their endless discussions. "Every worker," he said, "instead of drawing up and scribbling demands, must immediately and unconditionally begin to work." About this time the workers were told for the first time that strikes were "counterrevolutionary acts" and would be handled as such. Rácz and his aides saw the handwriting on the wall.

First the revolutionary councils in nonindustrial establishments were ordered dissolved. Then more and more local council leaders were arrested.

Many plants, certainly the most important ones, held by the revolutionaries long after the fighting ceased in Budapest's streets, were occupied by the Soviets. In the beginning the Russians were satisfied with military occupation. There were, for instance, dozens of their tanks in the vast yards of the Csepel industrial complex. They did not interfere with the strike, but let the workers sit idly in the workshops and allowed the workers' council to give orders. Reporters entered freely. When the strike continued, the Soviet troops became more aggressive in the idle plants, often participating in the arrests.

The Soviets did not let Kádár do all the talking. Major General K. Grebennik, commander of Soviet troops in Budapest, had frequent meetings with council representatives. He threatened and cajoled, warned about deportations and offered rewards, with no results. One of the workers' demands was the withdrawal of all troops from the factories. This, they said, was a precondition to talk about resuming work.

On December 6 the chairmen of the councils of two important plants, the Mávag and Ganz factories, were arrested. Rácz decided to act. On the same day he sent an ultimatum to Kádár to keep the many promises he had made or face the consequences. There was no answer.

On December 8, a Saturday, Ilona and I made a routine evening call at the council and immediately sensed that something unusual was in the works. What it was, we did not know. Our usual informants remained tight-lipped.

When Rácz, his hatchet face grimmer than usual, emerged from his cubicle, he brushed us aside. But then he seemed to ponder and finally asked my wife, the only woman in the group, to follow him to his private office. He seemed ill at ease, as if undecided what to do.

"We might need you tomorrow — besides it might be a story for you. After all, that is why you are here," he said in his gruff way.

He told Ilona to come and see him Sunday morning at eight at the Beyolannis factory, a former General Electric subsidiary which manufactured precision instruments. During the nation-alization of industry in the late 1940's it was named after a Greek Communist executed after the civil war in Greece.

"Come alone," he advised my wife. "You're a woman and they might prevent men from entering. When you are inside the gate just tell my men you have an appointment with me."

Back in the Duna we made plans for the next day. We still did not know what the workers were up to, but it must have been something important. It was decided that Ronny Farquhar of Reuters should drive my wife to the Beyolannis. He had an inconspicuous Skoda car with a Czech license plate.

The Beyolannis is a huge, modern plant behind thick walls in Budapest's twelfth district. On that Sunday a cordon of Kádár's militia surrounded the building and curious onlookers clustered around the corners, watching for something to happen.

Ronny, a quiet Scot, became hesitant. "You won't make it," he warned Ilona. "If you are lucky, they'll only turn you back, but you might get into serious trouble."

My wife knew from experience what it meant to get into the hands of the Communist secret police, but there are times when a reporter cannot flinch. It was decided that Ronny should wait for her around the corner. Then, trying to appear as casual as possible, she set out toward the gate. A policeman stopped her. Ilona told him she was a reporter and wanted to see what was going on. The policeman did not know what to do and escorted her to an officer who seemed to be in charge.

She showed him her press card. The officer pondered but in those days the police still had orders not to stop foreign report-ers. He shrugged: "You may try, if they let you in."

"They" did. The militia guarded the factory from the out-side, but the workers were the masters inside, behind the heavy, locked gates. Ilona was questioned through a little window on the gate, then inside again. Finally she was escorted upstairs where Rácz was waiting in one of the rooms. He did not waste time. There was apparently no time to waste.

"Look," he said, "they found out what we are up to: a general strike for Tuesday and Wednesday. This is our last chance, and our last weapon. Everything will stop on these two days, except electricity, gas, and water, and milk for the children and the hospitals. But they found it out. They raided our headquarters this morning and arrested everyone there. And they cut off all phone connections, our only means to give the order to strike."

My wife asked about his plans. He said he did not know. But he wanted to give her a declaration, the strike order. The world should know about it and if foreign radios repeated it, all the workers in Hungary would know what to do. He handed her the text and said good-bye. This was the last time any Western reporter saw Sándor Rácz.

Ilona reached Ronny's car without difficulty. He was sitting in the Skoda, biting his nails, wondering whether she would make it. The same morning I went to the council's headquarters to find it teeming with plainclothesmen. As Rácz had told my wife, they had arrested everyone they found there. I was not allowed to enter.

Back in the Duna there was bad news: no telephone connections with the West. Kádár was taking no chances: he had ordered a complete news blackout from the besieged city. We were desperate. We had the story — Ilona had gotten it at real risk — and now we could do nothing but just sit on it. Only a newsman could understand our misery. We kept on trying, pleading with operators, waiting for miracles. And a miracle did happen. Around eleven o'clock there was an incoming call: Reuters from London calling Farquhar. Ronny, holding the receiver, looked helpless and there were, it seemed, more freckles on his face than usual.

"Ilona, what shall I do? It's your story . . ."

"Go ahead," he was told. "It's tough luck, but the story must get out." Standing at his side, my wife translated Rácz's declaration, the appeal to the workers of the world to help, and the order to strike. Ronny repeated her words. Finally he was through. Then Reuters transferred the call to Ilona's London office.

"Bulletin," she said, and started to dictate: "A general strike was ordered today . . ." and then the line went dead. Somebody, belatedly, had discovered that despite every precaution the story had reached the free world. A few minutes later all Western radio stations began blaring the story back to Hungary, broadcasting in Hungarian the order to strike. It went on the whole day.

And so, through the Western broadcasts, the workers in Hungary learned about the strike order. The general strike was a complete success. Never before, I am sure, have the trade unions of any country organized such a strike. The council, though deprived of any means of communication in a revolt-torn country beleaguered by a foreign army, with its telephones cut off and its leaders either arrested or besieged in a factory, succeeded.

On Tuesday we watched how Kádár's men tried to keep a few streetcars running in the city by forcing conductors at pistol point to work. It did not last long: angry workers over-turned the trolleys. For two days the whole country was lame, but it was the beginning of the end. On December 11 Kádár gave Rácz the kiss of Judas: he asked him to come and continue their negotiations. The naive young man accepted the invitation and left his refuge in the Beyolannis where hundreds of workers were his bodyguards. When Rácz and Bali, his deputy, arrived on Parliament Square to call on Kádár, they were arrested. For two years nothing more was heard about them.

This is the first time the story of the December 11–12 general strike has been told. Both Rácz and Bali paid a heavy price for their role in this phase of passive resistance. They spent long years in prison, but now that they are free again, it can be explained how the strike was made possible.

The workers, the "elite of the proletariat," were the source of many of my dispatches. From them I heard for the first time the gruesome story that Hungarians were being deported to the Soviet Union. There had been rumors of deportations soon after November 4, while fighting was still going on in the streets. Then there was proof, still viewed with reservation by skeptical Western reporters, and finally came confirmation from the highest source, the top spokesman of the Kádár government.

My colleagues from the West needed confirmation because without that they would just not believe that in the twentieth century people were still being deported. I myself had few doubts. Anyone who had survived the Russian "liberation" eleven years earlier remembers how the Red Army produced fantastic numbers of so-called prisoners of war.

Surprisingly this is a little-known chapter of World War II. Because what happened in 1945 explains the deportations in 1956, it should be recalled. Many Magyars who went underground during the months of Nazism in Hungary, because they were Jews, honest anti-Nazis, or just plain patriots, believed that the Soviet soldiers would bring liberation for them individually, though they had no illusions that the country would be treated nicely for having sided with Hitler. I could not share this optimism and, unfortunately, I proved to be right.

Listening to the BBC and other Western radios during the war, I was always perplexed by the astronomic numbers of prisoners the Russians reported as having captured. They must be lying, I thought, because adding up one week's figures amounted to an army corps. The fall of Budapest, after a siege of almost three months, explained how this was done.

The Red Army obviously was under orders to produce a

certain number of prisoners every day. The most convenient way was to round up as many men as possible, regardless of the fact that they were civilians, or men persecuted by the Nazi regime, or even Communists. I know it because they caught me, too, not once but seven times. I always managed to escape because I was determined not to be dragged to Siberia. The story of my escapes has nothing to do with the revolution eleven years later, so it should suffice to mention that one night I spent what appeared to me to be hours in a large pipe under a highway, standing in ice mixed with water up to my chin and waiting until the column of prisoners from which I had escaped had been herded off by young Cossacks wielding their knouts. Another time I could escape because the Russian sentry who guarded our small group at a street corner while his comrades were searching a house for other victims, was decent enough to turn to the wall while he relieved himself. When he turned back, I was already running. He was a poor shot and I was running zigzag. A third time I sat on the snowy roof of the apartment house where we lived, having carefully pulled up the ladder through the attic window, while the Russians went from apartment to apartment rounding up their so-called prisoners of war. And a fourth time — I am less proud of that — my wife paid ransom: a bottle of red wine she borrowed somewhere to free me from my captor.

Some of the Russians, it seemed, were ashamed of what they were doing. They rounded up the men between eighteen and forty-five with some pretext. Usually it was *malinka robot*, a little work to do, and the first time I was deceived, too. Believing that it was *malinka robot*, I left the house with them the way I was: in civilian clothes and a warm pullover (there was no heat in the houses, of course, as there was no electricity or gas, and water for a few hours only) and the middle-aged Russian looked curiously at me. I had better get a coat, he said; it would be cold outside. I dismissed his advice: if it will be *robot*, I would not feel the cold, and *malinka* meant that I would be back soon. I was back, after two days and a sixty-mile walk.

After this experience it was understandable that I was more inclined to believe the rumors of deportations in 1956 than my colleagues from America or other civilized countries. Yet they had one good argument against it: after the war the Soviets needed manpower to rebuild what the Nazis had devastated. But in 1956?

They might have a point, I thought. I remembered the meek little janitor of the apartment house where my wife and I hid during the Nazi period, a real "proletarian" who was taken by the Russians the same day they took me. He returned seven years later, having helped "voluntarily" to rebuild what he did not destroy. Does history repeat itself? I asked myself.

I still do not know why they did it in 1956. The explanation cannot be punishment. True, there were some leaders of the workers and students among the deportees, but the overwhelming majority were plain citizens, young and not so young, herded at random into trains bound for the Soviet Union. The rumors gained powerful support by dozens of little scribbled notes given to me. They had been found by people who lived close to the railway, and had been thrown out somehow from the closed freight cars. Some of them were almost illegible; others had been written by men of education. They were brief, containing usually a terse message, a request, with telephone number and address added, that parents, a bride, or a girlfriend should be notified, and sometimes a brief reference to where and under what circumstances the man had been captured. Destination? Unknown.

I checked many of these messages, calling by telephone or personally on the addressee. The answer was in every case: yes, the son (or husband, or father) had disappeared on such and such a date and nothing had been heard of him since.

Some of us decided to confront the government with this evidence. A small group of foreign correspondents, my wife

and I among them, requested an appointment with István
Szirmai, chief of the Kádár government's press section. Szirmai
received us in the Parliament building. It was December 3, and
the man, generally known to be a "liberal" Communist, was
obviously ill at ease. We did not attack him directly with the
deportation issue. The newsman's tactics are different behind
the Iron Curtain. But finally one of us raised the question:
what about the deportations?

I must admit I was not too much interested in Szirmai's answer; obviously he had to deny it. That is what he did, but he
was evasive, uncertain, and I became very attentive. Then
something unprecedented happened: Szirmai "broke down,"
he admitted that there were deportations, "isolated cases" during the first chaotic days, but his government had asked the
Russians to return everybody and he had no doubts that this
would happen. I motioned my colleagues to leave before the
man realized what he had done. Back in the hotel we carefully
compared notes. There must be no mistake when we filed this
story.

It is characteristic that during and after the Czech occupation in 1968, the East Germans played a major role in the propaganda campaign against aspirations to freedom, just as they
did during the Hungarian revolution. Szirmai did not deny his
blunder in Hungary, where by then everybody knew about
the deportations, but the East German radio carried his denial
the next day, December 4, quoting Szirmai as having said that
he had never acknowledged the deportations simply because
there were none.

How many were deported nobody knew. At the headquarters of the workers the figure was around sixteen thousand, the
U.N. Special Committee on Hungary said there were "several
thousands." Many returned, some in a few weeks, others years
later, and many were arrested immediately after their return
by the Hungarian secret police as it was not in the regime's
interest to let these unfortunates go free and tell their story.

Yet a handful did escape. These few, returned by the Russians almost immediately, managed to escape to the West where they told their story to the U.N. Committee.

There was one significant difference between the deportations in 1945 and those in 1956. After the revolution Magyars were still on the warpath; theirs was not a broken, divided nation as it was after World War II, and a good number of deportees were freed before their sad train reached the Hungarian-Soviet border. The railwaymen cooperated, just as they did in Czechoslovakia in 1968. Trains were stopped with some pretext, usually during the night, the Russian guards were entertained until they got drunk, and then the freight cars were opened to free their inmates.

13

Noel Field, the Workers, and the Intellectuals

While the "Communist elite," workers and intellectuals, continued their remarkable passive resistance for months, there was a man who remained the apologist of Communism, though he was tortured by his comrades, and who stayed in a Communist country though he was free to go. He was the American Noel Haviland Field.

I met this strange man on December 28, 1956. It was, in a way, a sad encounter of two couples, Ilona and I on the one hand, and Noel and Hertha Field on the other. We were two Hungarians who had worked for years for American wireservices and who had been convicted by the Communists as traitors. The Fields were two Americans, imprisoned by the Communists whom they had served so loyally for years. During the hour we spent together we watched each other with curious eyes and, I admit, with the mutual sympathy of those who have survived the same ordeal.

There were three of us who went to see the Fields on a cold, snowy winter night. The third was Richard Kasischke, then AP's Vienna bureau chief, who came to Budapest to help with the coverage of the postrevolution period. We were the first and, as far as I know, the only Western reporters to meet Noel Field. None of our colleagues was permitted to see him afterwards.

The strange story of Noel Field, the American Quaker, former State Department specialist, friend of Alger Hiss, wartime collaborator of Allen Dulles and his hush-hush Office of Strategic Services (OSS), has been told in book form and in magazine articles. While Field was in a Communist prison in Budapest in 1951, Hede Massing, the self-confessed Communist spy, told the Senate Internal Security Subcommittee that she had recruited Noel for her Communist cell in 1934. Whittaker Chambers also confirmed that Field was a Communist, and it can be assumed that Josef Swiatlo, the Polish secret service officer who arrested Herman Field, Noel's brother, in 1949 and who defected in 1954, has told the CIA the same.

I was always baffled by the mysterious life of this man and especially by the still unexplained puzzle of why three members of his family crossed the Iron Curtain one by one shortly after Noel's disappearance in May 1949, only to be arrested themselves. They were his wife, Hertha, his brother Herman, and the Fields' adopted daughter, Erika Glaser Wallach. My visit to the Fields did not clarify the mystery, but it confirmed, if it needed confirmation, that Noel and Hertha were Communists. Whether they were card-carrying party members or not, is in my judgment irrelevant.

I had learned much about the Fields from Major Kretsmer, the AVH officer who handled my case. Exactly one year before Kretsmer interrogated me in Fö utca, he had been in charge of Noel Field's rehabilitation.

After the war the Fields lived in Europe, working for the Unitarian Service Committee, a relief organization. In May 1949 Noel left Switzerland for Prague, to collect material, he claimed, for a book he planned to write. After a week in Prague he was supposed to fly to Bratislava but he never arrived there. In July Hertha Field went to Prague to search for her husband and she disappeared on August 25. Three days earlier, on August 22, Herman Field, an architect, was believed to have boarded a plane in Warsaw for Prague. The plane arrived in the Czech capital without him. And finally, one year later, on August 26, 1950, Erika Glaser flew to Berlin and disappeared into the Soviet sector of the city.

It is difficult to understand the participants of this postwar mystery. Were they really so naive as to believe that somebody who was spirited away by the secret police of a Communist country could be found? Or did they hope for a secret reunion — not Herman, perhaps, but the wife and the adopted daughter? Were they lured by a false promise to rejoin Noel Field and live peacefully together ever after? Neither the Fields nor Major Kretsmer answered these questions.

The Communists needed Field to prove through him that the Americans and Tito, their "chained dog," had penetrated the ranks of honest Communists during the war years. They needed him more specifically to incriminate László Rajk and his codefendants in the most celebrated purge trial of 1949. He was needed to "prove" that the West had schemed during World War II to infiltrate the Communist parties of Eastern Europe and that Rajk in Hungary, Rudolf Slansky and Vladimir Clementis in Czechoslovakia, Traicho Kostov in Bulgaria, and a great many others, were Hitler's agents.

Who could have been more suitable to play this show role than Field, this American intellectual who indeed had known several of Rajk's codefendants during his OSS years? His task then had been to contact underground groups in Nazi-occupied territories, and Communists who had escaped Hitlerism and who were living in the West. But his timely appearance, like the entire staging of the Rajk trial, had been too conspicuously perfect. Why was Field behind the Iron Curtain just at that time? Was it pure coincidence that gave the Communists the excellent opportunity to get hold of him? Or was he himself lured somehow? To me, the latter seems very likely.

Field himself was never tried by the Hungarian Communists. His task was to incriminate the others, and he did so after his tormentors broke him. First he indignantly refused to "confess," but then he signed testimonies admitting that on instructions from Allen Dulles he had recruited Rajk and many others, either in French camps where members of the former International Brigade had been held after Franco's victory in the Spanish Civil War, or later in Switzerland, during World War II. But why was Field's incriminating testimony necessary? Wasn't it enough that Rajk and the countless other defendants in Communist purge trials in the Soviet Union and elsewhere confessed? The answer is obviously no, it was not enough. There needed to be others who confirmed the "crime," usually incriminating themselves, too.

Field signed everything and duly confessed as requested. Then he was discarded. While the others busily rehearsed their roles in this weird courtroom comedy, Field was kept in his cell. But on rare occasions he was summoned to his interrogator and on one of these occasions he was told that Tibor Szönyi, the former high-ranking Communist party functionary, had been sentenced to death on the basis of his testimony.

Field had met Szönyi in Switzerland during the war. The Rajk indictment said that Field "specialized in recruiting spies, from among so-called left-wing elements, and the various émigré espionage groups of different nationalities in Switzerland were subordinate to him." The indictment linked Rajk to Dulles through Szönyi and Field.

When the AVH officer casually informed Field that Szönyi had been sentenced to death, the American's conscience awoke. He knew that there was not a word of truth in his confession that he had "recruited" Szönyi in Geneva. He tried desperately to revoke his testimony. He pleaded and argued, in vain. Szönyi was hanged, together with Rajk.

After the execution the AVH had no need for the Fields. They were not tried, but they could not be released either, so they were kept for five years in the dreaded old and shabby Conti utca prison in Budapest. While they were there, the Communist governments of Hungary, Czechoslovakia, and Poland, replying to inquiries from Washington, blandly insisted that they knew nothing about the Fields. Then, after Stalin's death and when Imre Nagy became prime minister for the first time, the rehabilitation of Communist victims of the purge trials began. But the Fields were not convicts and for many months nobody remembered them. The couple was brought back to Fö utca only in March 1954 and both were put in cells on the same corridor, Noel occupying the cell that later housed me.

Noel lived a "luxurious" life and got VIP treatment. He had a small table, a simple wooden chair, and books, paper, and a pencil — all unheard-of luxuries for an intellectual deprived of such things for so many years. Here Noel wrote his new confessions for six months. He wrote them every afternoon in German, a language he spoke fluently. Otherwise he was treated as a number who had to stand close to the wall when the door of his cell was opened and fold his arms behind his back when led through the empty corridors. In the mornings he was escorted to his interrogator. There a secretary translated into Hungarian what he had written the previous day.

The investigation procedure in Communist countries is not a simple one. They want to know everything. The prisoner has to tell every detail of his life, report about every friend and acquaintance, reveal every secret thought or dream, until he stands naked there, completely at the mercy of the man who investigates his case.

Field declared that he was and remained a Communist despite his imprisonment. This is a respectable standpoint. A man of principles does not give up his conviction because of such trifling things as five years in prison without trial. But Field was a Communist with some reservations. He said he accepted the Marxist doctrine but not the necessity of violence, that the workers' class must resort to force to get rid of the exploiters. A true Communist will naturally smile at such naiveté, but this smile had no bad consequences in 1954 when Field's case was reexamined. They forgave him this deviation because he was considered a harmless idealist who already had paid a high price for his ideological shortcomings.

All this went smoothly. Major Kretsmer was interested in the truth only, and Field had no reason to hold back. But he had to prove that he was a true Communist and he succeeded. He told his interrogator that in 1944 he had suggested that the OSS form a "German committee of the West," with strong Communist participation. The suggestion was rejected; moreover, it was decided not to cooperate with German Communist underground groups, and Field immediately conveyed this vital information to the Communist underground in Germany. The AVH checked Field's story and Wilhelm Pieck, who was in Moscow during the war and later became East Germany's president, confirmed that it was true. The AVH decided to set the Fields free.

But before they were released, Kretsmer had to complete his review of the case and this took eight months. Meanwhile Field did not know what had happened to his wife. Hearing is the prisoner's most important sense. In spite of the complete isolation and iron discipline, sensitive prisoners frequently hear things that a free man would not. Despite heavy doors, the rubber covering of the corridors and the rule that everyone must whisper, Field became more and more convinced that he recognized his wife's steps in the corridor when a woman, taken to be interrogated, passed his cell.

Field was a timid man, afraid of learning the truth. Instead of asking directly, he wrote a "letter" to his interrogator and left it on his desk when, after the daily questioning, he was taken back to his cell. In this letter he asked the AVH officer whether his feeling was correct. He was told the next day that his wife was there indeed.

The Fields received the food of the privileged few during those eight months. Rolls instead of bread, bacon with their morning coffee, meat twice a day and occasionally fruit. Though they were not told so, they sensed during the last month that something would happen to them, that perhaps they would be freed. But they did not know, of course, what was going on in the outside world. They were never told that Swiatlo, the Polish secret police officer who came to Budapest to interrogate them, had defected and told the West what he knew about the Fields. The United States had sent strong notes, based on Swiatlo's story, to Poland and Hungary in September 1954, requesting information about the three Fields, Noel, Hertha, and Herman. Although it was known that Erika was in Russian hands, she was not an American citizen, so the United States had no legal basis to intervene on her behalf.

Instead of answering the notes, Poland released Herman on October 25, 1954, and Hungary freed Noel and Hertha on November 16. The case against them had been reviewed and "the conclusion was reached that charges could not be substantiated," a one-sentence communiqué of the Hungarian government said at midnight of that day.

The Fields were told only a few hours earlier that they were free. The couple was brought to a comfortable villa on the Sashegy, one of the hills on the Buda side of the Hungarian capital, a quiet, middle-class residential district. Then, for some days, the Fields were again on the front pages of the Western press. On November 18, two days after their release, Christian M. Ravndal, then the U.S. envoy to Hungary, and Donald Downs, first secretary of the legation, visited the couple. The next day, on November 19, Herman, having spent some weeks in a Polish hospital, arrived in Switzerland and was spirited away from Zurich airport by the American consul with Swiss police assistance. On November 27, Alger Hiss left prison after three and a half years. On Christmas Eve, Noel and Hertha asked for and were granted political asylum in Hungary. On

January 31, 1955, Ravndal, with legation counselor N. Spencer Barnes, visited the Fields again, for the second and last time.

Ravndal's first visit to the Fields' hideaway — they had asked the diplomat to respect their privacy and not to tell newsmen their address — provided him with little information about the couple's plans. The polite chat between them was not much more than beating around the bush. Both the legation and the Hungarian authorities had supplied the Fields with five years of newspapers, including copies of the *New York Times*, and what they read might have decided their future.

Then it became clear to them that while they were being grilled by the Hungarian secret police and while they were sitting in their prison cells, Whittaker Chambers and Hede Massing had testified that they knew Noel was a Communist. Although Mrs. Massing added that Noel Field had "balked" at treasonous acts, saying that he wanted to work for Stalin, but not while he was with the State Department, Field had good reason to believe that he might face trouble should he return to the United States.

In the course of Ravndal's first visit the Fields only asked for time to rest, to find out what was going on in the world. Noel also needed medical treatment because the years in prison had not helped his ulcer troubles. Though Ravndal was reluctant to prophesy, the diplomat had few if any illusions about Noel and so the couple's decision to seek asylum was no surprise. Ravndal's second visit to the Fields was only to obtain direct confirmation that they had decided voluntarily to remain in the Communist country where they had been kept in prison without trial.

The Fields, like all good Communists, did not like publicity. The legation in Budapest forwarded to them my request for an interview. One day in January 1955 I got a telephone call and someone who introduced herself as Noel's secretary said, "Mr. Field has no statement to make and, therefore, does not want to meet the press." I tried, of course, to get his address from the

Hungarian foreign ministry but was told that "Mr. Field is an American citizen and we think that you, as an American correspondent, should get his address from the legation."

Later in 1955 Erika was finally released from Vorkuta, the dreaded camp for political prisoners near the Arctic Circle. She had spent two and a half years in an East Berlin pretrial prison, and had been convicted for espionage and sentenced to death by a Soviet court-martial in 1952, but her sentence was later cut to fifteen years in prison. She worked on road and railroad construction and was told when released that the charges against her were "groundless." The Fields' stepdaughter, then thirty-three, returned to West Berlin in October 1955.

Meanwhile Noel and Hertha had settled down in Budapest. Their nice, pleasantly furnished, two-story house was on a remote street of the Sashegy, obviously chosen by the AVH to guarantee a quiet life for the Americans. They had a maid, and Noel took the bus to go to his downtown office where he supervised translations at the state-owned book publishing firm Corvina that specializes in publishing Hungarian books in foreign languages.

To learn the Fields' address, which had been a well-kept secret before the revolution, was no problem in December 1956. I drove the Volkswagen up the hill on snow-covered streets and we found the house without difficulty. I rang the bell and talked to the maid in Hungarian when she came to the gate. As she did not ask who we were, I did not volunteer the information. We were led to a comfortably heated living room on the ground floor, and then Hertha Field entered. She was not a little surprised when we told her who we were. She knew much about Ilona and me, including that we had been in prison, and her first question concerned what happened to our daughters while we were both in jail.

Probably her sympathy with someone who had shared a similar ordeal explains why she did not refuse us when I asked her to call her husband. She hesitated for a moment, but then agreed. Both Fields wore warm, dark-blue overalls, rather unusual clothing but very suitable in the heavily damaged, snowclad city that Budapest was then.

Most of the things I know about them they told me that evening. Speaking in low tones for about an hour, always calm and self-composed, Noel did not conceal his real sentiments, though he never called himself a Communist.

We talked first about his work with Corvina and Field told us with a little smile that he found it exasperating and would prefer to translate himself instead of correcting the translations of others. During the years he had acquired a remarkable command of the Hungarian language. Hertha had no permanent employment, but she helped her husband occasionally. They lived quietly and had a few friends whom they described as progressive intellectuals. They had toured Hungary repeatedly since their release, visiting Lake Balaton and cities throughout the country.

Field told us then that he had been in a hospital with ulcer troubles when the revolution broke out and spent the weeks of the revolt there. Whatever he "saw" was through the eyes of Hertha — and after the hour I spent with the couple I was convinced that throughout his married life Field had seen everything through his wife's eyes. Hertha Field was by far the stronger character of the two, a domineering personality and a clever woman whom neither the years nor prison could break. My impression was that she had converted Noel to Communism.

The Fields were remarkably cool when I asked them about Erika. They said with unmistakable indifference that they had no contact whatsoever with her.

The couple did not explain why they had chosen to stay in Hungary but from what they said it was clear that they wanted to end their storm-tossed lives in relative peace. I asked them about their passports and Field said they had none and did not need such documents, although they had not renounced their American citizenship and "always will be" Americans.

"You know," his wife added, "we are not young any more. We traveled much in our younger years, we still can go around in this country, and that is enough for us."

"I like to live here, it is exciting, and I want to watch how things will come out," Noel said.

Then he obviously thought it was his duty to make some statement. He said he supported János Kádár because Kádár "has saved this country from white terror."

I asked him with some surprise what evidence he had of "white terror," especially as he told me earlier he had not seen anything of the revolution.

Noel became hesitant; he realized he had made a mistake. "Oh, even in the hospital I felt it . . . and my wife told me so . . ." I did not press the question further.

On September 18, 1956, a month before the revolution broke out, Szabad Nép, then the official Communist party paper, published a letter to the editor by Noel Field, in which the American expressed "elation" over the prerevolution changes in Hungary, calling them "a turn toward humanitarianism, of which I am a living witness." It is understandable that Field, a "liberal" Communist who accepted the Marxist doctrine without the violence clause, enjoyed the refreshing, sparkling prerevolution climate in Hungary. In doing so he joined the many Communist intellectuals who were enthused by the same changes that elated Noel.

His second public utterance, broadcast by the government-controlled radio on June 26, 1957, seven months after the revolution, was a different matter.

In his letter to Szabad Nép, Field told the truth when he said he was a "witness" of the changes. Curiously, he used the same word in his 1957 radio message, a poor attempt to whitewash the Moscow-installed regime by repeating the trite "counterrevolutionary" charge, when he said: "I was a witness. . . . I lived through the rising and ensuing tragic days." This was, however, not true. He had told me personally that he had not been a "witness" because he was bedridden in a Budapest hospital throughout the weeks of the actual revolt.

During our visit Field impressed me as a cultured, refined man, and an inveterate daydreamer. He was led by a strong woman who had him completely under her thumbs. During the weeks between their release and the day they asked for asylum, the couple must have weighed their chances carefully. They compared the certainty of facing the music if they returned to the United States, with the possibility of getting imprisoned again in Hungary. The first was certain, the latter unlikely. The aging, tired man, the gaunt intellectual with thin white hair over the dome of his delicately shaped head, chose the illusory comfort of the second.

There is no doubt in my mind that the Fields were and remained Communists. That he was a "different" Communist and not the standard Moscowite type is neither unusual nor important. There are many of this kind, mostly idealistic intellectuals, though many of them became disillusioned sooner or later, as the impressive list shows, ranging from André Gide to Arthur Koestler, from Ignazio Silone to Howard Fast.

But the Field I met in December 1956 was not the same man who crossed the Iron Curtain in 1949. This Field did not want to play an active role in life any more. He was content with his relatively carefree life, his modest job with no politics involved, and with his comfortable house.

Field worked for the Corvina publishing house until his death on September 12, 1970. He had cancer. If anyone had doubts about his political beliefs, the Budapest announcement of his death clarified this point once and for all. It called Field "the known old fighter of the Communist movement."

The "old fighter" — he was sixty-six when he died — had not been used by the Hungarian government for propaganda purposes since his 1957 endorsement of Kádár. Whether he refused to lend his name to propaganda, we do not know. It is conceivable that the regime preferred to let the world forget about the man who was kept in a Communist prison for years without trial.

During the two months which followed the Russian onslaught on November 4, there were daily manifestations of passive resistance by individuals from all walks of life. I mention two which left a deep impression on me.

One day four Western newsmen were interviewing the manager of an important government-owned institution. The man was a veteran Communist who shall remain unnamed because he still occupies the same position. It was mid-November, the fighting in Budapest was over, and Nagy was in exile in the Yugoslav embassy. We talked about a number of things, including the way out of the present impasse, and the man mentioned several times "the prime minister," without naming him. It was a strange performance and I sensed that he wanted to convey some message. "Whom do you mean?" I asked. He replied: "Imre Nagy, of course. He is my prime minister."

This, in retrospect, is hard to explain. Szirmai risked his neck by admitting, without being really pressed, that there were deportations. The other man, sitting behind his high-salaried desk at the pleasure of the Kádár regime, spoke about Nagy, the "counterrevolutionary," as "his" prime minister, without caring to warn us reporters that he was "off the record," as is so frequently the case in the free world with much less justification.

The other happened much later, around mid-December. Sitting at my desk and working on a story one evening, the telephone rang. It was one of the long-distance operators, one of those nameless and faceless girls whose voice had become so familiar to me in the course of many years. She was casual and cool, almost matter-of-fact. "You might be interested to know that as of today your phone is being tapped again," she said. I played her game and thanked her briefly, without showing undue interest.

Why did she do it? She did not know me, certainly not personally, and before the revolt bugging of telephones had been a matter of course. But 1956 brought about a strange and unprecedented solidarity of virtually everyone, against the regime, against the Russians.

Though the workers' councils were outlawed after Rácz's arrest, the strikes were not immediately over. It took the government until early 1957 to induce all the workers to return, and only after using more terror tactics.

In the second half of December the emphasis shifted to the intellectuals, especially to the writers and journalists who were the last torchbearers of the revolution. Their role in the revolt had its ups and downs. Unquestionably, they were primarily responsible for the ferment and for the gradual undermining of the Rákosi-Gerö regimes before October 23. During the first phase of the revolt the writers had all the space they could dream of in the Hungarian newspapers and periodicals, and all the freedom they wanted to write as they pleased.

One of the few things I could save from those times was the November 2 issue of *Irodalmi Ujság*, the weekly of the Association of Writers. I think I should quote the first lines of a poem printed in that issue: "One Sentence on Tyranny" by Gyula Illyés, the greatest contemporary Hungarian essayist and poet. It was translated by Paul Tábori, a Hungarian writer living in London:

> *Where there's tyranny,*
> *there's tyranny,*
> *not only in the gun-barrel,*
> *not only in the prison cell.*

Illyés was never a Communist, but a left-leaning liberal even in prewar Hungary, and a kind and gentle humanitarian. After the war he maintained his independence, grudgingly respected by the regime, and Illyés, with many reservations, slowly made his peace with Communism.

During the war phase of the revolt understandably little was heard about the writers. This brief period belonged to those who fought with a gun in their hands. But the writers reappeared during the third phase of passive resistance and their role was probably as impressive as that of the workers. My personal contact with them was scanty, and this was my fault. Only once did I visit the headquarters of their association and on that day only a few were present.

An elderly little man received me. He was huddled in an old leather armchair, covered with a blanket to protect his fragile body from the icy wind which blew through the windows (they had been blown out during the fighting).

He said his name in a quiet voice and asked gently, almost paternally, in what way he could help me. Then, without waiting for questions, he started to talk. He was not angry, but sad. As a good Communist who had spent a lifetime in the "movement," he could neither understand nor condone the "rape of Hungary." There was a "literary strike," he said, and it would go on because the writers had tasted the intoxicating nectar of freedom and pledged never to lie again.

How long can this go on? I asked. He shrugged. "We may all die. You remember Benda's *La Trahison des Clercs?* We won't be traitors again. . . . I hope we won't."

Before leaving I apologized for not having caught his name. He was Zoltán Zelk, one of the most respected poets. A year later he was sentenced to a prison term.

I had long telephone conversations on many nights with Péter Veres, the great peasant writer, who died in 1970. He was not a Communist, but an apologist of the regime, a fellow traveler. I did not know him personally, but he called me one night because, he explained, there should be some record of what the writers were doing to save what could be saved. He called me several times, though I sent word to him that my telephone was tapped and he could get into trouble.

"Thank you for your message," he began the next night. "I really don't care. This is the least we can risk."

The writers were encouraged by the many manifestations of sympathy from the West, especially when these came from colleagues who were Communists themselves.

"Socialism, like freedom, cannot be carried on at the point of a bayonet. . . . When you fired during those October days, when Communist army tanks on command from Communist leaders butchered Communist workers, it was Socialism itself your bullets and gun shells were splinting to bits," Sartre and Vercors messaged from Paris to Moscow, and Howard Fast, the American, turned his back on Communism. These were only a few of those who protested, and all this was known to fellow writers in Hungary.

The Manifesto of Hungarian Intellectuals, issued on November 24, declared: "We, the intellectual workers of Hungary . . . associate ourselves with the heroes fighting for the freedom of our country. We accept all the consequences that our acts or our words may bring upon us: prison, deportation and, if necessary, death." This document was signed by one hundred and ten men and women, a glittering Who's Who, including such names as Zoltán Kodály, the composer; Péter Veres, president of the Writers' Association; and veteran Communist writers Tibor Déry, Lajos Kassák, and Gyula Háy.

Most of them had to face the consequences. József Gáli and Gyula Obersovszky, two lesser-known young writers, were sentenced to death in July 1957 and only the intervention of the International Pen Club saved their lives. Déry, Háy, Zelk, and several others were sent to prison.

The question was often asked: why did they do it? What caused Communist writers to turn against their regime, which guaranteed them a better, more carefree life than most writers enjoyed in the Western world.

I have no answer but to accept the title of a book written by such former Communists as Arthur Koestler, Ignazio Silone, Stephen Spender, and others: *The God That Failed*. The intellectual, it appears, who blindly accepts a religion, must go berserk if one day he is told that the god he worships is a fake, and that is what happened when Khrushchev denounced Stalin at the Twentieth Congress of the Soviet Communist party.

I had one indication that this theory was right. Miklós Gimes was a brilliant young newspaperman, a columnist and editorial writer of *Szabad Nép*, the Hungarian version of *Pravda*, and a Stalinist of the first magnitude during all the years of Stalinism. I knew him well. He was one of the few Communists whose company I enjoyed because of his intellectual brilliance. He intrigued me because he was a bright young man — he reminded me of the ice-cold figure of Saint-Just of the French revolution — convinced that Stalin could not be wrong.

In 1955 Gimes became a most bitter foe of the Communist system, with an almost unreasonable hatred against everyone who had anything to do with it including, I suspect, himself. I know there were strong efforts to save his life. But he could not be saved; he destroyed himself. He was executed together with Nagy, as was Saint-Just together with Robespierre.

Gimes, I believe, was the classic example of one extreme, of the blind believer who runs amuck when he recognizes that his god has failed him.

The writers celebrated a sad Christmas in 1956 by issuing their last manifesto. A crumpled copy of this document is one of my cherished possessions.

Out of two hundred and fifty writers assembled on that day only eight opposed *Solicitude and Creed*. It said:

"Here we stand on the blood-stained mound of the October War of Independence. Looking back on the past decade from this small hill, we see the people suffering because they were forced tyrannically to adopt a foreign way of life. Untold sufferings fill the Hungarian people with the ardent longing that their wounds be healed and that they become at last a nation. The spring that gushed forth from the depths on October 23 rose from this longing. As witnesses of this gushing geyser we must note with bitter hearts that the Soviet government made a historical mistake when it soiled the water of our spring with blood."

The manifesto marked the beginning of the end for me, too. On January 16, 1957, the Kádár government dissolved the Writers' Association. On the same day I left my country.

14

The Aftermath

To leave the country where I was born was a heartbreaking decision to make. Yet I had no alternative. To stay would have meant imprisonment once again for Ilona and me, and I could not have risked leaving our daughters without parents, possibly permanently.

Early in January 1957 it was obvious that the revolution was over, but I was stubborn. To me there was still a story to be told because the passive resistance of writers and intellectuals continued. But one night I had to admit defeat.

My wife, the two girls, and I were having dinner in our apartment when the telephone rang. It was a quiet, unemotional male voice. I recognized it immediately as the voice of a worker whom I had met almost nightly in November in the smoke-filled, shabby premises of the Greater Budapest Workers' Council. I never knew the man's name — there had been no formal introductions, and none were needed — but I remembered him well because he was different from the others. He appeared to be better educated than the others and was a thoroughly disciplined trade union organizer such as Sándor Rácz's amateurish outfit needed.

"You know who I am, don't you?" he started the conversation. I said yes.

"We understand that they plan to arrest you tonight. I would advise you and your wife not to stay in your apartment," the man said, and hung up.

I stood at my desk for a long minute and lit a cigarette automatically. What should we do, and what should I tell my family? I pondered.

"Well, who was it?" Ilona asked from the dining room. I had to go back to the dinner table and tell them about the call.

"The hole," Ilona said, and I nodded. The neighboring house was American property; Tom Rogers lived there with his family. At a recent dinner in their house a young American who had joined the legation just before the revolution broke out, jokingly mentioned how convenient it would be for us to find asylum next door should the need arise. Asylum was meant in the broad, nonlegal sense of the word: the homes of diplomats, except ambassadors' residences, do not enjoy extraterritorial immunity, but the Communist police would think twice before intruding.

Then someone recalled that there used to be a hole in the wire fence between the two houses to make communication easier between the Rogers children and ours. While we were in prison, the fence had been mended.

It should be opened again, the young attaché suggested. He thought it was a good joke and a party was dispatched with a flashlight and a wire cutter. "Mission accomplished," they laughingly reported a few minutes later, but I was not in the mood to laugh. This was the hole Ilona recalled that night.

There was no panic in our apartment, but we did not finish our dinner. In ten minutes, with a few small suitcases in our hands, we crawled quietly, Indian file, through the hole.

I knew that I had lost, that my argument about the journalist's duties had become hollow and that I had in fact outlived my usefulness as a reporter. When, two months earlier, we had sought refuge in the American legation, we did what dozens of other Western newsmen were doing. To seek asylum now was an individual act based on a vague, anonymous warning. There was no obvious danger in the streets and the situation was slowly returning to normal.

Only that normality could have been far more dangerous for Ilona and for me than were all the hazards of the revolution. When we were sent to prison in 1955, the charges against us were ridiculous. But now, as Ilona quietly explained during the night in the Rogers house, she could not again plead innocent to aiding and abetting the "enemy." Did not she encourage the "counterrevolutionaries" by translating Nehru's speech? And, more importantly, did she not help the general strike by smuggling out the strike appeal from the besieged Beyolannis factory?

Whether the warning saved us from arrest, there was no way of knowing. The next day Richard Kasischke, still in Budapest from Vienna, protested at the foreign ministry, where he was told that the ministry had no knowledge of any impending action against the Martons. The answer was expected because Communist secret police never notify a foreign ministry in advance of actions against a foreign correspondent, and seldom afterwards.

During the next few days there were little, mysterious hints indicating that the regime would not object if we left the country. No such thing can ever be said officially, of course, but early January 1957 was still a period of unusual candor and the country was still far from plunging back into Communist secrecy. One man went beyond the cautious hints and bluntly said the regime would welcome our departure.

"Don't you understand?" he asked me, with some frustration in his voice. "Our predecessors had some unpleasant experiences with you and your wife. To avoid a repetition the best thing for us would be to say good-bye and let you go. You may rest assured of one thing: never again will we accredit a

Hungarian citizen as a foreign correspondent." We should ask for regular passports, he advised, and added that things would go much more smoothly if AP sent another permanent correspondent to take my place and assure continuity of coverage.

Again, I had no choice. Had I preferred to join those more than two hundred thousand Hungarians who had "voted with their feet" and escaped to the West, I had missed the boat long before. The border had been sealed off since mid-December and very few, certainly not people with families, had succeeded in escaping. I agreed that we should apply for passports, and they were issued in a matter of days. Carl Hartman arrived to take over my office.

That last night Ilona and I were guests at a dinner given for us by the Rogerses. Ambassador Wailes and his wife were there with others from the legation. We had attended many such sad gatherings when friends had left and we remained behind, with no reasonable chance of meeting again. That night it was our turn.

Tom Rogers offered the toast. His words I still remember: "I say good-bye now. I also express the thanks of my country to this couple, who represented the free press of the world alone for so many years of darkness. They were brave and faithful to an idea that can be trampled into the dust for some time but will ultimately win."

The next morning, on January 16, 1957, the four of us, with whatever luggage we could carry, crammed into Tom Rogers's station wagon to cross the Iron Curtain. Sarah Rogers and her daughters waved us good-bye.

A few hours later we reached the border. Everything was back to "normal." The road was snowy and deserted and we were the only customers at the border station. The guards must have received instructions from Budapest because they gave only a cursory glance at our passports and did not touch any of our suitcases. The barrier was lifted and the car rolled slowly over the no-man's-land to Austria.

Tom Rogers stopped the car some fifty yards from the barrier. Without saying a word he took out from somewhere a
bottle of brandy and three small glasses. We drank in silence. I
got out of the car and walked slowly back to the barrier to take
a last look at my country, which I was now leaving for good.
What I saw could have been described as peaceful. The snow-
covered flatland with leafless trees flanking the deserted road in
the early January dusk, the small building of the frontier
guards, and the lowered barrier, a memento that it was the
border between two worlds. Peaceful, probably, for others.
During the brief minutes I was standing there alone, my
memory flashed back and what I saw was not peaceful at all:
the horrors of Nazism, of the war and the siege, then Communism, the prison, and the drama of the revolution.

I turned and walked back to the car. I left my emotions at
the barrier and was ready to start a new life.

The two and a half months we spent in Vienna was one of
the happiest periods of my life. I worked in the AP office in the
Austrian capital and enjoyed the colorful, gay life of the city I
had known so intimately since my early childhood. As a young
boy I had often accompanied my parents to Vienna, sometimes
only to attend a performance in the Hofoper, and dine and
spend the night in the Sacher. I knew every corner of this delightful baroque city and its restaurants and museums. I loved
its sleepy-eyed women and enjoyed talking the Viennese drawl
so abhorred by a "real" German. In 1957, coming from the
darkness and sadness of postrevolutionary Budapest, I felt unashamedly happy in Vienna and often walked to my office
humming and whistling. We had congenial social and professional companions, John and Molly McCormack, Seymour and
Steva Freidin, Robert Delaney, then with the U.S. Information
Agency, and his wife Mary, and of course the cheery staff of
the AP office.

Ilona, however, felt differently. Though once again a "lady" whose only chore was to stroll along Kärtnerstrasse while Juli and Kati attended an English-language elementary school for British and American children, she had felt uneasy in Vienna from the beginning. The city was too close to the Hungarian border. It was flooded with refugees and with rumors, not always pleasant ones, including sinister tales about refugees having been kidnapped and dragged back to Hungary. Ilona had uneasy nights and uneasy days, too. The formerly fearless reporter who crawled with me through the snow-covered streets of Buda in a hail of bullets during the 1945 siege of the city, who boldly went through the police cordon to keep a rendezvous with a labor leader, became a frightened woman, wife, and mother, so we decided to leave the friendly soil of Austria and to move to the United States. The decision would have been easier had we known that our son, to be born in a Washington suburb eight months later, had already begun his journey through life.

During the weeks in Vienna, my job was to sum up the tragic story of Hungary. Detached from daily events, I could concentrate on the broader questions which still torment so many men in the free world. One was the Kádár puzzle; the second, why the Russians chose to use naked force to oppress the revolt; and the third, could the revolt have ended differently had the West acted somehow? I do not claim to have found the answers to these questions, though they have kept my mind busy for years. Nor, I confess, did I learn much then or later from the men in Vienna and in the United States who were familiar with the Hungarian question in their official capacity.

Kádár, who is neither a Communist intellectual nor an apparatchik, has puzzled me and many other observers of the Hungarian scene ever since 1956. How can one understand and explain this man who on November 1, 1956, shook his fist in the face of the Soviet ambassador Andropov, saying that he would "go into the streets and fight your tanks with my bare hands," and then, on the same night, defect to the Russians? Some scholars, less familiar with Kádár, thought the answer was simple: he put on an act to deceive Nagy. Those who know him, including myself, dismiss this theory, however convenient it might be. Kádár has never been an actor. He is a simple man who probably could give an amazingly simple explanation of his metamorphosis if somebody asked him the question. It is hard to understand why it has never been asked by any of his Western interviewers.

A locksmith in his younger years, Kádár was active in the young workers' movement in Hungary between the two wars and spent two and a half years in prison when Admiral Miklós Horthy ruled in the country. When the Nazis invaded Hungary in 1944, Kádár was a trusted lieutenant of László Rajk, the leader of the Communist wing of the resistance, whom he helped to the gallows in 1949.

After the war Rákosi admitted Kádár into the inner sanctum: the party's Politbureau. In 1946 he became deputy first secretary of the party, and when Rajk was earmarked for doom, succeeded to the ministry of the interior in 1948. Rákosi trusted Kádár to such an extent that he gave him a delicate personal chore: to persuade Rajk to confess at his trial.

Kádár did not know that Rákosi would not keep his word and permit Rajk to live in the Soviet Union after the trial and that Rajk would be executed. I know from someone who was very close to Kádár that ten years later he did not know that Nagy would be executed either. Both were heavy blows for Kádár, but he was and is first and foremost a loyal party member for whom personal loyalty must be secondary.

This service to Rákosi did not save him, however, and Kádár, who was neither fish, nor flesh, nor good red herring, neither a Moscowite like Rákosi or Gerö of the ingroup, nor a red-white-green Communist like Rajk, was arrested in May 1951. The patently ludicrous charge against him was identical with that against Rajk: Titoism. His trial in December 1951 was secret and he was held in solitary confinement for three years. Kádár had a miserable time in prison before his trial. He was tortured and once when he complained about thirst, Vladimir Farkas, son of defense minister Mihály Farkas, a Soviet citizen on "loan" to the AVH, urinated into Kádár's mouth. The often-heard rumor that Kádár was castrated is not true.

Kádár gained his release in August 1954 during Nagy's first premiership. He became party secretary of the important thirteenth district of Budapest, a far cry from the high positions he had held earlier, but more than a man stigmatized as a traitor could normally hope for. Kádár remained in the background until July 18, 1956, when at a historic meeting of the party's Central Committee he played a dominant role in Rákosi's ouster in Mikoyan's presence and undoubtedly with Mikoyan's consent.

Kádár's attitude during the dramatic weeks between July and the outbreak of the revolution was characterized by his middle-of-the-road stand between the two extreme ideologies in the Communist party which drifted farther away from each other every day. He obviously could never join Gerö, who replaced Rákosi as first secretary, because Gerö was just a replica of the ousted dictator. After Rákosi's fall Kádár again became a member of the Politbureau and of the party secretariat, and on October 28, during the revolution, he replaced Gerö as first secretary.

There can be no doubt that Kádár betrayed Nagy on November 1, when he thought the revolution had run off the Marxist-Leninist rails. It took Kádár some time to decide whether to remain loyal to the man to whom he owed his freedom, or to adhere to the conservative concept of Communism. Kádár obviously needed both support and prodding and he got it from various quarters, including Ferenc Münnich, the veteran Communist who played the sinister role of a Svengali behind Kádár, and from Mikoyan and Suslov, whom Kádár had met on November 1 when the two Moscow emissaries had apparently recognized that there was no way of holding Nagy back from the course which led to the denunciation of the Warsaw Pact.

Kádár's movements on November 1 were never explained by him or by anybody else, but the facts soon became fairly well known. In the mid-morning of that day there was the enraged encounter with Ambassador Andropov in Nagy's presence. In the afternoon Kádár probably met Mikoyan and Suslov. In the evening, around 9:30, Kádár delivered a radio speech announcing the formation of the Hungarian Socialist Workers party, the new version of the defunct Communist party, with himself as first secretary. Immediately after Kádár's speech, Münnich ordered a government car to Parliament, drove to Kádár's apartment, and from there the two proceeded to the Soviet embassy. There, according to the driver, they changed cars and were driven away in a Russian military vehicle.

That was definitely the last time Kádár and Münnich were seen in Budapest, in spite of the special report of the U.N. Committee on Hungary which erroneously stated that they had been seen in Parliament again on November 2. Yet Nagy apparently refused to draw the consequences of Kádár's disappearance and Kádár's name was included in the November 3 list of cabinet members, issued only twelve hours before the Soviet attack.

Where the Russians took János Kádár became known three years later when Kádár accompanied Khrushchev to Uzhgorod, the capital of Soviet Carpatho-Ukraine in December 1959. There Kádár acknowledged in a speech that he and several others who had turned their back on Nagy, converged on Uzhgorod on November 1, 1956, to sit out the "period of transition," meaning the time required for the Soviets to crush the revolt.

Characteristically, many Hungarians, especially workers who had maintained a grudging affection for Kádár, refused to believe that he had betrayed the revolution. There were the usual fairy tales that he had been kidnapped, that he had tried to flee to Tito, and had been taken forcibly to Uzhgorod. However attractive, the stories were without foundation.

I believe one should recall some of the statements that Kádár made before and after November 4, 1956, because some of these have since disappeared in the mists of Communist "unhistory." The words Kádár used in speeches or in his talks with workers' delegates do not put this man into any of the pigeonholes to which some chroniclers have tried to consign him.

For instance, on November 1, announcing the formation of the new Communist party, Kádár said, "I do not hesitate to say that the leaders who prepared this uprising came from our ranks," meaning that they were Communists. He warned of what he called the danger of a counterrevolution, but he also said that Hungarians "have proved with their blood their intention to support unflinchingly the government's efforts to ensure the complete withdrawal of Soviet forces. We do not want to be dependent any longer."

His tone was not much different on November 4, the day of the Soviet onslaught, when, using a weak radio transmitter, he announced the formation of his new government. He said: "On October 23 a mass movement began in our country whose noble purpose was to make good the antiparty and antinational mistakes committed by Rákosi and his accomplices and to defend the national independence and sovereignty of Hungary. . . . Under any pretext, we will not tolerate the persecution of workers for having taken part in the most recent events. . . . We shall invite representatives of other parties to assume ministries."

On November 15, already firmly in control, talking to workers' delegates in Parliament, and faithfully reported in the government's newspapers, Kádár said: "We surrender the party's monopoly; we want a multiparty system and clean and honest elections. We know that this will not be easy because the workers' power can be destroyed not only by bullets but also by ballots. We must reckon with the fact that we might be thoroughly beaten at the elections. . . . Nagy never has been an enemy of our system and I see no reason why he should not resume a position in public life."

In addition Kádár made two statements which in my judgment should weigh in any assessment of this man. One he made in November 1962, when he boldly rephrased an old Communist dogma and said that "whoever is not against us is with us." This was a sharp and courageous reversal of the old Stalinist concept followed by Rákosi, that "whoever is not for us is against us." When the idea was translated into practice, it meant enormous changes in the lives of millions of Hungarians. In its practical application it meant the admission to higher education of qualified young people irrespective of their "social" origin, which previously had been the decisive factor. It meant the appointment of non-Communists to jobs previously reserved for party members and, perhaps most importantly, it often meant the opportunity to breathe more freely.

The other Kádár statement was far less significant, yet I believe it should not be ignored. A few days after Khrushchev's unexpected ouster in 1964, after his return to Budapest from a trip to Poland, Kádár was asked by an unusually inquisitive Hungarian newsman about the fallen Russian Communist chief. Kádár pondered and then said in a low and tormented voice that he would advise Hungarians not to be ashamed of their friendly feelings toward Khrushchev, whatever has happened to him. One may question the "friendly feelings" of Hungarians toward Khrushchev, yet what Kádár said was an unusual manifestation of personal loyalty, definitely unusual in the Communist world where even today continued friendly feelings toward a fallen leader may be dangerous. Somehow the exchange reminded me of Dean Acheson's famous words at a State Department press conference on January 25, 1950: "My friendship is not easily given or easily withdrawn. I do not intend to turn my back on Alger Hiss."

Kádár was undoubtedly Khrushchev's favorite satellite leader between 1956 and 1964. When Khrushchev and six Eastern European Communist leaders attended the U.N. General Assembly in 1960, I watched this little flock closely for weeks in the vast building on the East River. Khrushchev completely ignored most of them: Czechoslovakia's Antonin Novotny, Gheorghe Gheorghiu-Dej of Romania, Todor Zhivkov of Bulgaria, and Albania's Mehmet Shehu. He listened carefully, however, to Poland's Wladyslaw Gomulka and permitted him a certain leeway in conferring with other dignitaries, ranging from Cuba's Fidel Castro to Christian Herter, then the secretary of state.

Kádár's status clearly rested between those two extremes. Khrushchev overlooked the others, but always had a smile or a friendly pat for the shy Hungarian. Watching this strange group in a huddle in the lounges of the United Nations, one had the feeling that the ebullient Russian had a harem of six of whom Kádár was the favorite. The four others were discarded concubines and Gomulka was firmly in the position of the number-one wife.

Like all the others, Kádár addressed the General Assembly, but he became strangely apologetic in the concluding phrases of his speech. Defending his role in 1956 he said: "I personally have often been the target of attacks. I am a worker. Man can make mistakes and be in error. I did what I had to do."

This admittedly incomplete profile of Kádár cannot be completed without investigating briefly how the situation in Hungary has changed in the fourteen years of his rule. Kádár is not a Stalinist and does not like prisons because he has been imprisoned himself. But in 1957 and 1958 he did resort to the harshest Stalinist methods, including the frequent use of the gallows, to eradicate the lingering memory of October 1956. Within the

Communist system, which means the dictatorship of a small minority (and not the dictatorship of the working class, as the Communists claim), this was probably the only way to discourage Magyars from trying again what they had tried in 1956. The traumatic experience of the revolt was not forgotten and Hungarians now have an instinctive knowledge of where the limits of freedom lie.

One of Nagy's gravest political mistakes was that he let himself be pushed into bypassing a phase of evolution. His backers hoped to develop Hungary from a small component of the monolithic Moscow empire directly into an independent neutral country with a multiparty system, skipping the in-between phase of limited sovereignty within the Moscow bloc. This was, and remains, unacceptable to the Soviet leadership which has, one should acknowledge, since 1953 made concessions inconceivable under Stalin, by permitting the complete elimination of Moscowite bosses in every bloc country except East Germany, where Walter Ulbricht is still on top. In Hungary Kádár was chosen to be the nationalist-Communist leader and Khrushchev could not have found a man more faithful to the Soviet Union.

After 1958 and Nagy's execution, Kádár slowly and without fanfare committed himself to the road of political and economic liberalization with the result that in 1970 in Hungary there is more freedom, a fuller plate — Khrushchev called the post-1956 version of Hungarian Communism "goulash socialism" — and less evidence of police rule than in any other bloc country in Eastern Europe. The healing of the wounds of 1956 has reached the point where even suspicious critics of the regime acknowledge that Kádár has adopted some of the aims of the revolt and that the average Hungarian has more personal freedom than the citizen of any other Soviet bloc country, including Poland, Romania — a country which proclaimed its independence in foreign affairs, but domestically remains rigidly

Stalinist — and, since the ignominious end of the Dubcek era, Czechoslovakia.

Kádár himself is popular — however reluctantly one may use this word — probably more so among non-Communists than among party members. The non-Communists seem to remember that it was Kádár's "whoever is not against us is for us" policy which permitted them to participate if not in the political, then in the economic, social, and artistic life of the country. Most of these elements believe that the present live-and-let-live situation in Hungary depends on Kádár's ability to survive. Twice Kádár disappeared for weeks, first after Khrushchev's ouster in 1964 and again in 1968 when Dubcek was booted out. On both occasions there was grave concern that Kádár would be pushed aside as well. Nobody was dreaming about a change for the better — such dreams were killed in 1956 — but there was widespread anxiety that a man more to the left, perhaps an outright Stalinist, would replace Kádár.

It was well known in the State Department that Kádár played a special role in the Czechoslovak tragedy. In 1968, before the invasion of that country, his task was to plead with Dubcek, to warn him, to stop him at the last moment. Details of his mission are still obscure, but American specialists in Eastern European affairs seem to know that this was the purpose of Kádár's secret meeting with Dubcek on the Hungarian-Czech border forty-eight hours before the Soviet army moved into Czechoslovakia. Many say the meeting with Dubcek took place under orders from Moscow, but according to another theory Kádár acted on his own, reminding Dubcek of his own country's bitter experience of going too far too fast.

One year after the Czech invasion Kádár advised Dubcek's successor, Gustav Husak, how to dance on eggshells between the extreme conservatives and the Dubcek moderates. The Hungarian is an appropriate adviser because he has proved that it can be done. The Hungarian newspapers also echoed Kádár's advice and counseled "Kádárization" in Czechoslovakia, meaning reconciliation with former adversaries.

Kádár had cautioned Husak against hard-line excesses such as purges of progressives. During a visit to Prague in December 1969, the Hungarian lectured at a press conference on the virtues of conservative moderation. His remarks were faithfully reported in *Népszabadság,* the paper of the Hungarian Communist party, which openly warned Czech comrades against permitting ultraconservatives to pursue private vendettas against liberal elements. (This was also a clear indication of nervousness in Hungary about the course of events in Prague.)

Kádár and his aides are remarkably skillful and cautious in denying the Russians any potential excuse to interfere in Hungary. To mention only one example, the new economic concept in Hungary, which gives greater scope to competition and other market forces, is closely watched by the Soviets with grave skepticism and unconcealed suspicion. The plan, officially called the New Economic Mechanism, is virtually identical with that introduced by Dubcek, but too ostentatiously. For some time Moscow has been sending economists to Hungary to snoop around and find out what is really going on. The Russian experts are received in the ministries in Budapest with the greatest courtesy and are escorted with great reverence to the plants where the new system has been introduced. There they are told with a great flourish that without Soviet help economic progress would have been inconceivable and they are assured that the Hungarian economic experiment is in accordance with Marxist tenets. But that is about all the Russians ever learn and most of them return to their country more confused than ever.

The New Economic Mechanism may represent a giant step toward a consumer society, discarding the earlier sacrosanct system based on central planning. Going far beyond the cautious decentralization in the Soviet Union, it gives workers a share of the profit and permits competition among producers.

Prices of a great number of consumer goods were freed, though prices of basic foodstuffs, such as butter and milk, remained fixed. Imports are free of price controls. There is some inflation and housewives grumble, but probably no more so than elsewhere. Thousands of small enterprises, mostly in the service industries, were permitted to open workshops.

Commerce and industry are not the only fields where the scope of liberty has been gradually widened. A government decree, for instance, said that "every Hungarian citizen has the right to obtain a passport and travel abroad providing that he complies with conditions stated in the laws." Whatever this reservation means, this right to travel has no parallel elsewhere in Eastern Europe.

Consequently, more than a hundred thousand Hungarians travel to the West each year, though they could not do so without financial help from relatives and friends living abroad. The number of defections is negligible. The number of tourists visiting Hungary, including many former Hungarians, is far greater and might reach half a million a year, bringing badly needed foreign currency to the country.

There is much less to boast about politically and only few remember Kádár's promise to reintroduce the multiparty system. Though all candidates for Parliament belong to the Popular Front, a paper façade of the Communist party, in several constituencies the voter can now choose between two or more candidates. Parliament remains a rubber-stamping body, but there is now a question period and more and more members of the House venture to ask the ministers probing questions.

Kádár, I believe, discovered the only way to "coexist" with the Soviet Union, the senior partner of the bloc, and also to please his countrymen. To provoke the Soviet Union is to court disaster and this is well remembered by Hungarians. Kádár has turned out to be a realist whose job is to appease both the imperialist power in Moscow and the revolutionary movement at home. It is obviously too early to say whether he has succeeded, but the fact that he is still in power after fourteen years, and that he can walk on the streets and mingle with the people, the vast majority of whom are definitely not Communist, indicates a considerable degree of success. But I doubt that the Magyars have forgotten that on November 4, 1956, he came in on the backs of Soviet tanks.

15

"What Could We Have Done?"

Why the revolution took place and why the Russians suppressed it with force, and why the West did nothing, are extremely complex questions whose solutions must await the verdict of history. My own answers are based on endless discussions with Hungarians and others who were connected with the revolt, and on the study of documents available at the State Department and elsewhere, including the papers in the Dulles library at Princeton University.

Stalin's empire became a giant with feet of clay after the dictator's death in 1953. The weakening of the political center resulted in a slow loss of control of the satellites. Revolts usually break out in a period of relaxation when, for whatever reasons, a dictator loosens his iron grip. In 1956 this process was speeded up by Khrushchev's denunciation of Stalin's crimes at the Twentieth Party Congress. In at least two countries of Eastern Europe, Poland and Hungary, 1956 was a year of "liberalization." Many of Stalin's proconsuls were ousted, thousands of political prisoners were released and rehabilitated.

The peculiar aspect of the Hungarian revolution was that the privileged workers, students, and writers revolted. Many if not most of them were Communist party members and some were convinced Communists. The bourgeoisie and the farmers who had been really tormented and persecuted during the ten years before the revolt were suspicious, scared, and preferred to watch the drama from the sidelines. One of them acknowledged this in a book published in the United States four years after the revolution.

The author, József Kővágó, was a former army officer, engineer, anti-Nazi resistance leader, mayor of Budapest after the war, member of Parliament, Rákosi's prisoner, and finally, mayor of Budapest again for a few days during the revolt. He wrote in *You Are All Alone* that he had at first suspected a Moscow-planned plot and only "slowly but inevitably" had come to the conclusion that he too should take part in the revolt.

Kővágó was an extremely honest and brave man who could boast of having been jailed both by the Nazis and the Communists, and he was by no means alone in his hesitancy. We shall never know if the revolution might have turned out otherwise had Kővágó and other leaders pondered less and joined earlier.

"Liberalization," as the softening of the Communist dictatorship was called, permitted the revival of nationalism which caused rebellion in Poland and in Hungary in 1956, and in Czechoslovakia in 1968. This nationalism has gradually eroded the Soviet Union's political authority in Eastern Europe. Kremlinologist Zbigniew Brzezinski told an audience at the State Department during the Johnson era that nationalism has become the strongest force in Eastern Europe, stronger than ideology, stronger than the Communist parties themselves. "Eastern Europe is where the dream of Communist internationalism lies buried," Brzezinski said.

Not even the Magyars, whose history is crowded with rebellions against foreign domination and oppression, would have dared to revolt before Stalin's death. But when a dictatorship decides that it can relax its firm grip, the oppressed first dream about more freedom, then whisper about it, finally they shout, and intoxicated by their own screams, they revolt. That was what happened in Hungary in 1956.

After I arrived in the free world in 1957, I was appalled to hear from well-meaning non-Hungarians such a variety of superficial theories about why the revolt broke out. They did not consider the simple fact that Moscow itself encouraged, however unintentionally, the trend of liberalization and the rebirth of nationalism. I heard speculations that "unbearable" economic hardships caused the Magyars to revolt, and that Communist writers, permitted for the first time to visit Vienna, made unfavorable comparisons after their return to Budapest and thereby sparked the events of October. What nonsense! No Hungarian rebelled for economic reasons but virtually the entire nation was willing to fight against hopeless odds to gain freedom.

The second question, why the revolt was crushed with force, can really be answered simply: because the Soviet Union could not tolerate the defection of another one of its satellites. In 1948, when Yugoslavia fell into heresy and got away with it, I was convinced that only Stalin with his immense prestige and distaste for foreign adventure could have prevented the "disciplinary action" against Yugoslavia which, as is now known, the Soviet military requested. Stalin was never an international revolutionary like Trotsky, although, of course, this did not hinder him from grabbing whatever he could when the opportunity arose to do so without risk. He snatched the unhappy Baltic states with Hitler's blessing and extended Communist rule over Eastern Europe, thanks to a tacit agreement with the West which I will discuss later. But bringing Yugoslavia back into the fold would have meant a cruel guerrilla war, and Stalin was not anxious to wage it, especially in a period when he had the Berlin crisis on his hands.

What Stalin had tolerated unhappily in 1948, his far more adventurous successor, Khrushchev, could not tolerate in 1956.

The Communists do not know how to cope with dissent — if they did, they would not be Communists — and the only way they know to handle opposition is to suppress it.

In 1956 Moscow was caught as flat-footed as every other country. The 1953 East Berlin uprising was just an episode, though, in retrospect, it should have been a good warning of things to come. The changes in Poland in 1956 did not challenge that country's allegiance to the Soviet Union, so there was no strong repression. But in Hungary the Communist system collapsed, the party and its organs disintegrated, its new leader denounced the Warsaw Pact and proclaimed neutrality, and a whole nation went to war. The reaction of Moscow was to dispatch an entire army from the Carpathian Military District, commanded by General P. I. Batov. According to some American estimates thirteen thousand Hungarians died, while such a cautious neutral observer as Nehru said that twenty-five thousand Hungarians and seven thousand Russians were killed during the fighting.

Because the revolution came as a surprise, the decision in Moscow to use force in putting it down was neither immediate nor unanimous. During the Mikoyan-Suslov visits to Budapest, word had leaked out about the endless debates in the Kremlin on how to handle the revolt. Khrushchev himself, in a speech he made at the Budapest Mavag factory on December 2, 1959, acknowledged that the Russian Communist leaders were divided about the course to be followed. Those who were for ruthless intervention, led by Marshal G. Zhukov, gained the upper hand only when it became clear that Mikoyan and Suslov could not avert disaster, meaning the denunciation of the Warsaw Pact. According to all the accounts I heard in those days in Budapest, Khrushchev himself was at first inclined to let Hungary go and he had the powerful support of Mikoyan, while Suslov advocated a tough stance. There is good reason to believe that on October 29 Moscow had accepted the unpleasant fact that Hungary might become a second Yugoslavia. But three days later, on November 1, when the Nagy government went beyond the point of possible Soviet acceptance, the Kremlin agreed upon the course of military intervention and repression.

Khrushchev had not foreseen the ultimate effects of piecemeal reforms in the satellites, nor of his reconciliation with Tito, nor the impact of his denunciation of Stalin. But he could not tolerate two vital points in Nagy's final program: Hungary's secession from the Warsaw Pact linked to a declaration of neutrality, and the restoration of a multiparty system. No real Communist, and Nagy at that point could not be regarded as such, could accept the principle of a multiparty system, which, he must believe, is a perversion of Marxism. One should not forget that even Tito has firmly rejected the idea of having a Marxist-Socialist party in Yugoslavia. Khrushchev, who liked folksy comparisons, once told a group of visiting Frenchmen in 1956 that "to allow another party is the same as to permit of one's own free will a flea into one's shirt."

The question has been raised in several analyses: would Khrushchev have dared to send his armies into Hungary had there been no Suez crisis? A negative answer sounds attractive but I do not believe it would be correct. Of course the Suez incident helped protect the invasion of Hungary from world opinion because the West was bitterly divided and the United Nations was preoccupied with the Middle East. But I am convinced that after November 1, 1956, the Soviet Union had to act as an imperialist power and would have invaded even without a simultaneous Suez war. The 1968 military intervention in Czechoslovakia, when the Soviets used force with far less "justification" than they had in 1956, occurred when the West was not preoccupied with an internal quarrel.

The Soviets did not fear Western military countermeasures in 1956 nor in 1968 because they were firmly convinced that both Hungary and Czechoslovakia belonged within their sphere of influence which, in their vocabulary, is identical with sphere of domination. The harsh facts of geopolitics unfortunately justify Moscow's contention, together with the secret and not-so-secret wartime agreements between the Big Three.

This brings me to the question which still, twenty-five years after the war, makes the U.S. State Department jumpy: just what were those agreements between the Big Three to divide up the world?

In 1968 when it became clear that the United States would not go beyond tongue-lashing the Soviet Union for the invasion of Czechoslovakia, Dean Rusk, secretary of state of Presidents Kennedy and Johnson, heatedly protested that there never had been a pact nor even an "understanding" with Moscow on spheres of influence. The United States, Rusk stated, did not and does not recognize such spheres. He insisted that the Yalta conference endorsed the right of self-determination of every country to be liberated from Hitler's rule.

Rusk was technically correct. The popular contention that the nations of Eastern Europe were sold down the river at Yalta is wrong. In fact they were betrayed much earlier, in October 1944. The most celebrated chronicler of the era, Winston Churchill, says in his World War II memoirs that he himself proposed to Stalin a division of Eastern Europe.

Because of the many misconceptions of how this happened and why, I believe it is worthwhile to look back to October 1944. The quotations I use are partly from the volume of *Foreign Relations of the United States, 1944,* issued by the State Department, and partly from *Triumph and Tragedy,* the sixth volume of Churchill's narrative of World War II.

There is no doubt that Churchill had grave misgivings as early as 1943 about what was going to happen in Eastern Europe after the war. The "Former Naval Person," as he signed his messages to Roosevelt, frequently pleaded with the President of the United States to prevent that area of the world from fighting its way out of the frying pan into the fire, to be liberated from Hitler only to be subjugated by Stalin. Roosevelt ignored Churchill's warnings.

"Are we going to acquiesce in the communization of the Balkans?" Churchill asked Anthony Eden, his foreign secretary, in a bitter note on May 4, 1944.

By then Washington had made it quite clear to Churchill that it neither wanted to open a new front in the Balkans, nor would it agree to any postwar spheres of influence in the area. As Churchill remarked in his memoirs: "The first reactions of the State Department were cool. Mr. Hull was nervous of any suggestion that might appear to savour of the creation or acceptance of the idea of spheres of influence."

Cordell Hull, the secretary of state, was more than "nervous." Reporting on the Moscow foreign ministers' conference to the joint session of Congress on November 18, 1943, he made a major policy statement about the world he envisaged after Hitler's defeat: ". . . There will no longer be need for spheres of influence, for alliances, for balance of power or any other of the separate alliances through which, in the unhappy past, the nations strove to safeguard their security or to promote their interests." In retrospect one cannot fail to wonder at such a degree of naiveté. Ten years later John Foster Dulles concluded more alliances than the United States had ever had.

Churchill left London for Moscow on October 7, 1944. Roosevelt forbade Averell Harriman, his ambassador to the Russian capital, to participate in the Churchill-Stalin meetings except as an observer, which Harriman resented. President Roosevelt made it quite clear that he did not trust his two wartime allies. Harriman went to the airport to welcome Churchill on October 9 and wrote the same day to Roosevelt that the British prime minister "was disappointed that you did not make the discussions triangular by sending General Marshall or Stettinius or by giving me authority to participate, but that you had made it plain that I should be an observer only. Under the circumstances, he said that he thought it was better for me not to participate in his tête-à-tête talks with Stalin."

But Harriman was present at the historic occasion when Churchill and Stalin carved up Eastern Europe into spheres of influence. It happened at a 10 P.M. meeting in the Kremlin on October 9. It was an exclusive affair with only Stalin, Churchill, Eden, Molotov, Harriman, and two interpreters present. This is how Churchill described what happened:

"The moment was apt for business, so I said: 'Let us settle about our affairs in the Balkans,' " and he wrote out on a half-sheet of paper:

Romania: Russia 90 percent, the others 10 percent;

Greece: Britain (in accord with the USA) 90 percent, Russia 10 percent; Yugoslavia: 50–50 percent; Hungary: 50–50 percent (the percentage for Hungary was changed later to 75–25 percent in the Soviets' favor); Bulgaria: Russia 75 percent, the others 25 percent.

"I pushed this across to Stalin. . . . There was a slight pause. Then he took his blue pencil and made a large tick upon it, and passed it back to us. It was settled in no more time than it takes to set it down."

"Again there was a long silence," Churchill continued his reminiscence. "The pencilled paper lay in the centre of the table. At length I said: 'Might it not be thought rather cynical if it seemed we had disposed of these issues so fateful for millions of people, in such an offhand manner? Let us burn the paper.' 'No, you keep it,' said Stalin."

Was this a bad joke? Did Churchill believe that it would work? Can anybody believe that some neutral arbiter could successfully decide with a slide rule what the West's fifty percent interest in Yugoslavia would mean in practice? Could Churchill believe that the Red Army, by then deep on Hungarian soil, would ever permit the West to claim its twenty-five percent in that country, whatever that might mean in practical terms, or, vice versa, that the British and the Americans would grant Russia its ten percent in Greece? I submit that this arithmetical exercise in Stalin's Kremlin study was both childish and preposterous.

Yet perhaps Churchill had a good reason for proposing what appears to have been a cynical distribution of Eastern Europe. By then he must have known that Roosevelt, supported by no less an authority than George Marshall, would never agree to an invasion through the Balkans, Europe's "soft underbelly," and what he did was a last attempt to limit Stalin's control of that area. It was, of course, doomed to fail.

There was no such "division" made that night in the Kremlin concerning Poland and Czechoslovakia. These two were Nazi-occupied countries and Hitler's impending defeat was to return complete sovereignty to them, independent of domination by any great power. The Soviets, of course, did not see things this way. Every country they "liberated," whether allied Poland or enemy Hungary, shared the same fate, and no Western influence was to be tolerated in either.

If the United States knew about the deal in Moscow, there is no evidence of it, even though Harriman was present. In the many messages exchanged between Moscow and Washington during Churchill's stay in the Russian capital there was no word about the cynical percentages agreed to by the British prime minister and Stalin. On October 10, one day after the Kremlin pact, Harriman wrote to Roosevelt that, "On matters in the Balkans, Churchill and Eden will try to work out some sort of spheres of influence with the Russians." The same day, after a Kremlin luncheon at which Harriman sat next to Churchill and Stalin, he reported that Churchill had "prepared a draft of last night's discussions which is now being sent to you with certain modifications by Stalin. The most important change Stalin made related to the Balkans. After the sentence that tells of their talks regarding the Balkan countries, Churchill had included the words: 'having regard to our varying duty towards them.' The implication of this phrase was clearly a recognition of a sphere of influence of Russia and Britain in the several countries. Stalin crossed this phrase out and Churchill agreed. After lunch, talking across Churchill, I told Stalin that you would be very glad that he had eliminated this phrase."

Did Churchill and Stalin collude to hoodwink the sick man in the White House, to conceal from him that they had agreed the previous night on the fate of the Balkans? Only they could have answered the question and they did not.

On October 11, the following day, Churchill drafted a letter to Stalin which he did not send, "deeming it wiser to let well alone," as he remarked in his memoirs. But he included the draft in his book: "These percentages which I have put down are no more than a method by which in our thoughts we can see how near we are together. . . . As I said, they would be considered crude, and even callous, if they were exposed to the scrutiny of the foreign offices and diplomats all over the world. Therefore they could not be the basis of any public document, certainly not at the present time. They might however be a good guide for the conduct of our affairs." What a curious example of secret diplomacy.

Also on October 11 Roosevelt replied to Harriman's October 9 message on the envoy's participation in the bilateral summit. "In regard to your participation in current conferences between Churchill and Stalin it is, of course, inadvisable for you to attempt to break into tête-à-têtes." And on the same day the President, in another message to Harriman, made it again unmistakably clear how limited his interest was in the future of Eastern Europe. He wrote: "My active interest in the present time in the Balkan area is that such steps as are practicable should be taken to insure against the Balkans getting us into a future international war."

On the same day and on October 12 several messages tried to assure Roosevelt that nothing really appalling had been agreed upon between Churchill and Stalin. On October 11 Harriman

messaged that "in regard to the Balkan countries and Hungary
. . . Churchill had been using the unpopular term 'spheres of
influence,' but as Eden describes his objectives, it is [sic] to
work out a practical agreement on how the problems of each
country are going to be dealt with." On the same day Churchill did a little whitewashing in a separate message to the American President: "It is absolutely necessary that we should try to
get a common mind about the Balkans, so that we may prevent
civil war breaking out in several countries when probably you
and I would be in sympathy with one side and U.J. [Uncle Joe,
meaning Stalin] with the other." In another message Harriman
told Roosevelt that "Eden and Molotov agreed that the Allied
Control Commissions should be under Russian commanders
during the period of hostilities but that hereafter the Control
Commissions should be made genuinely tripartite with equal
authority of each member but with Soviet chairmanship."
Molotov's promise, of course, was never kept and the American and British elements of the Allied Control Commissions in
Eastern Europe remained impotent observers of the complete
communization of those countries.

Nothing illustrates this involuntary impotence better than a
bitter report sent by Major General John A. Crane, American
representative on the Allied Control Commission in Bulgaria,
to the Joint Chiefs of Staff on February 4, 1946, long after the
"period of hostilities" when the commissions should have been
made "genuinely tripartite."

"Ever since our arrival here we have been in a most humiliat-
ing position," wrote General Crane. "Restrictions put on our
movement . . . have made us and America the laughingstock
not only of the Russians but of the Bulgarians. . . . For the
first time in my life I have had to hang my head with shame
that my country should permit such treatment of her representatives. . . . It infuriates me to have to go with my hat in
hand and beg the Russians: 'Please, Sir, may I bring a plane

next week, may I bring Private Jones to my detachment. Please, Sir, can I bring ten bags of coffee, two field telephones. Please, Sir, may I go to London the day after tomorrow.'

"These peoples, both Russians and Bulgarians, have respect for one thing, and that is force. Every time we compromise with them and give them anything, we lose. I am afraid we are following the policy of appeasement of the late Mr. Chamberlain," the general's report concluded. Dozens of similar though perhaps more diplomatic reports were written from all Communist capitals where unhappy American generals experienced the same treatment — and the same indifference in Washington.

Finally, on October 12 Churchill explained the situation to his cabinet from Moscow. "The system of percentages," he wrote, "is not intended to be more than a guide, and of course in no way commits the U.S., nor does it attempt to set up a rigid system of spheres of interest." In the same letter Churchill singled out Hungary when, in an obvious attempt to explain why he agreed to a 75–25 percent change of the original 50–50 of the spheres in that country, he said: "As it is the Soviet armies which are obtaining control of Hungary, it would be natural that a major share of influence should rest with them, subject of course to agreement with Great Britain and probably the U.S., who, though not actually operating in Hungary, must view it as Central European and not a Balkan state." It may be a small consolation for the Hungarians that Britain's wartime leader recognized what every schoolboy knew, that Hungary was neither geographically nor otherwise in the Balkans.

Whatever the explanations coming from Moscow, Washington did not believe them and insisted that no spheres of influence could be tolerated in the postwar world. A State Department "briefing paper," prepared for the 1945 Yalta Conference of the Big Three, said that the 1943 Moscow foreign ministers' conference "definitely rejected the spheres of influence idea. . . . Any arrangement suggestive of spheres of influence can-

not but militate against the establishment and effective func-
tioning of a broader system of general security," meaning obviously the United Nations. Nevertheless, the briefing paper
added with some resignation, "the evolution of events in recent
months indicates that the British and Soviet governments are in
fact operating under such an arrangement."

Although everybody in Washington, beginning with Hull
and ending with Rusk, has vehemently protested against
spheres of influence, it should not be forgotten that the United
States itself set the example with the 1823 Monroe Doctrine.
Stalin always had a healthy respect for the Monroe Doctrine
and I firmly believe that he would have never agreed to Khrushchev's 1962 gamble of smuggling missiles into Cuba.

Words, however, have different meanings in the two halves
of the world. President Kennedy forced Khrushchev to withdraw his missiles because Cuba, whatever government it had,
remained in America's sphere of influence. But apart from the
abortive Bay of Pigs adventure, the United States made no serious effort to get rid of Castro's Communist regime in Cuba. In
the Communist vocabulary, on the other hand, to belong to
Russia's sphere of influence means complete subordination, as
Hungary in 1956 and Czechoslovakia in 1968 have proved.

Although spheres of influence, as Rusk's statement showed,
remained taboo in Washington, there is no way of escaping the
hard fact that such spheres are a reality. Simplifications are
sometimes in order: American reluctance to go to war to save
Hungarians or Czechs who are fighting for freedom, and Soviet willingness to lose face and withdraw the missiles from
Cuba instead of risking war, mean nothing less than the tacit
acknowledgment that Hungary and Czechoslovakia are in the
Soviet orbit, and Cuba in the United States sphere of interest,
whatever Imre Nagy, Alexander Dubcek, or Fidel Castro might
think about it.

Many pragmatic writers who could afford to be less hypo-
critical than apparently the politicians or diplomats must be,

openly concede that spheres of influence are not only tough facts of life but can be, "if properly defined, the best diplomatic formula we have in the present state of world affairs for working out a bearable compromise between the giant states," as James Reston put it in a *New York Times* column after the Soviet aggression against Czechoslovakia.

The spheres of influence doctrine, said Reston, "is a device for keeping the great powers from getting into critical disputes in areas where one or the other feels it must risk war to defend its vital interests. It is not a fair doctrine," Reston admitted, "for it puts the small neighbors at a serious disadvantage with the giants, but it is a practical formula for minimizing the tensions between the nations that have the power to start a world war."

"Whether we like it or not," Reston continued, "the world is coming back to power politics (what other kind are there?), to the balance of power, and to spheres of influence. It has never really departed from them. . . . The trouble is not that Moscow and Washington have defined their spheres of influence, but that they haven't. They have not agreed on what a sphere of influence is and what it isn't, or where their respective spheres lie, but this is probably coming in the next phase of U.S.-Soviet relations."

Concerning Reston's prophecy, I have my doubts. Neither the United States nor Soviet Russia can afford the burst of outrage from all quarters that would inevitably follow if they agreed publicly on how to divide the world among themselves. A secret agreement, a convenient device of an earlier era, would not remain secret for long.

Walter Lippmann endorsed the spheres of influence doctrine several years before Reston. "Recognition of spheres of influence," he wrote, "is a true alternative of globalism. It is the alternative to Communist globalism which proclaims a universal revolution. It is the alternative to anti-Communist globalism which promises to fight anti-Communist wars everywhere.

... The acceptance of spheres of influence has been the dominant foundation of the détente in Europe between the Soviet Union and the West. Eventually it will provide the formula for coexistence between Red China and the United States."

One question remains to be discussed and I do it with a heavy heart. Could the revolt have ended differently had the West raised a finger to help?

Obviously I do not know the answer and anybody who claims he does is irresponsible. Based on the Churchill-Stalin deal of 1944, the Soviets considered Hungary as belonging in their backyard.

Yet — and this must be stressed — this neither explains nor excuses the West's depressingly negative attitude during the few days when something could have been done, between October 23, the outbreak of the revolution, and November 4, the day of the Soviet onslaught. It is a sad matter of historic record that virtually nothing was done.

I should make it quite clear that by "something" I do not mean military intervention. There might have been a few daydreamers in Hungary who turned their heads toward the sky waiting for American paratroopers to be dropped, but I did not meet any, though I talked to many hundreds from all walks of life during those dramatic weeks. None of the serious workers of Csepel whom I admired so much ever raised the question when talking to me: "Where are the GIs? When do they arrive?" But I did hear time and again the question: "Where is Hammarskjöld? Why doesn't he come?" and also: "What are the Western diplomats doing?" I had no answer then. I am afraid I have no answers today either.

A Black Panther leader once said that violence is as American as apple pie. He might have been right but I would add that so is the feeling of guilt. During my weeks in Vienna and for years in Washington, the humble and the mighty asked me the self-tormenting question: "What could we have done?"

Two years after our arrival to the United States we moved to another house. On the first Saturday in this new house I was working in the yard when the mailman came. When I thanked him, he looked at me and asked, "What accent?" I explained that I came from Hungary, a little red in the face that a brief "thank you" should be enough for him to detect a foreign accent. The mailman fidgeted with the bundle of mail in his hands and then asked the question which I have heard so many times before: "What could we have done?"

My answer to the mailman was the same one I have given on university campuses and at the State Department. "You should have done something, and you did nothing."

In a strongly worded *mea culpa*, the House Committee on Foreign Affairs called the West's failure to help Hungarians "the lost opportunity of our generation." The committee's statement was a bitter charge, accusing the Eisenhower administration of sitting on its hands. And there is much truth in it.

The domestic circumstances in the United States at the time were tragically unfortunate for Hungary. The revolt broke out only two weeks before the national elections in the United States, and on November 3, some twelve hours before the Russian onslaught on Budapest, John Foster Dulles, the man responsible for shaping America's foreign affairs, was operated on for cancer at Walter Reed Hospital.

The transcript of the State Department press briefing on November 4 is interesting reading, though it is a bitter pill for a Hungarian. The briefing was held by Lincoln White, then the Department's press spokesman, at Walter Reed at 3:10 in the afternoon. The transcript was five pages long, double spaced — and no question was asked about Hungary, and White had nothing to volunteer. It was the day the Russians attacked Budapest after having kidnapped General Maléter, and the day Cardinal Mindszenty found refuge in the U.S. legation. It was a Sunday and there was no press briefing at the White House.

Do the elections, sickness, and preoccupation with Suez explain the almost fatalistic do-nothing reaction in Washington, or the disinterest of my Washington press colleagues on November 4, the day when the wires from Europe carried little else but Nagy's frantic appeals from Budapest? They might explain it, but hardly justify it. A great power cannot afford to turn its back to the world, even temporarily.

There is no doubt in my mind that the United States was completely unprepared for the revolt, despite the many signs which strongly indicated that something might erupt in Hungary. If evidence is needed that Washington was off-guard, there is some. Since the summer of 1956 there had been no American minister in Budapest, so the legation was without a master during those exciting months of the ferment.

For about a week the legal Hungarian government of Imre Nagy waited in vain for some diplomatic support from the West, primarily, of course, from the United States. Nagy's appeal to the United Nations, proclaiming his country's neutrality and asking that "the defense of this neutrality by the Four Great Powers . . . be put on the agenda" reached the United Nations at 12:27 P.M. of November 1, two and a half days before the Red Army struck. Yet nothing happened during those days. The august body on the East River could not extricate itself from the Suez debate, and there was not a word from Washington.

Finally, in the afternoon of November 3, on the insistence of some delegations, but not that of the United States, the Security Council met to discuss Nagy's appeal. There was, however, no discussion. The Yugoslav delegate moved for an adjournment because negotiations on the withdrawal of Russian troops had already started between the Soviet Union and Hungary. That was all right from a Yugoslav; nobody would have expected anything else from him. But it was hardly to be expected that Henry Cabot Lodge, the United States delegate, would support the proposal. "We believe," Lodge said, "that adjournment for a day or two would give a real opportunity to the Hungarian government to carry out its announced desire to arrange for an orderly and immediate evacuation of all the Soviet troops." Did Lodge really believe in such an "opportunity"?

Anthony Eden gave a devastating assessment in his book *Full Circle* in 1960. "Five days passed without any Council meeting on Hungary, despite repeated attempts by ourselves and others to bring one about. The U.S. representative was reluctant, and voiced his suspicion that we were urging the Hungarian situation to divert attention from Suez. The U.S. government appeared in no hurry to move. Their attitude provided a damaging contrast to the alacrity they were showing in arraigning the French and ourselves." Though Eden, whose political career was broken by the Suez debacle, was hardly an unbiased observer, his facts are correct.

Many years later Lodge conceded that the West left Hungary in the lurch. In an interview on February 16, 1965, deposited among the Dulles papers at Princeton, he said that ". . . the United Nations failed on Hungary — so did the United States, incidentally, and so did everybody else." But Lodge apparently felt he should explain his role ten years earlier: "It looked as though, at that time, you couldn't rectify the brutal actions taken with regard to Hungary without starting World War III. There didn't seem any way to do it except to put in troops. And I must say, with the advantage of hindsight, it still seems to me that was a realistic judgment. It was dreadful, a dreadful thing."

To put in troops, as Lodge said, would have been of course one of the alternatives, but, as I said, nobody in Hungary really expected it. But, to use the answer I so often gave in those years, "something" could have been done which would have been more effective than the appalling procrastination at the United Nations and the confusion at the State Department. Could not Washington have instructed Charles Bohlen, then the ambassador to Moscow, to visit the Russian foreign ministry, preferably together with his British and French colleagues, and declare there in unmistakable terms that the Big Three had received and accepted Nagy's declaration of neutrality and then strongly advise that the Soviet Union do likewise? Such concerted action, I believe, could have been arranged despite Washington, London, and Paris sulking at each other. Would it have worked? It may have, considering the split in the Kremlin on November 1 and the outraged reaction of the non-ruling Communist parties in Western Europe to the first Soviet intervention in Hungary on October 23. Moreover, there was no risk in such a diplomatic move — but "Chip" Bohlen received no instructions and the Soviets must have been convinced that the United States really did not care.

"The side which is willing to run greater risks — or which can make its opponent believe that it is prepared to do so — gains a psychological advantage," wrote Henry A. Kissinger, now President Nixon's top foreign policy adviser, in his *The Necessity of Choice*.

"During the Suez crisis," Kissinger went on, "the Soviet Union threatened obliquely to launch rocket attacks against London and Paris, despite the fact that it would almost certainly have lost an all-out war. During the Hungarian revolution the West, though it was far stronger, was not willing to make similar threats against the U.S.S.R. . . . The diplomatic position of the Soviet Union has been greatly enhanced by its ability to shift to its opponents the risks and uncertainties of countermoves."

Two more aspects of the Western role in 1956 should be discussed. One is the charge that the Republicans, especially Dulles, had encouraged the Hungarians to rebel by too much loose talk about liberation. The other is the role of Dag Hammarskjöld, secretary general of the United Nations.

Many of Dulles's rhetorical notions became part of the American political vocabulary, such as "agonizing reappraisal," "massive retaliation," the "positive loyalty" of other nations, and also, unfortunately, "rollback" and "liberation." "Liberation for the satellites," wrote Adlai Stevenson scornfully in *This Week* magazine on February 28, 1960, "may have been a good vote catcher for the Republican candidates, but the tragic fate of the Hungarian rebellion demonstrated its fraudulence as a policy."

Whether it was a good vote catcher, I cannot say. I can, however, dispel one misconception: slogans such as rollback and liberation were at best only a secondary incentive in Hungary in October 1956. Many Hungarians doubtless knew what Dulles and several others had said because their words were faithfully reported in the Hungarian broadcasts of Western propaganda radios. But it would be an insult to suggest that the Western broadcasts prompted the Magyars to rebel. With their thousand-year history in the "most draughty place in Europe" (as Sándor Hunyadi, a writer in the first half of the century, put it), Hungarians can differentiate between rhetoric and reality.

Dulles used the word "rollback" for the first time in his December 11, 1952, speech in Denver before the National Council of Churches. He recalled the period when the United States was founded and said that "during those early days the tide of despotism was high. We exercised a tremendous influence in *rolling it back*. Today, when the tide of despotism is high again, we instinctively try to meet it again by appealing to men's love of liberty and freedom." In the same speech he also talked about liberation. "If our free people will dramatically show that freedom provides the qualities of spirit, of mind and of action needed to lead the way to world order, to observance of human rights, to practice of the Golden Rule, then freedom will become again the force that puts despotism to rout. Then a new era of *liberation* will be ushered in.

"During the recent political campaign there was discussion about the policy of 'liberation.' Some were frightened by this idea, feeling that it meant war. . . . The influence of freedom cannot be contained, it is all-pervading. No Iron Curtain of the despots . . . can prevent moral and spiritual forces from penetrating into the minds and souls of those under the ruthless control of the Soviet Communist structure." (Italics added.)

Among Dulles's personal papers at Princeton I found a draft of his October 27, 1956, speech before the Dallas Council on World Affairs. In the draft prepared by a speech writer Dulles had inserted in his own handwriting the following sentence, which replaced a much shorter and weaker one: "The heroic people of Hungary challenge the murderous fire of Red Army tanks. These patriots value liberty more than life itself, and all who peacefully enjoy liberty have a solemn duty to seek by all truly helpful means, that those who now die for freedom will not have died in vain." This, one has to admit, was an admirably diplomatic sentence as everybody can read whatever he likes into the phrase "all truly helpful means."

But Dulles was careful. In the same draft he struck out the following sentence which could have discouraged the Hungarians: "It would not help the captive peoples if we were to go to war to liberate them. They would be the first to be annihilated."

At a press conference in Augusta, Georgia, on December 2, 1956, when the revolt in Hungary was over, Dulles was reminded of his 1952 Denver speech about rollback and liberation and was asked whether he thought it had encouraged Hungarians to rise. He replied: "In all of the statements that were made by President Eisenhower and by me, we constantly emphasized that liberation would have to be brought about as an evolutionary process, and we did not encourage violent revolution because we did not see how violent revolution would prevail." One should ask, I believe, why did he not speak about "evolutionary processes" in Denver in 1952? This more moderate position would have spared him and the Republicans from much criticism.

Dulles's 1956 year-end statement, issued on December 28, contained a beautiful obituary of the Hungarian revolution. "The future belongs to those who exercise their God given right to believe, to think and to choose," he said. "That has been most dramatically demonstrated by the heroic people of Hungary. Despite eleven years of Soviet indoctrination, the people rebel and thousands contribute their life blood so the torch of liberty burns bright for all to see." One cannot fail to ask whether this epitaph was on Dean Acheson's mind when he contemptuously said about Dulles (*New York Times Book Review*, October 12, 1969) that "he was a psalm-singing Presbyterian Wall Street lawyer."

Even many years after the Hungarian uprising the question of guilt in general and Dulles's rollback slogan in particular was on the minds of several men who had been active in political and diplomatic life in 1956. Among the Dulles papers at Princeton I found a series of interviews given in 1965, nine years after the revolt.

Richard M. Nixon, then Eisenhower's Vice President, said: "On the Hungarian situation . . . it may have led to the hard line Dulles took against the British and the French. We couldn't, on the one hand, complain about the Soviets intervening in Hungary, and on the other hand approve of the British and French picking that particular time to intervene against Nasser."

Averell Harriman, a Democrat, recalled events in 1956 in his usual straightforward manner. "I violently disagreed with his [Dulles's] liberation policy. I thought this was a very ill-advised form of playing domestic politics with international problems. I was gravely concerned that the Eastern Europeans would misinterpret it, that they would consider that we could do something, to go in and help them free themselves. . . . I do feel that the emphasis on liberation and the way it was used in broadcasts through Eastern Europe did have an influence on the people behind the Iron Curtain." Harriman also recalled that in a television debate with Dulles during the 1952 campaign "I warned him that if he pursued his liberation policy it would encourage uprisings and lead to the death of brave people."

Charles Yost, former U.S. ambassador to the United Nations, acknowledged that, "I think, in retrospect, that one of the mistakes of the Republican Party platform in 1952 [was] that they emphasized — I forget the exact terms — but they implied the possibility of liberation and rollback."

Veteran diplomat Robert D. Murphy, former under secretary of state, said: "We just were boxed. Even some of the Swiss at that point, who have not been noted for their great bravery, said: 'For God's sake, for once let's show some courage!' Well, now, what did that mean? How do you show that courage? Because I don't have the slightest doubt that any intervention on our part would have meant confrontation militarily with the Soviet Union. I am sure they did not want to enter Hungary. I am sure this was the last thing they wanted to do. But once they took the decision, they had to go in all out."

The day the revolution broke out Dulles was in Dallas as the guest of Wiley T. Buchanan, ambassador to Luxembourg and chief of protocol during the Eisenhower era. "The only thing that I can think of that I really personally disagreed with his [Dulles's] policy was that I felt then and now that we should have gone in to help the Hungarians," Buchanan said in the interview. "I heard Foster Dulles say on several occasions: 'If the Iron Curtain ever starts crumbling, it will go all the way and it will go quickly.' I still feel in my own mind that it was a mistake not to aid the Hungarians and that this possibly could have started the 'crumbling.' "

Llewellyn Thompson, one of the great American Kremlinologists and in 1956 the ambassador to Austria, spoke about another important aspect of the problems of those times. "It was quite clear that communications weren't adequate in time, that the [State] Department in the early tense days was operating on the basis of information of developments of the day before. And this was true of the debates in the United Nations. I would listen in Vienna to those [discussions] late at night on the radio and find that they were talking about conditions that had already changed."

Thompson gave an interesting illustration of how Washington was hopelessly limping behind the daily changes in Hungary in connection with Ambassador Wailes, who was hastily and belatedly dispatched to Budapest to take over the legation. Wailes, Thompson recalled, passed through Vienna on his way to Hungary "and I asked him what his instructions were about presenting his credentials. He was told just to go to Budapest and wait, not to present them till he was told to do so. I felt very strongly that if he didn't get in the next day or two and present them immediately, he would never have an opportunity. And, so, I insisted that we get in touch with the Department and we telephoned. We didn't reach anyone very high up, but he merely repeated the instruction. So he [Wailes] went in, and then they instructed him to present them, but by that time it was too late. The government had been overthrown and it was quite clear that he wasn't going to be able to present them to the succeeding government."

Edward L. Freers, in 1956 director of the Office of Eastern European Affairs at the State Department, said that Dulles "was anxious to keep our posture that we were for the 'liberation of the captive peoples' of Eastern Europe as a public posture, but, as a practical measure of foreign policy, [we should] do our best to loosen the ties between the regimes of that area rather than bring about an overthrow of the Communist regimes." Freers said he had the impression that Dulles "backed away" from the concept of massive retaliation. "He had discarded massive retaliation as an effective instrument of policy . . . recognizing the lessons of the Hungarian situation. Now I know there are people who think that he would have been ready, had Suez not occurred, to use power in the Hungarian situation. But none of this ever came to my attention." Freers also said he did not think Dulles's rollback and liberation slogans had encouraged the Hungarians. "I did not think this was a major influence. The Hungarian and the Polish uprisings stemmed from basically domestic considerations, and since the Hungarian uprising wasn't organized, there was no indication that anybody in any organized way expected any assistance from the West."

Felix von Eckardt, the veteran German diplomat and Konrad Adenauer's confidant was also interviewed for the Dulles papers. His words were recorded in German; the translation is mine. "I do not think," he said, "that Dulles ever believed in using military means to achieve a rollback. I never heard anything like this from him. I do not think Dulles ever believed he could use military measures to force the Soviets to pull back." It was, von Eckardt said, "a great disappointment for us when the world's attention was turned away from Hungary because of Suez." When finally the United States voted with Russia on the Suez issue in the United Nations, "we [Germans] felt that Dulles's firm position toward the Soviet Union was destroyed, that this vote represented the spectacular end of the rollback policy."

I am convinced that many Hungarians were more distressed by Dag Hammarskjöld's apparent lack of interest in their country's fate than by the "failure" of the United States to send in its troops. When will Hammarskjöld come? Why does he not come? These questions were asked every day of the revolt by factory workers and by writers, by men carrying arms and by others watching the drama from a safe distance. To whatever category they belonged, they firmly believed that it was the secretary general's duty to rush to the spot where a great power had so obviously violated the U.N. Charter. Some of the young revolutionaries had an almost religious faith that Hammarskjöld would descend from heaven like the archangel Gabriel, the herald of good news and comfort. He never did, of course, and it is small wonder that when the Soviets concluded their dirty work, Hungarian disillusionment with the United Nations was complete.

Among the Dulles papers I found a routine exchange of messages between Hammarskjöld and the secretary of state which became significant only because it helped me to recall what a former high-ranking U.N. diplomat had told me in 1957 about the secretary general.

On November 3, 1956, the day Dulles was operated on for cancer, Hammarskjöld sent him a telegram expressing appreciation "for your role and leadership in the present Middle East crisis," wasting no word on the simultaneous Hungarian crisis. Dulles was more circumspect in his reply on November 15. The United Nations, he said, "owe you a great debt for the role you are playing in helping to advance the cause of peace with justice in the Middle East *and Hungary*" (italics mine). One should probably not attach too much significance to such messages, yet it might very well be that Hammarskjöld did not mention Hungary in his telegram because he did not want to remember this tragedy which the United Nations had so successfully ignored.

I watched Hammarskjöld in later years and had some grudging admiration for this strange man after his dignified answer to Khrushchev's rude attacks on him during the 1960 General Assembly session. But I could never forget, nor forgive, his one great deficiency which obviously forced him to brush aside the Hungarian question in 1956.

Shortly after I arrived in the United States I had lunch one day in New York with Povl Bang-Jensen, the Danish diplomat and then senior political officer of the United Nations who committed suicide under mysterious circumstances in 1959. I had met him once before, in Vienna, where as secretary of the U.N. Special Committee on Hungary he heard witnesses, mostly Hungarian refugees.

During the lunch we naturally spoke about Hungary and I

told him how disappointed I had been with the impotence of the United Nations. Bang-Jensen pondered before he replied. After the lunch I immediately jotted down what he said and can quote him now with a fair amount of accuracy.

"One of the troubles was Hammarskjöld's inability to deal with two problems simultaneously," Bang-Jensen said. The secretary general, he explained, could not be blamed for that; it was an inborn deficiency. "When the two major crises, Hungary and Suez, erupted at the same time, Hammarskjöld had to decide which came first, and which he should shelve. Nobody was close enough to him to know what agonies he went through before he made the decision, but he made it, and Hungary was dropped."

Bang-Jensen, who impressed me as a man of strong opinion, said this matter-of-factly, without a trace of bitterness, as a physician would talk about a patient's unusual illness. This conversation between us took place in the spring of 1957, well before the Danish diplomat's celebrated clash with Hammarskjöld when Bang-Jensen refused to surrender the names of anonymous witnesses who had testified about events in Hungary in 1956 under the condition that their names should not be available at the United Nations, where Russian and other Communist country personnel had access to them.

Epilogue: Journey's End

For the last fourteen years I have done my best to keep track of developments in my old country. I have read thousands of accounts by colleagues who have toured Hungary. I talk to diplomats, Americans and others, who have served in Budapest, and occasionally to the limited number of Hungarians who visit the United States and whom I knew in earlier years. The 1970 picture I have formed is admittedly sketchy.

Understandably, I was most interested in the daily life of my former compatriots. Materially and as far as personal freedom is concerned, they are better off than they were before the revolt. Magyars prefer not to speak about 1956, when they paid a high price for proving that a small nation can rebel against Communist oppression. They do not talk about it because there will be no repeat performance because neither they nor their present rulers have forgotten the lesson of 1956. Kádár, it appears, keeps this lesson in mind. He has given his people more freedom and more consumer goods than Hungarians expected, and has transformed his rule into the most tolerant one in Eastern Europe.

What the Russians did in 1956 was easy to explain. The Soviet Union is the only colonial empire in the second half of the twentieth century and recognizes nothing but the harsh logic of power politics. Their leaders behind the thick walls of the Kremlin probably had a good laugh when after 1956 the United States kept punishing little Hungary for the Red Army's aggression by withholding for years recognition of the Kádár government. After so many years of reporting on often unsavory issues of foreign policy, I can even understand that the Soviets could not think of another way to deal with the uprising.

There are, however, cruelties I can neither understand nor forgive: the senseless murders of Nagy, General Maléter, and so many others. The sanctity and inviolability of the guest is a principle which has been respected all over the world since ancient times. Nagy was given a written safe conduct; Maléter was invited to the Soviet headquarters. Had they studied Machiavelli, they would not have walked into the trap set for them by the Russians.

Milovan Djilas said in 1956 in his *The Storm in Eastern Europe* (*New Leader*, November 19) that between the Polish and Hungarian revolts, although they happened almost simultaneously, "there lies a whole epoch. The changes in Poland mean a triumph of national Communism, which is a different form of what we had already seen in Yugoslavia. The Hungarian uprising is something more, a new phenomenon, perhaps no less meaningful than the French or Russian revolutions. . . . [It] blazed the path which sooner or later other Communist countries must follow. The wound which the Hungarian revolution inflicted on Communism, can never be healed."

The maverick Yugoslav, a Communist who became the harshest critic of Communism, may have been right.

One day, during the roughest period of my time in prison, when I shuffled back to my cell after endless hours of interrogation, I thought I heard from far away an orchestra playing a familiar tune. I listened incredulously: the imaginary orchestra played again and again the same few bars from Antonin Dvorak's *New World* Symphony.

Hallucinations are not unusual in mentally and physically exhausted prisoners. For weeks I kept hearing the sweet melody and asked myself: why the *New World?* Music has played an important role in my life, but Mozart and Beethoven were my favorites, not Dvorak.

In April 1957, flying across the Atlantic to America for the first time, I suddenly remembered my hallucination. I was soaring toward the New World which one day would be my new country. I looked up into the ocean of blueness. The sky, I thought. I can look up at the sky as a free man. Never again will it be forbidden to me.

Index